Gender, Social Structure and Empowerment

Gender, Social Structure and Empowerment

Status Report of Women in India

SANGEETA BHARADWAJ-BADAL

RAWAT PUBLICATIONS
Jaipur • New Delhi • Bangalore • Mumbai • Hyderabad • Guwahati

ISBN 81-316-0239-7

Published by
Prem Rawat for **Rawat Publications**
Satyam Apts, Sector 3, Jawahar Nagar, Jaipur 302 004 (India)
Phone: 0141 265 1748 / 7006 Fax: 0141 265 1748
E-mail: info@rawatbooks.com
Website: www.rawatbooks.com

New Delhi Office
4858/24, Ansari Road, Daryaganj, New Delhi 110 002
Phone: 011 2326 3290

Also at Bangalore, Mumbai, Hyderabad and Guwahati

Typeset by Rawat Computers, Jaipur
Printed at Chaman Enterprises, New Delhi

Contents

Preface

A considerable body of literature has emerged documenting the unequal status of women in relation to men in India. Despite tremendous improvements in health, well-being, literacy levels, life expectancy, and labor force participation for women, their status relative to men is still far from equal. India, like many other third world nations, has been following the development model which focuses mainly on the generation of economic growth, with the belief that benefits of economic growth would eventually spread throughout the various strata of society. But despite the tremendous economic growth, many continue to suffer both economically and socially. The social costs are being borne primarily by the most disadvantaged and backward sections of the society, among which women are the major sufferers. The purpose of this research will be to assess the impact of cultural, social, and economic processes on the well-being and status of women in India.

Most studies on women's status focus on *status* as a unitary construct and search for a universal explanation of the low status of women. Recognizing the inadequacies of such research the present study focuses on the multi-dimensionality of the concept and argues that the complexity of the phenomena makes it necessary to conceptualize status broadly in terms of its economic, social, and political dimensions. The contrasting performance of specific states/districts on each dimension clearly indicates that the dynamic and variable nature of women's status cannot be captured by any one dimension. Further, a structural approach is used to analyze the regional variations in women's position in India across each dimension because such a framework, stressing economic context and sociocultural factors, reveals the complex and multilayered nature of the processes that affect women's position. It is observed that women's status is affected by kinship structures, development levels, and social stratification, which vary over space and time individually and in interaction with each other. It is this variation that leads to differences in women's position from one region of India to another.

The findings of the study suggest that it is important to recognize the mutual interdependence of gender relations, development levels, and social stratification without underestimating the full significance of each in Indian society. In some cases kinship patterns interact with economic development to produce major spatial variations in women's status, and in others, it is the development levels and social stratification that has the greatest influence. For instance, kinship structures appear to be the most powerful factor in affecting women's economic status, while the social dimension of women's status is greatly affected by the varying development levels. And finally, political socialization appears to have the largest impact on women's political status. This reiterates not only the independence of these dimensions but also the important role of 'place' in the constitution of gender differences in India.

In this research I use quantitative techniques to assess women's position on different scales—State and District-level, and in different sociospatial contexts—North, South, and the East India. The study documents women's position along the social, economic and political dimensions, thus providing a "sweeping view" of women's status for the whole of India.

This study is primarily based on the 1981 cross-sectional data of the Indian District Database (IDD). The IDD has been compiled from Census Data and a variety of secondary data sources by the Center on Population, Gender and Social Inequality, University of Maryland, USA. To my knowledge this is the only database of its kind that houses Indian population data at the district level and includes a wide array of measures pertaining to social, political, and economic dimensions. In order to do this process-oriented research numerous socioeconomic variables were needed, but several are available only for the 1981 census. Though an effort was made to add 1991 census data to the IDD in the year 2003, such a comprehensive list of variables, as used in this study, are not available for the 1991 census. Hence, this makes this study as current as possible based on the availability of district level data from India. In spite of the limitations of the data, the results of this study seem meaningful in the context of the social/historical realities of women's lives in different parts of India even today. Moreover, such a detailed empirical analysis of the whole of the country can be very useful in designing general policies on an all-India level or at a more local level—the district-level.

Acknowledgements

This research would not have been completed without the support, encouragement, and intellectual insights of my teachers, friends, and colleagues. I am grateful to my PhD advisor, Robert H. Stoddard, Professor Emeritus, Department of Geography and Anthropology, University of Nebraska Lincoln (UNL), for all his personal and professional mentoring over the last few years. He offered incredible insight into the history and geography of India. Stimulating discussions with him helped me to better articulate the theoretical framework for my research. A very special thanks to J. Clark Archer, Professor of Geography and Anthropology at UNL, for guiding me through the difficult and sometimes frustrating path of quantitative analysis. His thoughtful guidance, critical analysis, and provocative comments on many drafts of this work helped improve this research. I sincerely appreciate the intellectual and moral support I received from David Wishart, Chair, Department of Geography and Anthropology at UNL. My work has also been heavily influenced by Robert Hitchcock, Professor of Anthropology at Michigan State University, who offered courses which led me to think about gender issues in development. I also wish to thank Prof. Douglas Amedeo for his wit and wisdom, which kept my spirits up. I extend my sincere thanks to S.L. Sharma, Professor and Chair (retd.) at the Department of Sociology, Panjab University, Chandigarh for his invaluable comments on this book. I would also like to thank the Association of American Geographers for the Robert D. Hodson and Paul Voras Ph.D. Dissertation Grant. Thanks also to Patrick Guiberson for his assistance in producing the figures and tables for this research.

This work would never have been possible without the constant support of my parents, Shyama and M.P. Bharadwaj, retired professors from Panjab University, Chandigarh, who raised our son Nishant all the years that my husband and I were in graduate school. Many thanks to both of them for their unconditional love and support. Also I wish to thank my husband, Vijay, for his continuous support, encouragement, and advice which helped me through many crises and kept me focused on my work. I dedicate this work to my husband, my parents, and our children Nishant and Rohan.

The support of all my friends was invaluable. The continued support of my very special and close friend Beth Ritter, Associate Professor of Anthropology at University of Nebraska Omaha, was much needed during this long journey through graduate school and after. She and her husband, Alan Osborn, made Lincoln, Nebraska, a "home away from home" for both my husband and I. It would be impossible ever to convey our gratitude adequately for everything that they have done for us. I would also like to thank Sally Stoddard for including my husband and I in their family get-togethers and for her friendship through all these years.

List of Tables

List of Figures and Maps

Figures

Maps

1

Introduction

Scope of the Project

The declaration of the *International Women's Year* by United Nations in 1975 and subsequently the *Women's Decade* in 1975–85 focused world attention on issues of sexual inequality. It was realized that:

> throughout the world, the poorest people in the community are predominantly women and their dependent children. Women, on the whole, often work for no pay at all and, if they are paid, they usually earn far less than men. Two-thirds of the illiterate people in the world are women. Women face increasing levels of violence, because of their gender...
>
> Eugenia Piza Lopez, Coordinator,
> Oxfam Gender and Development Unit, 1993

By the end of the *Women's Decade* a considerable body of literature had built up documenting the unequal status of women in relation to men, but little change, if any, could be seen in the overwhelming subordination of women throughout the world. A need for providing a theoretical framework to the issue of women's oppression, which was constructed differently in different cultural settings, led to a rethinking of the issues of gender inequality instead of accepting gender roles as natural and essential (Forbes, 1996). New issues emerged in feminist studies and new methods were developed to explore the links between social processes and spatial patterns.

Though gender bias exists in every country, nowhere is this inequality more evident than in some South Asian countries, with India being one of them. Dowry deaths, cases of ameneocentesis and abortions in the quest of male children, and low ratio of females to males in the Indian population are just some indicators of the low valuation and relative neglect of the health and well-being of women in the country. The present study is an effort to understand the gender inequality in India and explore the causes for variations in women's status from one part of the country to another.

India, like many other Third World nations, has been following the development model which focuses mainly on the generation of economic growth, with the belief that rapid industrialization and structural transformation would eventually spread the benefits of growth throughout the various strata of society. But despite the growth in GNP figures the country continues to suffer both economically and socially, and the social costs are being borne by the most disadvantaged and backward sections of the society. Among the disadvantaged groups women are considered as major sufferers (Corbridge, 1991; Dreze and Sen, 1995; Bennett, 1992).

On the one hand, national statistics indicate that literacy levels for women have increased in the last two decades, more and more women are joining the paid labor force, and life expectancy for women has increased in India. But, on the other hand, numerous academic studies, UN reports, and official documents of Government of India look beyond these *absolute* gains for women and demonstrate the inequitable and sometimes widening gaps between men and women in life expectancy, economic activity, literacy and education, access to healthcare, and political voice. The United Nation's *Human Development Report 1991* (United Nations, 1991: 31) states that families in India's rural

Punjab spend more than twice as much on the medical care of male infants than on female infants. Women typically work up to 15 hours more per week in rural India than men. The official 1981 census shows that, of the rural working age population, only 16 per cent of women were economically active compared with 53 per cent of men (Bennett, 1992).

Is the persistence of female-male gaps in human development in India indicative of the low status assigned to women in that cultural setting? Are the various gender ideologies rooted in the different kinship structures, leading to a subordinate status of women in India? Does economic development interact with kinship patterns to produce spatial variations in gender relations in India? Do these structural processes affect women's status differently in different parts of India? In other words, does 'place' play a role in the constitution of gender differences in India?

The purpose of this research will be to address these and other related questions, and to assess the impact of cultural, social, and economic processes on the well-being and status of women in India.

Theoretical Considerations

Feminist academicians, both inside and outside geography, have focused on the subordination of women and tried to explore the basis for women's inferior status. Such an understanding, it is believed, is essential as it would lay the guidelines for what needs to be done to achieve a society where gender ceases to be a defining factor (Rubin 1976, rpt. 1990). Drawing inspiration from the women's movement in the 1960s, the earlier feminist studies used the "add and stir" strategy to make women visible. Under this phase, which has been called Liberal Feminism or Feminist Empiricism (Harding, 1986), feminist work focused on the gender roles rather than gender relations and explained women's subordination in the social system in relation to their roles as housewives or mothers (Johnston et al., 1994). Following this largely empirical tradition, the early feminist geographical research aimed to portray spatial variations in women's status around the world by taking up extensive mapping exercises (see Literature Review). Counting women was, and continues to be, an important part of geographical research (McLafferty and Preston,

1991) with a goal of producing a "less biased description of the world by including women" (Mattingly and Falconer-Al-Hindi, 1995: 429).

In the 1970s, moving beyond this documentation of women's lives, feminist analyses sought to uncover the theoretical basis of women's subordination. Taking its cue from the Marxian thought, Socialist Feminism evolved as a "major paradigm in feminist thought and strategy" (Philipson and Hansen, 1990). The two most conspicuous theoretical approaches that have held sway over many socialist feminists to this date are: "the dual systems theory" and the "sex/gender system". The dual systems approach focuses on two autonomous systems: the system of male domination, often termed as *patriarchy*, and the system of mode of production, in most cases *capitalism*, that interact to lead to women's subordination and oppression (Young, 1980; Philipson and Hansen, 1990). According to Zillah Eisenstein (1977, rpt. 1990: 134):

> the mutual dependence of patriarchy and capitalism assumes not only the malleability of patriarchy to the needs of capital but also the malleability of capital to the needs of patriarchy. ... When one states that capitalism needs patriarchy in order to operate efficiently, one is really noting that male supremacy, as a system of sexual hierarchy, supplies capitalism (and systems previous to it) with the necessary order and control; this patriarchal system of control is necessary to the smooth functioning of the society and the economic system and hence should not be undermined.

Though this "vast theoretical synthesis" (Ehrenreich, 1984, rpt. 1990: 268) provided many socialist feminists with a theory that combined the two traditions, Marxism and Feminism, it soon became apparent that this dualistic theory failed to really show how these systems reinforced each other to be a source of women's oppression (Philipson and Hansen, 1990: 18–19). The dual system theory focused on the sexual division of labor between the men and women, suggesting that women's unpaid labor in the home was essential for the maintenance of the patriarchal-capitalist structure (Morgen, 1990; Ehrenreich, 1984, rpt. 1990), and it is this issue of men's control over women's labor in connivance with capitalism that is the cause of their oppression (Young, 1980). But this explanation seems obsolete in today's reality where more and more women are joining the labor force (Philipson and Hansen, 1990; Ehrenreich, 1984, rpt. 1990). As Ehrenreich (1984, rpt. 1990: 272) explains:

> If women's work were as essential to the status quo as socialist-feminist theory argued, capitalism would have been seriously weakened by this withdrawal of women's labor (from home). Yet no one is arguing, for example, that the decline of American productivity is due to unironed shirts and cold breakfasts. Nor has any sector of capital come forth and offered to restore the male family wage so that women can get back to their housework.

Hence, this goes to show that the genesis of women's oppression does not lie in the analysis of capitalism or the patriarchy/capitalism link that the dual system theorists proposed. It was felt that in their efforts to create a mega-theory the socialist feminists had created a "functional fantasy" (i.e., patriarchy functions to reinforce capitalism, and capitalism functions to support patriarchy) (Van Allen, 1984, rpt. 1990: 293) which narrowly conceives of all social relations as falling under the overarching system of economic production (Young, 1980; Rubin, 1976, rpt. 1990). It unduly problematizes the issues of family, procreation, and sexuality and labels them as 'modes of reproduction', isomorphic to the Marxist 'modes of production', attempting to make women central to the Marxist categories of thought and strategy.

Moreover, the dual systems approach takes an ahistoric view of patriarchy, suggesting that the "law of the father"—i.e., patriarchy—has operated in a historically uniform manner universally (Mitchell, 1974), keeping the spheres of women's and men's lives separate to "protect the sexual hierarchy of society" (Eisenstein, 1979: 25). The criticism of this viewpoint has been twofold: (a) the separation of the spheres into the 'public' and the 'private' is a form of gender relations peculiar to capitalist industrialization and thus should not be taken as a transhistoric truth (Young, 1980; Philipson and Hansen, 1990), and (b) projecting the existence of patriarchy universally fails to take into consideration those societies where different forms of kinship and gender hierarchies have been present (Rubin, 1976, rpt. 1990). For instance, large parts of society in the south Indian state of Kerala have a matrilineal organization.

The dissatisfaction with the purely economic explanations of women's subordination and the ahistorical and undifferentiating character of the dual systems theory led anthropologist Gayle Rubin (1976, rpt. 1990) to search for women's subordinate status in the myriad of kinship structures, which vary over space and time, and produce equally variable gender systems in which people of that society operate. Using the works of Claude Levi-Strauss and Sigmund Freud as the conceptual tools, she builds the "descriptions of the part of social life that is the locus of the oppression of women" and defines it as the "sex/gender system" (Rubin, 1976, rpt. 1990: 74). According to her, the society transforms the biological distinction between male and female into gendered identities "who in turn reproduce their society's particular sex/gender system" (Philipson and Hansen, 1990). Gender ideologies are rooted in the kinship structures which are the "observable and empirical forms of sex/gender systems" (Rubin, 1976, rpt. 1990: 82) as can be seen in the marriage systems, the ownership rights to property, or terms of descent. These are just some of the mechanisms of the gender system by which particular conventions of the gender differences are produced and maintained. Rubin expands on Levi-Strauss's, (1969) work to incorporate a theory of women's subordination in the marriage systems where the women are exchanged as gift[1] between the two groups of men. Such an exchange of women creates a wide network of relations. But due to its very nature it is the men who are the beneficiaries of such exchanges. As Rubin (1976, rpt. 1990: 86) points out:

> If it is the women who are being transacted, then it is the men who give and take them who are linked, the women being a conduit of a relationship rather than a partner to it … . And it is the partners, not the presents, upon whom reciprocal exchange confers its quasi-magical power of social linkage.

This, then, is the origin of women's subordination which is perpetuated through kinship structures. Support for this argument can be found in Jamison's study of ancient India (1996: 207) where she explains marriage to be the "fundamental exchange relation ... linking the males of the Aryan community in both horizontal and vertical bonds". The custom of "Kanyadaan", gift of the father or some other elder male member to the groom at the time of marriage, still continues in the modern day India.

The present work extends from Rubin's sex/gender theory, wherein I try to conceptualize the position of women in relation to the different kinship structures present in India and then add other explanatory variables in an effort to fully comprehend the reasons for spatial variations in the status of women in India. The extant literature indicates that though the family structures are predominantly patriarchal in most parts of the India, there are clear interregional differences in kinship structures which have a significant impact on the status of women (Basu, 1992; Kishor, 1993; Malhotra et al., 1995). The North Indian kinship system is characterized by patrilocal exogamy for females (where affinal and consanguineal ties are considered mutually exclusive and so women are married outside the village) (Kishor, 1993; Malhotra et al., 1995; Basu, 1992), and by inheritance of property primarily by male members. As a result of this, women in the North are less likely to be independent which in turn affects their status inside and outside the home. The kinship system in southern India, on the other hand, can be broadly characterized by intra-kin marriages and endogamy (i.e., marriages within the village), and women can sometimes inherit property. Hence, women in South India are able to maintain closer ties to their natal kin which strengthens their position in the household and outside.[2]

Other than these two major types of kinship organizations, there is a third system in the eastern zone, where the cultural organization is different from both the North and South. Some traits of the eastern pattern of social organization are similar to the South-East Asian cultural groups. The population of this region is divided into various clans and tribes and some of the tribes are divided into exogamous clans (i.e., persons must marry outside the clan). In such family structures, both husband and wife work to support the family and women enjoy a considerable amount of freedom. Hence, it can be expected that the cultural roots of the differences in women's status in India perhaps can be traced to the differences in the kinship structures prevalent in different parts of the country (Basu, 1992).

The purely cultural explanations, though extremely important, cannot suffice as the sole explanation for women's subordinate status in a society. As Rubin suggests, "a full-bodied analysis of women" in any society must include an exploration of the economic and political arrangements under which women exist (1976, rpt. 1990: 107). Hence, moving beyond the cultural explanation, I include the 'development levels' as another explanatory factor in understanding women's status in India.

India has made considerable economic progress in nearly all the sectors since its independence in 1947. The introduction of economic reforms and the adoption of liberalization packages by the Indian government since 1991 have led to a reasonably high growth rate of above 5 per cent in recent years (World Bank Report, 1995; Dreze and Sen, 1995; Corbridge, 1991). There has been significant industrial and agricultural growth and tremendous improvements in the infrastructural sectors of transport and power. But the economic development is not uniform throughout the country. There are marked variations in development levels from one region of the country to another. For instance, in 1991 the per capita income of Bihar was US $161, whereas the figure was $544 for Punjab (World Bank Report, 1995: 41). Similarly, levels of urbanization vary from state to state, with Maharashtra having nearly 40 per cent of its population in urban areas in 1991, and the corresponding figure for Assam being just 11 per cent (World Bank Report, 1995: 41). Similarly, the indicators of social development, such as female literacy or female life expectancy at birth, show striking contrasts among different states and regions in India. The present study explores the effects of these varying development levels on women's position and analyzes whether varying development levels lead to variations in gender relations, which subsequently affect women's status differently in various parts of the country.

Other than the kinship structures and the development levels, agricultural practices and social stratification are also included to see their individual and combined effects on female status in India. Due to large variations in all these structural factors, it is expected that the lives of women in different regions vary greatly. Large differences in women's roles between North and South India, between higher caste and lower caste groups, between different religious groups, and between urban and rural communities are expected. As Malhotra et al. (1995: 282) point out "gender inequalities ... in India are neither invariable nor monolithic". The position of women varies from place to place with the variations in the structural aspects of the Indian society, such as the kinship structure, development levels, and social stratification. The present study focuses on this spatial unevenness in gender differences and attempts to explore how the particularity of place affects, and is affected by, the structural processes, which in turn affects the status of women throughout the country.

Methodological Issues

Paralleling the changes in the feminist thought there has been a search for an appropriate research method. Initially, when feminist geography emerged in the 1970s, the method of making women visible was by "counting women to show that women count" (Mattingly and Falkoner-Al-Hindi, 1995: 429). But very soon, arguing against the supposed 'objectivity' and 'neutrality' of the positivist method, the feminist critics pointed out that "significant aspects of human existence and experience are not amenable to quantitative description and analysis" (Mattingly and Falkoner-Al-Hindi, 1995: 428; see also Buttimer, 1976; Olsson, 1980). The methodological controversies have been going on for over two decades now with both the camps asserting their positions and view points (Hodge, 1995) (see the special 'Focus' on this issue in *The Professional Geographer*, November 1995).

In this research I use quantitative techniques to assess women's position on different scales (Chapter 2 draws broad generalizations at a state level, while the other chapters use district[3] as the unit of analysis), and in different sociospatial contexts (the whole of India is divided into the North, South, and the East). The study documents women's position along the social, economic and political dimensions, thus providing a "sweeping view" of women's status for the whole of India. Though the critics of the quantitative methods have questioned this approach saying that it de-emphasizes 'relatedness' and 'connection' with the subject and are abstract generalizations of the phenomena being studied (Mies, 1991), yet one must consider the enormity of the task. It would be impossible for me to make a 'living connection' (McLafferty, 1995: 438) with the 400 million women in India. The aim here is to analyze spatial associations between the various structural factors and reveal the broad differences in women's lives, perhaps setting a stage for more localized, small-scale studies, and also providing information for policy-making. Though I realize that there are great differences between women from one region of India to the other, there are still some "shared experiences ... (which) ... can be represented" (McLafferty, 1995: 437). As Raju (1994) found in her study of female workforce participation in urban India, the participation rate of non-scheduled caste[4] women is closely related to the scheduled caste females but do not show such a relationship with their male counterpart (the non-scheduled caste males). This indicates that women in India, irrespective of their varying positions in the social hierarchy, "behave as a cohesive body and respond to demand for labor in a similar manner" (Raju, 1994: 22).

Though it is difficult to quantify the elements of the abstract concepts such as social systems, or development levels, or social differentiation, and many a times the information in the census or other statistical sources is not collected specifically for the purposes of studying gender relations and roles (Duncan, 1991), a careful attempt is made to select variables that closely represent the concept. For instance, marriage systems are a good representation of the kinship patterns (Rubin, 1976, rpt. 1990), hence patrilocal exogamy, the indicator that characterizes marriage system in most parts of north India, is used to denote the kinship patterns in the region. Similarly, indicators for 'development' and social stratification are selected to represent these concepts as accurately as possible.

Literature Review

Various aspects of women's status and well-being have been studied by sociologists, anthropologists, economists, and geographers. During the 1950s and 1960s, women's concerns were often subsumed in research on economic development. It was believed that rapid economic growth would benefit all equally. The 1970s saw a questioning of this growth model. The pioneering work of Boserup (1970) underlined the different impact of development on women and men. Her study pointed to evidence that many development projects not only ignored women but actually undermined their economic opportunities and independence. Some studies indicated that women's traditional sources of livelihood are disrupted without a sex-equitable redistribution of the new economic and social resources generated by economic growth (United Nations, 1980; Papanek, 1976; Tinker and Bramsen, 1976). This led to a recognition of an urgent need to document women's suffering, invisibility, and subordination, and to explore causes of women's secondary status.

Efforts were made by various scholars (Dixon, 1976; Van Dusen and Sheldon, 1976; Lee and Shultz, 1982; Andrews, 1982; United Nations, 1995) to construct a gender-related development index: an index that could *measure* the concept of status-of-women and be used as a tool for policy prescription. Along with efforts to construct a gender-related development index many studies focused on documenting women's subordinate position in society. Seager and Olson (1986), Shortridge (1987), Gibson and Fast (1986), and Sivard (1985) mapped the forms of this subordination, thus providing illustrations of spatial variation in the lives of women globally. Other works focused on the differences in the status of women and men, in countries or regions (Andrews, 1982; Lee, Stewart, and Winter, 1979; Lee and Shultz, 1982; Holcomb et al., 1990; and Holcomb and Jones, 1990; Duncan, 1989, 1991). These studies were more descriptive in nature rather than being grounded firmly in social theory. Others (Momsen and Townsend, 1987; Brydon and Chant, 1989) attempted a theoretically-based analysis of women's subordination using case-studies from various countries. But these studies have been criticized for their ethnocentric assumptions and their failure to establish a link between "global processes and local geographical variations in gender relations" (McDowell, 1993: 164–65).

In India the first comprehensive report providing information about different aspects of women's lives was published by Government of India in 1974 (Committee on the Status of Women in India, (CSWI) 1974). This report was followed by a volume *Status of Women in India: A Synopsis of the Report of the National Committee on the Status of Women, 1971–1974* (Indian Council of Social Science Research (ICSSR) 1975) and a statistical report (Department of Social Welfare, 1978) presenting data on various issues concerning women. Since then, there have been many descriptive studies from a liberal feminist perspective (Desai, 1977; Wadley, 1977; Jain, 1975; de Souza, 1975; Bhasin, 1972; Nanda, 1976; Stein, 1988; Jacobson, 1976–77; Mandelbaum, 1988; Shukla, 1988) depicting the role of women in the traditional Indian social system. Moving away from the passive-victim stereotype of the Indian women, studies have focused on the agency of women and their resistance movements (Forbes, 1981; Omvedt, 1980; Calman, 1992; Kumar, 1993, 1995). Continuing in the same tradition, Jeffery and Jeffery (1996) focused on women's agency and addressed the interplay of social structures and women's daily lives in rural Bijnor (in Uttar Pradesh). Using a biographical approach they showed how women creatively carve out spaces for themselves under powerful sociocultural constraints.

Focusing on the sociocultural aspects of women's lives, scholars have attempted to understand the interactions between class and gender in India (Mies, 1980; Liddle and Joshi, 1986; Mason, 1989; and Sharma, 1985). Caldwell (1982) and Goode (1963) suggest that a rise in economic position has an egalitarian effect by providing women access to key resources such as education and employment and by altering traditional family systems, thus freeing women from many patriarchal constraints. However, other studies (Safilios-Rothschild, 1980, 1982) have shown that women from lower socioeconomic strata exhibit greater sexual freedom and higher labor force participation, indicating a negative relationship between class and patriarchy. This view is supported by some studies done on India (Sundaram, 1989; Papanek, 1979; Miller, 1981; and Sharma, 1980) which show that women withdraw from the Indian labor market when affluence increases. There are others (Mason, 1989; and Sharma,

1985) who argue that this interaction of class and gender only means a difference in the domain rather than the degree of female oppression. However, all these studies fail to recognize the significance of the spatial unevenness and geographic variation in these structural processes and their varying impacts on female status. In some studies the connections between 'development' and change in women's position in the society have been implied (Sharma, 1985; Mukhopadhyay, 1984), but they have not been specifically studied. None of the above mentioned studies attempts to relate women's position to the place-to-place variations in gender relations and patterns of development in India. Moreover, most of these focus on only one dimension of *status* by either stressing the social or the economic dimension.

Several studies on women in India have tried to analyze the position of women in a 'vacuum', that is, without allowing for the possibility of contradictions or correlations among different aspects of gender inequality. For instance, Basu (1992) in her study of demographic behavior and status of Indian women, fails to bring out the individual relationships between indicators of women's status and demographic outcomes. Hate (1969) and Rao (1983), on the other hand, describe the change in status of Indian women in absolute terms without any comparison to men. The validity of studying women as an isolated category has been questioned by Bradley and Khor (1993), Mead (1948) and Singh (1975). Building on the ideas of these challengers, the present study analyzes women's status by focusing on the interrelationships and dynamics of different dimensions of status, and by looking beyond the *absolute* gains for women to their position *relative* to men in that society.

Organization of the Study

Since the study is concerned with explaining the regional variations in the status of women in India, my overall approach is first to focus on the complex nature of women's status. After understanding the multidimensionality of the concept, I move on to analyze the combined effects of structural factors, such as patriarchy, kinship patterns, development levels, agricultural practices, and social stratification, on women's position in India. Attention is also focused on the issue of place-to-place variations in these structural factors and whether they influence women's status differently in different regions of India.

All the 25 states and 7 union territories[5] in India are included in the study. The analyses are done on a district level, except for those variables where the data are available only on a state level. State level data are used in Chapter 2 to identify the various dimensions of women's status and to provide an overall picture of women in different states of India. Once the broad patterns are established, the focus shifts to the district level in the subsequent chapters.

Chapter 2 explores the concept of *status of women* in an Indian context. In recognition of the complex nature of the concept, a wide range of indicators illustrating the overall patterns of inequality between women and men are chosen for study. The Principal Components Analysis is used to empirically derive the various dimensions of *status*. The interrelationships among the dimensions of *status of women* identified are explored to facilitate a better understanding of the complexity of the concept.

Based on the implications of the Principal Components Analysis, Chapters 3 through 5 explore the status of women in the economic, social, and political realms by analyzing the effects of various social processes on women's position in Indian society. The relationships between the variables are explored using Linear Regression. Linear Regression is used here as an exploratory device to reveal patterns and interrelationships between variables identified theoretically, not as a rigid linear process of testing hypotheses. This process involves questioning and in some cases even revising the theoretical concepts, rather than the mere testing of the data (McLafferty, 1995; Lawson, 1995).

Chapter 3 examines the economic dimension of women's status by focusing on the female labor force participation rate in India. The individual and combined effects of the structural factors on women's labor force participation (both urban and rural) are examined, as are the regional variations in these economic and non-economic factors which lead to spatial unevenness in women's work participation rate.

Chapter 4 focuses on the social aspect of women's status and analyzes spatial inequalities in the levels of female literacy in India. This chapter articulates how various structural constraints and opportunities, both economic and cultural, interact to produce and shape patterns of female literacy in India.

Chapter 5 analyzes the issues related to the political dimension of women's status. Using female voter participation as a surrogate measure of women's political status, attention focuses on regional differences in women's participation in the state apparatus, and the factors that lead to a higher level of female voter participation in one part of the country versus another.

Finally, Chapter 6 summarizes the findings of the study, and discusses some policy implications. Conclusions are made about the particularities of place and their significance in the construction of 'gender' in different parts of India along the various dimensions. The study closes with comments on possible future directions for research.

Notes

1. Gift-exchange was one of the most important features in the primitive societies. It was a way to create social links between the members of different groups and held societies together in the absence of any "Specialized Government Institutions" (Levi-Strauss, 1969).
2. Basu (1992) explains the differences in marriage practices of the North and South in terms of the differences in their economies from ancient times. According to her, the primarily pastoral economy in the North made it imperative for the families to draw on external alliances to strengthen their positions, whereas, in the South the support of already-related kin was crucial for the survival of a largely agricultural economy.
3. Districts are administrative units directly below the state level. See Maps 2a and 2b in Appendix 1.
4. The Constitution of India refers to certain groups of people as the 'Scheduled Castes'. These groups are given special consideration under the constitution.
5. See Map 1 in Appendix 1.

2

Measuring the Position of Women

The Status-of-Women Index

A greater awareness of the sexual inequality around the world has led to a rapid proliferation of literature concerning gender inequality and, more specifically, concerning the determinants of the status of women (Mascia-Lees, 1984: 1). Efforts were made to document women's suffering, invisibility, and subordination, and to explore the causes of women's secondary status. Such efforts yielded many new but often "competing and even contradictory hypotheses" concerning the determinants of the status of women (Mascia-Lees, 1984: 1). One reason for this confusion may be that researchers investigating the issue of status have been working from different methodological and theoretical orientations (Mascia-Lees, 1984: 1), but perhaps a more pertinent reason is that status is a complex multidimensional concept which is hard to define and even harder to measure. Most early efforts at understanding and measuring the status of women focused on status as a unitary construct, and tried to search for a unicausal explanation of the low status of women (Mascia-Lees, 1984). But the inadequacies of this research led scholars (see Quinn, 1977; Whyte, 1978; Mascia-Lees, 1984; Bradley and Khor, 1996) to question the search for a universal measure of women's status, and instead to focus on its complex nature. This chapter attempts to understand and analyze the status of women in present-day India by focusing on the multidimensionality of the concept and exploring the sub-national variations in women's position.

Following Zelditch (1968), and Bradley and Khor (1993: 348–49), "*status* can be defined as a phenomenon that emerges from social organization, through a process of differentiation and evaluation, rather than as an outgrowth of any intrinsic or natural characteristics of persons *per se*". Bradley and Khor (1993) conceptualize status in terms of its economic, political, and social dimensions. Similar conceptualization of status earlier had led Schlegel (1977) and Whyte (1978) to define status in terms of three dimensions and nine scales respectively. Thus, it is clear that instead of treating status as a unitary construct which can be measured by a composite index, it probably is more appropriate to address the multidimensionality of women's status and measure the position of women across various scales.

In this study, status is broadly defined in terms of economic, political, and social dimensions. The interrelationships between these dimensions are explored using a number of variables. Finally, the cartographic representations of the variables and dimensions help in the understanding of regional variations in the status of women in India.

The Search for an Index

Efforts have been made by various scholars to construct a gender-related development index—an index that could *measure* the concept of 'status-of-women' cross-nationally and perhaps be used as a tool for policy prescription. Early attempts to construct an index of the status of women were made by Dixon (1976) and Van Dusen and Sheldon (1976). Their basic premise was that equality would occur only with the abolition of the social division of labor based on gender. The indicators were derived from the following spheres of women's activities: sexual relationships, reproduction, homemaking and child care, economic production, and political decision-making.

There were other efforts to measure the *absolute* or *relative* status of women in specific countries (Lee and Shultz, 1982) or cross-nationally (Andrews, 1982; United Nations, 1995), but most operational indexes excluded one or more dimensions of *status*. For instance, Lee and Shultz (1982) included economic and social indicators in their composite index, but completely ignored the political dimension of women's status. On the other hand, Andrews (1982) did consider political-legal, economic and social indicators to be equally important in the construction of an index, but problems of cross-national comparability of political-legal and economic indicators made it difficult for her to include them in the operationalization of an index. Hence, her index was based only on social indicators, such as female life expectancy, literacy and fertility. The much talked about Gender-related Development Index (GDI) proposed by United Nations (1995) is a merger of economic and social indicators, but fails to include the political dimension. The GDI is the average of three indices: life expectancy, educational attainment, and adjusted GDP per capita. It measures the disparity between the achievements of males and females in a society and imposes a penalty for inequality. Therefore, the greater the gender disparity, the lower will be the country's GDI.

Some scholars (Whyte, 1978; Mascia-Lees, 1984) have found intercorrelations among several of the variables used in the construction of their indexes. According to them, the relationship between indicators renders a composite summary index inadequate to fully operationalize the concept of status of women. Whyte (1978) found nine scales of status, each representing a different aspect of the position of women, and concluded that there is no single predictor of women's status. Mascia-Lees (1984) constructed four status indices, each dealing with a particular sphere of women's lives: political, economic, educational, and family spheres. She examined interrelationships among these indexes and found that women's overall status cannot be treated merely as a linear combination of the four indexes. Instead the four indexes clearly underlie two major dimensions of women's status: an economic dimension comprising of the economic index, and a second dimension comprising of women's political, educational and family status. Although Mascia-Lees (1984) found no statistically significant correlation between the two higher dimensions, she did find that several variables in the four indexes are correlated to each other.

The above mentioned cross-national studies (Whyte, 1978; Mascia-Lees, 1984) make it amply clear that the status of women is not a unitary concept which can be measured by a single composite index. But these studies do not draw a distinction between the public and private domain of women's lives and also fail to capture the interrelationships at the level of indicators. To overcome these problems Bradley and Khor (1993) presented a conceptual multipleindicator model for cross-national research, focusing on the multidimensionality of women's status and the web of interrelationships among dimensions (political, social and economic) and domains (public referring to the 'outside' and private, the 'inside'), but they did not operationalize it.

The generalizations from the cross-national models and studies remain tentative unless corroborated by similar findings in particular societies because the configuration of status, i.e., relationships among dimensions could vary from society to society. In the present study the findings from the cross-national studies (see Whyte, 1978; and Mascia-Lees, 1984) and the conceptual model proposed for cross-national research on status of women (see Bradley and Khor, 1993) is tested within India. Empirical exploration of these relationships helps in the assessment of the applicability of their findings and the generality of explanations.

Data and Methodology

The purpose of this chapter is to identify factors which influence levels and spatial variations in women's status in the Indian social structure. The analysis is done on a state level primarily using the 1991 census data for all the 23 states and seven union territories in India.[1]

Study with states as the territorial unit has one major drawback. It does not yield very detailed results from a social point of view, as characteristics ascribed to entire states can be largely the result of conditions in one or two major cities (Smith, 1973). This tends to obscure subtle regional patterns produced by highly localized historical and cultural factors. The analysis on a district level would have been a more reasonable way of viewing variations, but due to unavailability of data for all the variables on a district level I have used the state as a unit for determining broad regional trends across the entire nation. Moreover, the generalizations derived from this inter-state level analysis may point to important factors influencing status within particular geographical settings. Certain aspects of women's status, like their legal and political standing in society, are greatly affected by state and national level governmental policies. This impact of state programs and policies on the social well-being of women can be brought out in a state-level analysis, even though there may be differences in women's status within these areas based on sub-cultural, class, or ethnic differences (Mascia-Lees, 1984).

In recognition of the complex multivariate nature of the concept of status, a wide range of different indicator variables have been chosen so as to represent as closely as possible the scope of status patterns discussed above. The three major realms selected for assessing the status of women are employment, education and health, and political participation. Under each of these headings several variables are included. The variables selected for the various dimensions are listed in Table 2.1.

Table 2.1

Status Dimensions

Economic	*Political*	*Social*
1. Women's Share of the Labor Force (PFW)	1. Female Voters (FVOTE)	1. Female Literates (FLIT)
2. Sectoral Distribution of Female Labor Force (FPRIM, FSEC, FTERT)	2. Women Elected to Parliament (FLOK)	2. Primary School Enrolment (FENROL)
3. Female Labor Force Participation Rate (FLFPR)	3. Sexual Harassment in Public Places (FHAR)	3. Sex Ratio (SEXRTO)
4. Ratio of Female to Male Non-Agricultural wages (NAGWG)*	4. Violence Against Women in Homes, Dowry Deaths and Abuse (DOWRY and ABUSE)	4. Average Age of Marriage (FMARRY)

* The indicator could not be included in the Principal Components Analysis due to unavailability of data for all the states and union territories. However, it is included in the correlation analysis.

Note: The procedure of calculation for each variable is presented in Appendix 2.

The first step is to perform a correlation analysis to examine the univariate relationships between individual variables. The matrix of correlation coefficients (Table 2.2) indicates that for most of the variables related to women's employment—female share of the labor force (PFW), females in primary, secondary and tertiary sectors (FPRIM, FSEC, FTERT), and total female workers (FLFPR)—the states covary in a markedly similar manner. In other words, all these variables have high correlations with each other. Even though the variables measuring women's participation in secondary and tertiary sectors (FSEC and FTERT) are negatively correlated to the others in this group, the relationships between them and the other variables in this group is significantly stronger than their relationship to any other variables in the data-set. Similarly, indicators related to women's social development—female literates (FLIT), female enrolment in primary schools (FENROL), and average age of marriage for females (FMARRY)—or to their political well-being—per cent females who participated in the election process (FVOTE), females elected to the House of People in the Indian Parliament (FLOK), and violence against women (ABUSE, DWRY)—tend to convey similarly clustered covariations. This shows that there are strong linkages among certain variables which form subsets within the larger set of indicators.

The next step then is to examine whether the interrelated variables align themselves into components, or smaller numbers of hypothetical variables. The Principal Components Analysis is used as an exploratory device to search for the minimum number of hypothetical variables or underlying *dimensions* of women's status. Table 2.3 shows that almost 80 per cent of the total variance is attributable to the first four factors. Since the first three factors account for over 70 per cent with the fourth factor accounting for only 8.1 per cent of the total variance, a three-factor model is chosen for the purposes of this study.

In addition to identifying the minimum number of factors that can account for the observed correlations, it is important to explore the relationships between the dimensions. For example, in many studies of women's status there is an unexamined assumption that increased labor force participation of women automatically leads to a higher overall status for women (Bradley

Table 2.2

Univariate Relationships between Individual Variables

	ABUSE	DWRY	FHAR	FLOK	FVOTE	FENROL	FLIT	FMARRY	SEXRTO	PFW	FPRIM	FSEC	FTERT	FLFPR	NAGWG
ABUSE	1														
DWRY	0.3452	1													
FHAR	–0.1095	0.3164	1												
FLOK	0.4412*	0.6952**	–0.0844	1											
FVOTE	–0.4206*	–0.4527*	0.0988	–0.5815**	1										
FENROL	–0.1267	–0.2308	0.1668	–0.5196**	0.4428*	1									
FLIT	–0.2135	–0.2591	0.2304	–0.5120	0.4030*	0.7812**	1								
FMARRY	–0.4743**	–0.4945**	0.0563	–0.6661**	0.3644*	0.6424**	0.5987**	1							
SEXRTO	0.0517	–0.2384	0.0624	–0.1366	–0.1715	0.1446	0.047	–0.0133	1						
PFW	0.1358	–0.3667*	–0.0208	–0.2793	0.0084	0.0206	–0.252	0.2024	0.4473*	1					
FPRIM	0.1725	–0.0176	–0.2292	0.176	–0.2078	–0.4386*	–0.6852**	–0.2458	0.3421	0.7171**	1				
FSEC	–0.0761	–0.1145	0.0686	–0.13111	0.3475	0.3421	0.5633**	0.053	0.0367	–0.5362**	–0.7829**	1			
FTERT	–0.1884	0.0603	0.2614	–0.1743	0.1413	0.4294*	0.6611**	0.2871	–0.4367*	–0.7098**	–0.9780**	0.6360**	1		
FLFPR	0.1354	–0.3496	–0.2259	–0.2695	0.0185	0.0169	–0.272	0.2278	0.3148	0.9752**	0.6833**	–0.5665**	–0.6577**	1	
NAGWG	–0.1625	–0.3655	–0.3135	–0.2025	–0.3429	0.0203	0.1805	0.3078	0.1929	0.0017	–0.0519	–0.2257	0.1648	–0.0308	1

* –Significance Level 0.05, ** –Significance Level 0.01 (2-tailed).

and Khor, 1993). In other words, if women are doing well in the economic dimension it is assumed that they likely are doing well in other spheres of their lives. It is important to test whether the dimensions covary by looking at the intercorrelations between the conceptual dimensions of status. A mathematical approach to this issue can be followed by using an oblique rotation[2] and calculating the correlation between the dimensions. The Factor Correlation Matrix (Table 2.4) indicates near-zero correlations between the dimensions which confirms that the resulting factors are orthogonal.

Table 2.3

Per cent Variance Attributable to Each Factor

Factor	*Eigenvalue*	*Per cent of Variance*	*Cumulative per cent*
1	4.95901	35.4	35.4
2	3.70940	26.5	61.9
3	1.27051	9.1	71.0
4	1.13573	8.1	79.1
5	1.07068	7.6	86.8
6	0.53708	3.8	90.6
7	0.47266	3.4	94.0
8	0.26033	1.9	95.8
9	0.18617	1.3	97.2
10	0.14030	1.0	98.2
11	0.12594	0.9	99.1
12	0.12162	0.9	99.9
13	0.01057	0.1	100.0
14	0.00000	0.0	100.0

Table 2.4

Factor Correlation Matrix (from oblimin rotation)

	Factor1	*Factor 2*	*Factor3*
Factor 1	1.00000		
Factor 2	0.06959	1.00000	
Factor 3	0.10773	0.12818	1.00000

Hence, "knowledge of where women are located relative to one dimension would not predict with much reliability where women would be located relative to other dimensions" (Bradley and Khor, 1993: 357–8). Keeping this in view, simpler orthogonal rotation using Varimax has been used to enhance the interpretability of the factors.

The Varimax Rotated Factor Pattern Matrix (Table 2.5) shows that Factor 1 can be termed the economic dimension of women's status, and is composed mainly of female share of the labor force (PFW), total female workers (FLFPR), females in tertiary sector (FTERT), females in secondary sector (FSEC), and females in primary sector (FPRIM), with FTERT and FSEC having signs opposite of the other three. This indicates the bipolar nature of this dimension. In other words, states with higher percentage of females in the primary sector (FPRIM) tend to have lower percentages of females in the secondary (FSEC) and tertiary (FTERT) sectors.

Table 2.5

Rotated Factor Matrix

	Factor 1	*Factor 2*	*Factor 3*
PFW	0.92755	0.22722	0.08818
FPRIM	0.90870	–0.24140	–0.21881
FTERT	–0.90162	0.23358	0.15422
FLFPR	0.89119	0.23852	0.01297
FSEC	–0.67296	0.19651	0.34967
FLOK	–0.07437	–0.88371	–0.11933
FMARRY	–0.03001	0.82772	0.10118
DWRY	–0.24441	–0.78673	0.13883
FVOTE	–0.08505	0.66717	0.16929
ABUSE	0.20535	–0.61573	0.36106
FLIT	–0.48245	0.58185	0.52651
FENROL	–0.19460	0.59235	0.60459
SEXRTO	0.51434	0.08225	0.56966
FHAR	–0.23671	–0.08107	0.49210

Factor 2 can clearly be interpreted as a political dimension of women's status, as it represents issues and activities concerning power and control exercised over women in a patriarchal society (Bradley and Khor, 1993). The variables that load the highest on this dimension are females elected to political office (FLOK), average age of marriage for females (FMARRY),[3] rate of dowry deaths (DWRY), rate of abuse by husband and his family (ABUSE), and per cent females who participated in the 1996 Lok Sabha (House of People) election (FVOTE). FMARRY and FVOTE covary in one direction, whereas FLOK, DWRY and ABUSE are negatively signed on this dimension. This dimension, like the first one, is also bipolar in nature. This means that in states where the average age of marriage for females (FMARRY) and female participation in the political process (FVOTE) is high, the per cent of females elected to political positions (FLOK) is low and also violence against women (DWRY, ABUSE) tends to diminish. A high positive score, in this case, denotes high political status for women.

Finally, Factor 3 is comprised of female enrolment in primary schools (FENROL), sex ratio (SEXRTO) and female literates (FLIT), with these variables covarying in the same direction. This is referred to as the social dimension of women's status, with high positive scores indicating a high social status of women.

After identifying the underlying dimensions of women's position in the Indian social structure, it is appropriate to examine women's status with respect to a particular dimension across the states. Factor scores (Table 2.6) for each state on each component indicate the standardized value on a variable multiplied by the component loading for that variable. Thus, if a state has high values for the variables with large loadings on the component, then that state should have a high factor score value on the component (Johnston, 1992). For instance, the state of Kerala has high female literacy and female enrolment in primary schools, and these two variables have high loadings (0.52651 and 0.60459) on the social dimension. Hence, Kerala has a high positive score on the social dimension of women's status (1.58228). In order to more easily visualize the position of a state along a dimension, the scores have been standardized to a 0–100 scale (Table 2.7), so that the region with the highest status in a particular dimension has a score of 100, while the one with lowest status has a score of zero.[4] These scores are then mapped to see the geographical pattern of status of women in different status dimensions.

Table 2.6
Factor Scores

	Name	Factor 1 Economic	Factor 2 Political	Factor 3 Social
1.	Jammu & Kashmir	–98.00000	–98.00000	–98.00000
2.	Kerala	–0.30833	0.92815	1.58228
3.	Lakshadweep	–1.65492	0.93848	0.36351
4.	Goa	–0.29833	0.69674	0.57357
5.	Pondicherry	–0.47298	–0.11245	2.57125
6.	Punjab	–1.58376	–0.03401	–0.77220
7.	Rajasthan	0.65536	–1.77864	–0.97010
8.	Uttar Pradesh	–0.34341	–1.76485	–1.07174
9.	Haryana	–0.69995	–1.10645	–0.43962
10.	Gujarat	0.44005	–0.75965	0.18773
11.	Daman and Diu	–0.31624	0.94728	0.95567
12.	Dadra & Nagar Haveli	1.50979	0.45188	–0.18795
13.	Delhi	–2.07096	–0.84724	0.52571
14.	Himachal Pradesh	1.08960	0.00321	0.65438
15.	Chandigarh	–2.07096	0.79625	–0.81006
16.	Bihar	0.09947	–0.91189	–1.94713
17.	Andaman & Nicobar Islands	–1.41057	0.51550	–0.46472
18.	West Bengal	–0.64333	–0.57903	0.12408
19.	Assam	–98.00000	–98.00000	98.00000
20.	Arunachal Pradesh	0.72791	0.59146	–1.60155
21.	Manipur	0.87015	1.12082	0.06807
22.	Mizoram	0.81349	1.55875	0.02545
23.	Tripura	–0.08888	0.35013	–0.28765
24.	Orissa	0.29780	–0.66958	–0.40033
25.	Meghalaya	0.90403	0.89228	–0.12553
26.	Sikkim	0.37050	1.07284	–0.97448
27.	Nagaland	0.88546	1.50776	–0.84840
28.	Andhra Pradesh	0.85198	–1.00917	0.56864
29.	Karanataka	0.51803	–0.62301	0.61211
30.	Maharashtra	0.87169	–1.65559	2.18988
31.	Madhya Pradesh	0.77622	–1.17735	–0.35122
32.	Tamil Nadu	0.53733	0.65730	0.25133

The values for the states of Jammu & Kashmir and Assam (–98.00) indicate missing data.

Table 2.7
State Values on Three Dimensions

	Economic Dimension	
	Name	*Scale 1*
1.	Dadra & Nagar Haveli	100.00
2.	Himachal Pradesh	89.05
3.	Meghalaya	84.21
4.	Nagaland	83.73
5.	Maharashtra	83.37
6.	Manipur	83.33
7.	Andhra Pradesh	82.86
8.	Mizoram	81.85
9.	Madhya Pradesh	80.88
10.	Arunachal Pradesh	79.62
11.	Rajasthan	77.73
12.	Tamil Nadu	74.66
13.	Karanataka	74.15
14.	Gujarat	72.12
15.	Sikkim	70.31
16.	Orissa	68.41
17.	Bihar	63.24
18.	Tripura	58.34
19.	Goa	52.88
20.	Kerala	52.62
21.	Daman & Diu	52.41
22.	Uttar Pradesh	51.70
23.	Pondicherry	48.32
24.	West Bengal	43.89
25.	Haryana	42.41
26.	Andaman & Nicobar Islands	23.89
27.	Punjab	19.38
28.	Lakshadweep	17.52
29.	Chandigarh	6.68
30.	Delhi	0.00

Cont'd...

Cont'd...

	Political Dimension	
	Name	*Scale 2*
1.	Mizoram	100.00
2.	Nagaland	98.47
3.	Manipur	86.88
4.	Sikkim	85.44
5.	Daman & Diu	81.68
6.	Lakshadweep	81.41
7.	Kerala	81.10
8.	Meghalaya	80.03
9.	Chandigarh	77.16
10.	Goa	74.17
11.	Tamil Nadu	72.99
12.	Arunachal Pradesh	71.02
13.	Andaman & Nicobar Islands	68.74
14.	Dadra & Nagar Haveli	66.83
15.	Tripura	63.79
16.	Himachal Pradesh	53.39
17.	Punjab	52.28
18.	Pondicherry	49.92
19.	West Bengal	35.94
20.	Karanataka	34.63
21.	Orissa	33.23
22.	Gujarat	30.53
23.	Delhi	27.91
24.	Bihar	25.97
25.	Andhra Pradesh	23.06
26.	Haryana	20.14
27.	Madhya Pradesh	18.02
28.	Maharashtra	3.69
29.	Uttar Pradesh	0.41
30.	Rajasthan	0.00

Cont'd...

Cont'd...

Social Dimension		
	Name	*Scale 3*
1.	Pondicherry	100.00
2.	Maharashtra	91.56
3.	Kerala	78.11
4.	Daman & Diu	64.24
5.	Himachal Pradesh	57.58
6.	Karanataka	56.64
7.	Goa	55.77
8.	Andhra Pradesh	55.68
9.	Delhi	54.73
10.	Lakshadweep	51.14
11.	Tamil Nadu	48.66
12.	Gujarat	47.25
13.	West Bengal	45.84
14.	Manipur	44.60
15.	Mizoram	43.66
16.	Meghalaya	40.32
17.	Dadra & Nagar Haveli	38.93
18.	Tripura	36.73
19.	Madhya Pradesh	35.32
20.	Orissa	34.23
21.	Haryana	33.36
22.	Andaman & Nicobar Islands	32.81
23.	Punjab	26.00
24.	Chandigarh	25.17
25.	Nagaland	24.32
26.	Rajasthan	21.62
27.	Sikkim	21.53
28.	Uttar Pradesh	19.37
29.	Arunachal Pradesh	7.65
30.	Bihar	0.00

Findings

The Economic Dimension

Before discussing the cartographic display of this factor, it is important to note the dissonant character of this dimension. This dimension was defined as the economic one because all the variables that had loadings exceeding ±0.5 pertain to women's participation in the economic sector, with the largest of these (PFW) accounting for nearly 89 per cent of the variable's original variance. From the signs of the loadings we can interpret that states having higher proportions of females in the workforce, especially in the primary sector, have lesser shares of women employed in the secondary or tertiary sector. This shows that there are two distinct clusters of states: one group has very few women in the workforce but the majority of those employed are in the secondary and tertiary sectors, whereas the second group of states has a higher proportion of economically active women, but the majority of them are in the agricultural sector. Hence, the question is whether employment of women in secondary and tertiary activities suggests a higher status for them, even if overall participation of women in the workforce is extremely low. Or, is higher participation in the workforce, even if it is in the agricultural sector, better for women?

The values for the states of Jammu & Kashmir and Assam (–98.00) indicate missing data.

The extant literature (Horton, 1996; Anker and Hein, 1986) indicates that as the level of development increases women's share of the non-agricultural workforce will increase. Accordingly, the movement of women out of the rural subsistence realm into the industrialized labor force is expected to raise their standard of living and have a positive impact on their status. But on the other hand, some studies (Boserup, 1970; Chinchilla, 1977; Mascia-Lees, 1984) point out that the displacement of women from the traditional productive labor force has often had a negative impact on their status position. Not all women who are displaced from the agricultural sector can be absorbed in the industrial sector, due to their low educational and skill levels. In this situation a small increase in industrial and service sector employment is an insufficient compensation for the larger number of traditional jobs that are eliminated (Mascia-Lees, 1984). However, if women's employment-shift out of agriculture and into services and industry is considered an improvement, then most northern states would rate highly. For instance, Punjab has 65 per cent of its women workers in the secondary and tertiary sector and would show a scaled value of 81 (by subtracting the state value from 100; see Table 2.7). Similarly Haryana (58), West Bengal (57), and Uttar Pradesh (49) would have high values. Whereas, most southern and western states would not do well on this scale.

The point to note, however, is that in most of the northern states, very few females are in the regular workforce (less than 10% of women are considered main workers, i.e., women who work for 6 months or more in a year). In such a situation, having a higher proportion of working females in the secondary and tertiary sectors does little to suggest that women as a group are doing better economically in northern India. According to Chinchilla (1977: 55–56):

> Lacking adequate employment outside of the home and lacking sufficient income into the home ... industrial growth, once the liberal panacea to poverty and backward ideas about "women's place", becomes linked to increased poverty and feudal patriarchy.

For instance, in Punjab, only 2.79 per cent of the females are main workers, so 97 per cent are out of, or marginally involved in, the workforce. Of those working regularly, about 66 per cent are in the secondary and tertiary sector. In terms of absolute numbers, it means that out of the total female population in Punjab only 1.84 per cent of females are in the non-agricultural sector and 0.96 per cent are in the primary sector. In contrast, the southern states, such as Karnataka and Tamil Nadu, have more than 22 per cent of their female population in the regular workforce, but only one-fourth of these are working in the non-agricultural sector. But, in absolute numbers, this means that about 5 per cent of female population is in the non-agricultural sector and more than 17 per cent in the agricultural sector. This shows that even if employment of women in the secondary and tertiary sectors is considered positive, the South Indian states are doing better than the northern states. In addition, they have a higher proportion of women working in the agricultural sector. Hence, for the purpose of this study female workforce participation rate is used as the criteria for judging the economic status of women and a scale is constructed accordingly, with states with higher proportions of gainfully employed females ranking high on a 0–100 scale.

In the economic dimension (see Table 2.7) the Union Territory of Dadra and Nagar Haveli has the highest score (100), followed closely by the states of Himachal Pradesh, Meghalaya, Maharashtra, Manipur and Andhra Pradesh. Delhi scores the lowest, with the Union Territory of Chandigarh and the state of Punjab not far behind. Map 4[5] indicates that women are doing well economically in the states of Maharashtra, Andhra Pradesh, Madhya Pradesh and Rajasthan. Similarly the north-eastern states of Meghalaya, Nagaland, Manipur, and Mizoram also score high (>81) on the scale. These states are followed closely by Tamil Nadu (74.65) and Karnataka (74.15). Such a finding comes as no surprise as the majority of the southern and eastern states have high proportions of women in the workforce, with more women as regular/main workers and a lesser proportion as marginal workers. The surprising entries in this category are the northern states of Himachal Pradesh (89) and Rajasthan (77) which, compared to others in this category, have fewer female main workers and a higher proportion of female marginal workers and still score high on the economic dimension. This may be due to the fact that both Himachal Pradesh and Rajasthan have nearly 90 per cent of their female main workers employed in the primary sector. This provides them with a distinct advantage on this scale, where higher participation in the primary sector is considered 'good'.

The state of Gujarat in the west, Bihar and Orissa in the east, Kerala in the south, and Tripura and Sikkim in the north-east occupy intermediate positions. The first three of these have fewer women working on regular wages and high proportions of female marginal workers. Kerala has fewer women in the workforce, probably due to the sluggish industrial and agricultural growth, and furthermore, the fact that the majority of these (>60%) are in the tertiary sector drags this state down on this scale. Sikkim and Tripura have fewer women in the workforce both as main and marginal workers. This is especially the case with Tripura where only 10 per cent of the females are classified as main workers, and 3.62 per cent as marginal workers. Moreover, nearly 27 per cent of the main workers are in the non-agricultural sector which further pulls it down on this scale.

The whole of the northern belt, extending from Punjab in the north-west to West Bengal in the east, has low values on the economic dimension. As mentioned earlier, the reasons are: low female work participation and high incidence of marginal workers. Punjab and Haryana have very low female work participation rates, possibly due to the culturally induced withdrawal of women from the workforce with improvements in family income (Nagraj, 1989: 115; Nayyar, 1989: 239), or possibly due to lack of labor demand in the highly mechanized agriculture practiced in these "Green Revolution" states (Raju, 1994). On the other hand, Uttar Pradesh and West Bengal are characterized by depressed economic conditions, low agricultural development, higher population pressure and cultural barriers against entry of women into the workforce.

The Political Dimension

This dimension, like the economic dimension, is bi-polar in nature. Females elected to the Lok Sabha (House of People) (FLOK), rate of dowry deaths (DWRY), and rate of abuse (ABUSE) load negatively (see Table 2.5) on this dimension, whereas average age of marriage (FMARRY) and per cent females who voted in the Lok Sabha elections (FVOTE) load positively. This duality in the dimension indicates that states with larger numbers of females elected to political positions tend to have higher female abuse rate, fewer females participating in the electoral process, and lower average age of marriage. On the other hand, states where females vote in larger numbers the average age of marriage is higher and the abuse rate is lower, but fewer females are elected to political offices. This finding is contrary to the widely held belief that an increase in the number of women elected to the political office will positively affect the political status of women. Also, it is puzzling to see that states with a higher voter turnout (both male and female) have fewer women elected to political offices. A look at the data reveals that this negative relationship between per cent voter turnout and females elected to political positions is contributed in large part by the northeastern states where the voter turnout is very high but no women have contested or won any seats in the 1996 Lok Sabha (House of People) elections. For instance, Nagaland, Sikkim, and Mizoram have very high voter turnout (>73%) but did not have any female contestants for the Lok Sabha (House of People) seats. On the other hand, Tripura, Meghalaya and Manipur did have women candidates but women did not win the elections. One reason for fewer women contesting elections in this largely tribal region could be that most of these states have seen prolonged tribal protest movements against the massive expropriation of their resources and intensified exploitation (Dikshit, 1995). In such periods of unrest and ongoing violence it is unlikely for women to run for elective office, even though they may vote in high proportions.

If women-in-elected-positions is considered 'good' for the political status of women, most of the states with high rates of dowry deaths and abuse will rank high on the 0–100 scale. For instance, in the states of Rajasthan, Uttar Pradesh and Haryana more than 10 per cent of the Lok Sabha seats are won by women, but these states are also characterized by high rates of abuse, low average age of marriage, and fewer female voters. Hence, for the purpose of this study, per cent of women voters is considered an indicator of political status of women and a scale is constructed accordingly with states having larger proportions of women voters ranking high on the 0–100 scale (see Table 2.7).

Most of the northeastern states and Kerala in the south rank high (above 80) on this dimension. In all these states the number of females who exercise their franchise is high, average age of marriage for females is above 19 years, and crimes against women are negligible. Tamil Nadu in the south and Punjab and Himachal Pradesh in the north follow in the next category with values between 52 and 72. The per cent of female voters in these states is reasonably high (>57%), with high average age of marriage and low reported crimes against women. Except Punjab, none of the states in the top 50 values (see Table 2.7) has women elected to the 1996 Lok Sabha.

West Bengal and Orissa in the east, Bihar in the north, Gujarat in the west, and Karnataka in the south have low values on this scale (rank 25–35). Though West Bengal has a high percentage of women voters (80.86%), it does not perform well on this scale due to low mean age of marriage (16 years), reasonably high abuse rate (5.74 women abused per 1,00,000 females), and high percentage of women candidates elected to Lok Sabha seats. Bihar, Orissa, and Karnataka have fewer women voters (between 50% and 55%), low average age of marriage (between 15 and 17), and larger share of parliament seats won by women candidates. Gujarat has a high average age of marriage (above 18 years) but the per cent of female voters is very low in this state (29.64%), dragging it down on this scale.

The states which do the worst on the political dimension (values below 25) are Andhra Pradesh in the south, Maharashtra in the west, and Haryana, Uttar Pradesh, Madhya Pradesh, and Rajasthan in the north. In all of these states, except Maharashtra, women candidates have won more than 10 per cent of the seats in the Lok Sabha, which explains their low statistical values. Maharashtra, Rajasthan and Uttar Pradesh have fewer women voters (between 36% and 47%), low average age of marriage (15.7–16.8 years), and a very high abuse rate, all of which lead to the concentration of these states at the lower end of this scale.

It is important to note that measurement error poses a particular problem in this dimension, especially with respect to the data on rate of abuse (abuse by husband and his family). A careful interpretation of this data is needed, as it can be very misleading because all the cases of abuse are not reported accurately due to low social and cultural valuation of women in India. Moreover, in some states where women are economically and socially advanced, the reporting of crimes is better (for instance, the western and southern states), making those states look worse than others. A look at the map (Map 5) makes this clear. The state of Punjab ranks quite high on the scale (52) despite the fact that it does not have an extraordinarily high percentage of female voters (61%) (women voters being the positive factor on this dimension). In fact, about 7 per cent of the Lok Sabha seats in the state were won by female candidates, which should have dragged this state lower on this scale. But this is not the case probably due to very low reporting of crimes committed against women in the state. On the other hand,

Maharashtra, which is traditionally considered a 'good' state for women, has the lowest value, in large part due to the higher incidence of crime reporting in the state. The data on dowry deaths can be considered more reliable as it is a serious crime because it results in death of a woman and, hence, is likely to be reported accurately.

The Social Dimension

Scores on component 3 (social dimension) form a more complicated geographical pattern (Map 6). The regions are not as clearly divided into north and south as they were in the first dimension. The Union Territory of Pondicherry ranks the highest on this scale, followed closely by Maharashtra and Kerala. These states have high literacy, high primary school enrolment for females, and a more balanced sex ratio.

The second group is comprised of Andhra Pradesh and Karnataka in the south, and Himachal Pradesh and Delhi in the north. In all these states, except Andhra Pradesh, female literacy levels are above the national average. Andhra Pradesh scores 55 because of its high sex ratio and reasonably high female enrolment in primary institutions. The sex ratio in all these states is above the national average of 927 females per 1000 males, except for Delhi which has a figure of 827 females per 1000 males. But despite a very low sex ratio, Delhi scores 54, possibly due to its high female literacy and female enrolment in primary schools.

The prejudice against women is probably affecting the social status of women in states like Punjab, Haryana, West Bengal, Orissa, Madhya Pradesh, and Gujarat. Orissa and Madhya Pradesh, have female literacy levels and female enrolment below the national average leading to lower scores on the social scale (score 34 and 35 respectively). Similarly, Punjab, Haryana, and West Bengal have very low sex ratios, dragging them down on this scale.

The situation is even worse in Rajasthan, Uttar Pradesh, and Bihar, which scores the lowest on the social scale. Low cultural valuation and poverty (see Map 7) combine to exacerbate the problem in states like Uttar Pradesh, Bihar, Orissa, Madhya Pradesh, and West Bengal. Poor families do not educate their daughters as their labor is essential for the survival of the household. Moreover, educating a girl-child is not deemed necessary as the future economic security of the family does not depend on the daughter. The daughter will eventually move into another family after marriage and any economic benefit from her earnings will accrue to the family she is married into (Bennett, 1992).

The preceding discussion clearly suggests that all the three dimensions are independent from each other and are integral to the analysis of women's status.

Conclusion

This chapter explores the complex multidimensional concept of status of women and the regional variations in women's status in India. In recognition of the complex nature of the concept of status, a wide range of different variables were chosen to represent as closely as possible the different dimensions of status. The dimensions were empirically determined based on the patterns assumed by the variables. The scores on these dimensions were then used to scale states from 0 to 100. One general conclusion which can be drawn involves the existence of three major independent dimensions of inter-state variations in the status of women. The first dimension clearly shows that female employment is the most crucial factor influencing the economic status of women. As the Indian economy is primarily rural, female participation in the primary sector plays an important role in determining women's economic status. The southern states do well on this dimension because of their high female work participation rates. The second dimension represents issues and activities concerning power and control over women. This identifies those states where female participation in the electoral process is high and violence against women in the domestic sphere is low. The northeastern part of India does well on this scale with most central states ranking low. Finally, the third dimension has to do with social well-being of women measured by literacy and primary school enrolment. The western and southern states of Maharashtra, Kerala, Karnataka and Andhra Pradesh do well on this dimension. Most of these states are designated as the dynamic regions of India with high levels of urbanization and industrialization, and a well-developed infrastructure (Sengupta, 1968).

The independence of these three dimensions is highlighted by the contrasting performance of specific states. For instance, Maharashtra ranks high (83) on the economic dimension but does poorly on the political dimension (3). Similarly, Kerala drops from score 78 on the social scale to 52 on the economic scale, Pondicherry scores 100 on the social scale but drops to 49 on the political scale, and Andhra Pradesh scores high (82) on economic dimension but sinks low on the political scale (23).

A purely apriory index construction technique may be appealing from a stand-point of influencing policy or goal oriented perspectives, but a deductive approach is likely to miss certain variations and unexpectedly dissolve relationships among variables. An extensive analysis of such relationships can only be possible when we talk about the status of women relative to different dimensions. Based on the results of this chapter the following chapters explore the status of women in individual dimensions.

Notes

1. The states of Assam and Jammu & Kashmir are not included due to missing data.
2. I used the Direct Oblimin oblique rotation method as it does not arbitrarily impose the restriction that factors be uncorrelated. Its advantage over orthogonal rotation is that after making oblique rotations, if the resulting factors are orthogonal, then it is clear that the orthogonality of the factors is not an artifact of the method of rotation.
3. Average age of marriage (FMARRY) was initially included as an indicator of social dimension (see Table 2.1) but the principal components analysis indicates its greater association with the 2nd dimension.
4. The states are ranked using the formula proposed by Gould and White (1974: 66):

$$\text{Scale Score of a State} = \frac{|\text{Raw Score of the State} - \text{Largest Regional Score}|}{\text{Largest Regional Score} - \text{Smallest Regional Score}} \times 100$$

5. All the maps are presented in Appendix 1.

3

The Economic Status of Women

As a result of increased economic development, more and more women are entering the labor force in India. A majority of these (nearly 80%) are concentrated in the primary sector, while the proportions of women working in the secondary and tertiary sectors continue to be low (Registrar General and Census Commissioner, 1991). Some see this increased participation in the primary sector as an indication of women's disadvantaged position in the Indian economy and insist that mere wage labor does not guarantee a shift of balance in power relations between genders (Bennett, 1992; Ahmed-Ghosh, 1994; Sharma, 1980; Cornwell and Chou, 1986; Sathar et al., 1988 and Sharma, 1985). Others suggest that participation in and of itself is important, especially in the early stages of development, and leads to higher economic status for women and consolidation of their position within the family (Duvvury, 1989; Banerjee, 1988; Miller, 1981 and Safilios-Rothschild, 1982). Keeping in view that very few females in India are in the workforce (22%), with a sizeable portion of these engaged in the primary sector, participation of females in any type of economic activity is considered positive and taken as an indicator of the economic status of women in this study. The participation of women in paid work does not completely reverse the gender roles leading to equality between genders, but it does mean an improvement in women's capacity to negotiate and improve their positions 'inside' and 'outside' the home (Duncan, 1991).

There are major differences in female labor force participation rates from different socioeconomic groups and among various regions within India. The regional variations in female participation are usually linked to class and caste divisions in Indian society. Studies (Sundaram, 1989) have indicated that women from lower socioeconomic strata have a higher participation in the workforce due to relaxation of the taboos against working outside the home for wages, but with increasing affluence and social status women in India withdraw from the labor force. Others have tried to explain variations in female participation as related to the performance of local economies, suggesting that higher levels of development generally lead to a decline in the participation of women, at least initially (Presser and Kishor, 1991). While some others have related female participation in the workforce to the agricultural practices (Bardhan, 1974, 1988), explaining that the plow-based agricultural production excludes women from the workforce, but the labor-intensive rice cultivation encourages female participation in the labor force. But a comprehensive approach to understanding variations in female labor force participation by including economic and sociocultural factors has yet to be made. Moreover, the processes behind this differentiation need to be understood. For instance, do kinship structures affect women differently in different parts of India? Are these related to regional variations in levels of development? What are the effects of these factors, individual and combined, on female labor force participation rate? The present chapter deals with these questions and tries to explain the combined effects of kinship structures, economic development, agricultural pattern, social stratification, and religion on female labor force participation in India.

Background

There have been several attempts to understand the regional variations in female workforce participation in India on a state level. Sundaram (1989) related the female labor force participation rate to fertility rates, indicators of prosperity measured by average asset base of the household (land/ livestock/non-farm business equipment), and average levels of living (monthly per capita expenditure). He found that high fertility levels and high living standards inhibit the participation of women in economic activities, but average asset base of the household positively affects female labor force participation by providing women access to self-employment within the household. His study, though statistically significant, focuses only on the economic factors, completely ignoring the cultural basis for differential participation rates. Similarly other studies (Gulati, 1975; Reddy, 1975; Dholakia and Dholakia, 1978 and Acharya, 1996) have attempted to understand regional variations in female work participation rates on a state level by relating female labor force participation rates to per capita income, agro-climatic conditions, agricultural productivity, land tenure systems, cropping patterns, literacy, proportion of scheduled caste and tribal population, and male work participation rates, but the results are mixed at best. Many of these studies found no consistent relationship between any of the variables and female workforce participation rate, whereas, some did indicate a negative correlation between male earnings and female participation (Sinha, 1975) and agricultural productivity and female participation rate (Reddy, 1975) on the one hand, and a positive relationship between household expenditure and female participation in economic activities on the other (Acharya, 1996).

Other studies have tried to explain female participation in the workforce as a function of sociocultural factors like the 'purdah' system (seclusion of females) (Beteille, 1975; Abdullah and Ziedenstein, 1982). This explanation does not hold uniformly for the whole country as women in South India participate in the labor force in larger numbers despite the prevalence of some forms of seclusion.

A majority of the studies mentioned above focus either exclusively on the economic explanation or on the effects of cultural factors on female workforce participation, with little attempt to compare the two. Moreover, state-wise analyses are too aggregated to reveal the finer patterns, so the associations identified remain suggestive at best (Duvvury, 1989 and Kishor, 1993). There are some micro-level studies focusing either on one or two states (Acharya, 1996; Parthasarthy and Rama Rao, 1974; Sawant and Dewan, 1979; Jain, 1985) or on the urban centers (Raju, 1994), but it is difficult to draw generalizations for the whole of India on the basis of these isolated cases.

The present study, therefore, aims to fill the gaps by including both economic and non-economic factors in an attempt to identify and explain the wide regional differences in female work participation rates in India on a district level.[1] My thesis is that regional variations in female labor force participation in India can be explained by region-specific economic or sociocultural constraints, such as, kinship structure, economic development, and social differentiation.

Data and Methodology

This study is primarily based on the 1981 cross-sectional data of the Indian Development District Database (IDDD) (Vanneman and Barnes, 1992). The reasons for using the 1981 data are twofold: first of all, availability of such a large number of variables on a district level for the whole of India is problematic. The IDDD has been compiled from census data and a variety of secondary data sources by the Center on Population, Gender and Social Inequality, University of Maryland. Such a comprehensive database is not available for the 1991 Census. Secondly, it is important to understand the social and economic processes that affect gender relations in India and how variations in these processes can lead to variations in gender relations in different parts of India, which in turn have an impact on the female labor force participation. In order to do this process-oriented research numerous socioeconomic variables are needed, but several are available only for the 1981 Census. Female labor force participation rate is included as a dependent variable and a range of independent variables, for each explanatory factor, have been identified.

The *female labor force participation rate* (FLFPR) is measured as share of female workers out of the total female population:

$$\text{FLFPR} = \frac{\text{Female Workers}}{\text{Total Female Population}} \times 100$$

Female workers comprise the main and the marginal workers[2] in the Indian labor force.

Area under Rice: Physical land conditions are an important factor influencing women's involvement in paid labor force (Basu, 1992). For instance, it is widely believed that in India, female labor force participation is higher in areas where labor-intensive wet-rice cultivation is practiced than in the areas where wheat is the main crop (Bardhan, 1974, 1988; Miller, 1981; and Moore, 1973). Thus, female labor force participation rate is expected to be higher in the areas of rice cultivation. The area devoted to rice is calculated as:

$$\text{RICE} = \frac{\text{Area under rice in each district}}{\text{Area under 37 major crops}^{3}} \times 100$$

Patriarchal Kinship Organization: As described in Chapter 1, kinship patterns vary among the northern, southern, and the eastern parts of India. The North Indian kinship system is considered unfavorable for the status of women, thus, lowering their participation rates in the 'outside' activities. On the other hand, under the prevalent kinship structure in southern India women are able to maintain closer ties to their natal kin which strengthens their position in the household and outside, making it easier for them to participate in economic activities outside the home.

Other than these two major types of kinship organizations, there is a third system in the eastern zone, whose traits of social organization are similar to the South-East Asian cultural groups. These groups differentiate themselves sharply from the other populations in terms of their physical, materialistic and social characteristics (Karve, 1968). For instance, some of the tribes are divided into exogamous clans (i.e., a person must marry outside the clan) where the married couple start an independent family. Thus, a married woman has considerable control over her life, unlike the joint family system of the North where the newly married woman is thrown into an unknown circle (Karve, 1968;

Basu, 1992). Another instance is the *Khasi* tribe of Assam, a matrilineal group where all the ancestral property is passed on through the mother's clan. The family structure among *Khasis* is similar to the one described above with more autonomy for the woman (Karve, 1968). In economic terms then this should translate to more women participating in the labor force in the eastern region of India.

It is difficult to quantify the elements forming patriarchal social systems; moreover, the information in the census or other statistical sources is not collected specifically for the purposes of studying gender relations and roles (Duncan, 1991). Hence, the variables identified here may be inadequate to capture some aspects of kinship patterns and structures, but in the absence of better data, the following indicators are used as measures of kinship structures in India:

1. *Females married under the age of 20 years (MAR19F):* In patriarchal systems men's honor is tied to women's purity and considerable effort is made to ensure that women do not involve themselves with the outside world, especially the world of men (Basu, 1992). One way of exerting control over women is by marrying them early to ensure their chastity and purity (Malhotra et al., 1995). Early marriage combined with an exogamous system may lead to fewer women participating in the paid labor force. Hence, early marriage can be used as a determinant of economic worth of women. MAR19F is measured as:

$$\text{MAR19F} = \frac{\text{Females Married in Age Group 10–19}}{\text{Total Female Population in Age Group 10–19}} \times 100$$

2. *Patrilocal exogamy:* Exogamous systems are likely to have a negative impact on the social status of women. Various studies indicate that in India females migrate as a consequence of marriage whereas males migrate largely in search of jobs (Malhotra et al., 1995; Kishor, 1993; Premi, 1979; Libbee and Sopher, 1975). A measure of exogamy can be derived by calculating the migration rate for females as compared to males:

$$\text{MIGR} = \frac{\text{Number of females not born in their district of enumeration}}{\text{Number of males not born in their district of enumeration}}$$

The higher the MIGR ratio, the greater the patriarchal control of women, leading to lesser participation in the labor force.

3. *Proportion of females in high-paid jobs:* Participation of women in high status full-time jobs is important for allowing social mobility for women. This also leads to a relatively more independent and unconventional lifestyle, breaking down the patriarchal domination of men over women. The participation of women in high-paid jobs is calculated as:

$$\text{HIGH} = \frac{\text{Number of Women Employed as Doctors and Teachers}}{\text{Total Female Workers}} \times 100$$

   The number of women employed in medicine and education is considered as an indicator of high-paid jobs as these are the occupations that women have traditionally been employed in.

4. *Crimes against women:* Patriarchal domination seeks to establish power over the lives of women, their labor, and their sexuality. In situations where patriarchal lifestyle norms are breaking down, for instance, where women move out into the labor force, gender differentials are reinforced by male violence against women at home, at the workplace, or while journeying to work (Duncan, 1991; Walby, 1986, 1989). Studies indicate that regions with higher female labor force participation also show higher levels of male domestic and non-domestic violence towards women. Inside the home, the major reasons for domestic violence are sexual possessiveness, demands over labor, and control over household finances, while the 'outside' is essentially 'policed' by men (Duncan, 1991; Center for Criminology, 1990; Valentine, 1989; HMSO, 1989; Painter, 1991). Violence against women is measured as:

$$\text{CRIME} = \frac{\text{Total Incidence of Crime Against Women}}{\text{Total Female Population}} \times 100{,}000$$

The crime statistics have been taken from the National Crime Records Bureau of India (1996). The data for this variable are available only at a state level, so the state-level values are applied to the districts. This was done to include all the available information about this indicator.

Social Stratification: Variations in female labor force participation have been explained partly by the varying presence of Scheduled Castes and Scheduled Tribe[4] populations in India (Rao, 1978; Raju, 1994; Sahoo and Mahanty, 1978). It has been suggested that women from these lower castes (bottom of the social hierarchy) or tribal societies (kin-based and socially unstratified) have higher labor force participation rates partly due to the relaxation of social taboos against engaging in public activity. But other studies indicate that scheduled castes and tribes conform broadly to the behavioral patterns of the dominant castes in the region (Das, 1976; Raju, 1994) and hence, the differences in factors that explain female participation tend to cut across caste differences (Raju, 1994; Miller, 1981). The following indicators are used as measures of social differentiation in India: (a) the per cent of scheduled castes in a district, and (b) per cent scheduled tribe population. And finally, (c) per cent population that is Muslim is also included as an indicator. The tendency to seclude women from public domains and strict patriarchal controls exercised by confining women to traditional familial roles are some of the key characteristics of Muslim society and culture. These traditions depress Muslim women's participation in economic activities outside the home. It is expected that regions with large concentrations of Muslim population will have lower female labor force participation rates.

Development (Social and Economic): Studies in India have shown that with increased levels of economic development female labor force participation declines, at least initially (Kishor, 1993; Presser and Kishor, 1991; Pampel and Tanaka, 1986). As mentioned before (see Chapter 2), increasing levels of development could lessen the number of jobs available to women in the agricultural sector. This displacement of women from the traditional productive labor force often has a negative impact on their status as these women cannot always be absorbed in the industrial and service sectors due to their low educational and skill levels.

Thus, an increase in non-agricultural sector employment is considered to be an insufficient compensation for the number of traditional jobs that are eliminated (Boserup, 1970; Chinchilla, 1977; Mascia-Lees, 1984). In other words, increased development may lower the economic status of women, at least initially.

In this study economic development is measured by (a) agricultural productivity per farm worker in 1,000s of 1970 rupees[5] (PROD), (b) urbanization (URBZ), i.e., per cent of population living in urban areas, and (c) male labor force participation rate (MLFPR) i.e., per cent of male workers (main + marginal) from the total male population.

Social development is measured by female literacy (FLIT: per cent of females who are iiterate from female population above the age of 5). Studies (Anker and Hein, 1986; Acharya, 1996) suggest that the relationship between female literacy and labor force participation may be a U-shaped one. Increased level of education may not necessarily improve the participation rate of women in the labor market. In fact, according to Acharya (1996: 50) "illiterate enter the labor market in largest proportions followed by the just literate and then the middle school graduates" in India. Hence, female literacy is expected to show a negative relationship to female labor force participation.

Regional Variables: Dummy variables are used in this cross-sectional research to estimate differences between regions and to evaluate whether region moderates the effects of other explanatory variables. As discussed previously, there are three major kinship zones in India: the North, the South, and the East. Similar differences across regions can be observed for nearly all the variables included in this study. For instance, there are wide regional variations in agricultural practices and patterns, female literacy levels, crimes against women, and development patterns. In order to assess the impact of regional variations on female labor force participation, three dummy variables are chosen: North, South and East.[6]

Findings

I begin by identifying gross differences in female labor force participation rates across regions of India. Then I build progressively more complex models predicting female labor force participation rates. First of all an attempt is made to examine whether the regional differences in FLFPR persist when we control for each independent variable. Next, I use the dummy variable regression format to estimate region-specific effects for all the variables in the regression model.

A look at the descriptive statistics (Table 3.1) reveals the following basic pattern: female participation in economic activities is the highest in the South, followed by East, and the North India. The difference between the North and the East is negligible, probably due to close cultural contact between the Austro-Asiatic Tribes of the East and Aryans from the North, leading to structural adaptations of the kinship organization and religion (Karve, 1968). Map 8, showing female labor force participation, confirms the above findings. There is a clear North-South distinction in terms of female labor force participation rate. The Northeastern region also indicates high female participation. Many of the districts in the belt stretching from the Northwest (Punjab state) to the east (West Bengal state) have very low female participation in economic activities. A detailed district-wise analysis follows.

Table 3.1

Average Female Labor Force Participation Rate by Regions: 1981

Region	*Average Female Labor Force Participation Rate (in per cent)*
East	19.41
North	19.38
South	28.55

The picture becomes clearer by the presentation of zero-order correlation coefficients for the dummy variables, the independent variables, and the dependent variable, FLFPR (Table 3.2). All the kinship variables, except crimes against women (CRIME), show a strong negative effect on the female labor force participation rate, though the relationship with early marriage (MAR19F) is not significant. The positive relationship with rate of crime is expected as regions having higher 'outside' participation by women may witness the reinforcement of patriarchal norms by

Table 3.2

Bivariate Correlations (All India)

	FLFPR	RICE	MAR19F	MIGR	HIGH	CRIME	SPC	STP	MUSL	PROD	URBZ	MLFPR	FLIT	NORTH	SOUTH
FLFPR	1														
RICE	–0.0582	1													
MAR19F	–0.0649	–0.1879**	1												
MIGR	–0.4190**	–0.0504	0.4659**	1											
HIGH	–0.5618**	–0.0086	–0.3472**	–0.0804	1										
CRIME	0.2243**	–0.2955**	0.2458**	–0.1049*	–0.1117*	1									
SPC	–0.4177**	–0.0855	0.3117**	–0.2620**	0.1260*	–0.0993	1								
STP	0.4442	0.1330*	–0.0863	–0.2668**	–0.2190**	0.1098*	–0.4479**	1							
MUSL	–0.1	0.1104*	–0.1665**	0.0214	0.0745	–0.1818**	–0.2666**	–0.1505**	1						
PROD	–0.4510**	–0.536	–0.2746**	–0.0432	0.5596**	–0.1639**	0.2753**	–0.2543**	–0.0889	1					
URBZ	–0.2600**	–0.0767	-2574**	–0.3184**	0.5931**	0.1406**	–0.083	–0.1484**	0.0322	0.1563**	1				
MLFPR	0.5117**	–0.0262	–0.0628	–0.3539**	–0.2317**	0.0733	–0.1216*	0.2808**	–0.0606	–0.0914	–0.1031*	1			
FLIT	–0.1203*	0.1325*	–0.6156**	–0.4181**	0.4923**	–0.1230*	-1823**	–0.08568	–0.0851	–0.2796**	0.5240**	–0.2888**	1		
NORTH	–0.2461**	0.3366**	0.3628**	0.3886**	0.0608	0.1808**	0.2098**	–0.075	0.0502	0.0868	–0.1376**	–0.1757**	–0.4457**	1	
SOUTH	0.3080**	0.0403	–0.2562**	–0.3102**	–0.0561	–0.064	–0.2445**	–0.0943	–0.0372	–0.0674	0.1843**	–0.1642**	0.4427**	–0.7982	1

* –Significance Level 0.05, ** –Significance Level 0.01 (2-tailed).

increasing sexual violence against women inside and outside the home. Female labor force participation also is negatively affected by the scheduled caste (SCP) and Muslim population (MUSL), though the latter is not significant, but exhibits a positive relationship to scheduled tribe population (STP). This is probably due to a significantly different cultural pattern than the Hindu-Brahminic north, and a strong Christian presence among some of these populations. The relationship to Muslim population, though negative, turns out to be statistically non-significant probably due to the few outlying districts (see Figure 3.1) in the Muslim-dominated Kashmir region, of Jammu and Kashmir state which has a sizeable proportion of females engaged in economic activities.

Figure 3.1

Female Labor Force Participation and Muslim Population

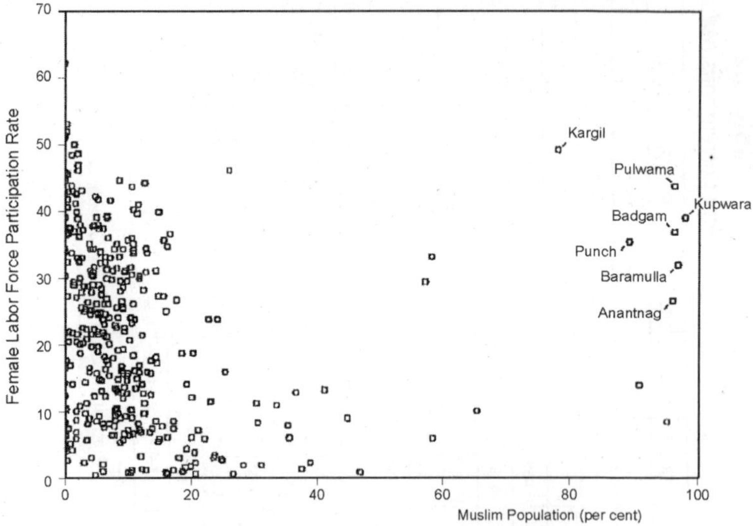

Source: 1981 Indian Development District Database (IDDD).

All the development indicators, except male labor force participation, exhibit a negative relationship to female workforce participation, indicating that districts with high agricultural productivity, high levels of urbanization, and high female literacy are expected to have lower workforce participation by women.

The scatter diagrams for the first two variables (Figure 3.2 for agricultural productivity and Figure 3.3 for urbanization levels) confirm the above mentioned relationships. A few districts in Punjab (Figure 3.2) have a very high agricultural productivity but

Figure 3.2

Female Labor Force Participation and Agricultural Productivity

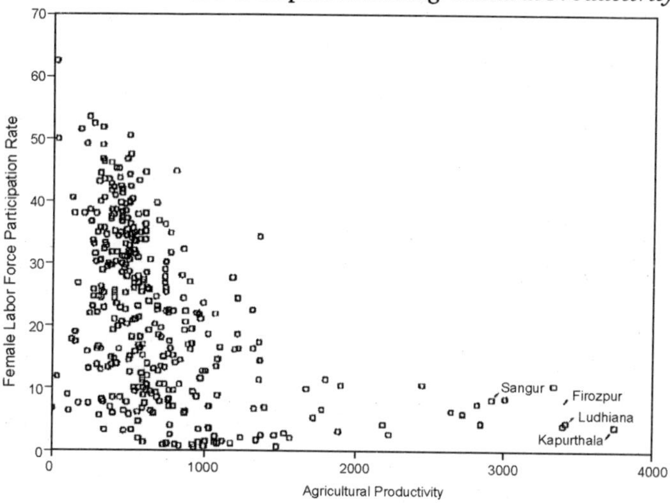

Source: 1981 Indian Development District Database (IDDD).

a very low female labor force participation rate, possibly due to the prevalence of a cultural pattern that lowers the cultural worth of women. Similarly, the highly urbanized regions of India, the four metropolitan areas of Bombay, Calcutta, Madras, and Delhi, have very low female participation in economic activities (Figure 3.3) affecting the relationship negatively. The lack of appropriate skills and education, coupled with the sociocultural constraints, limits women's employment in the modern sector non-agricultural employment (Anker and Hein, 1986; Raju, 1994). Surprisingly, the area under rice cultivation (RICE) has a negative bearing on female work participation, though the correlation is not statistically significant. This is contrary to the widely held belief that in India female labor force participation is higher in areas where labor-intensive wet-rice cultivation is practiced. A look at the scatter diagram (Figure 3.4) shows that a few districts having almost 100 per cent of their cultivable area under rice have very

Figure 3.3

Female Labor Force Participation and Urbanization Levels

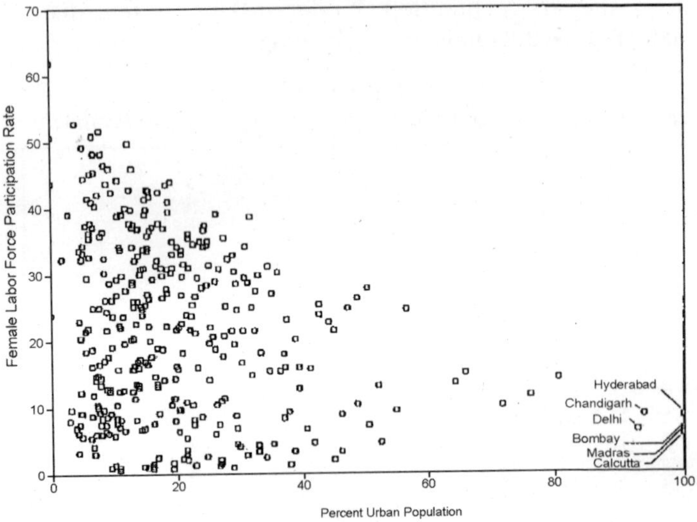

Source: 1981 Indian Development District Database (IDDD).

Figure 3.4

Female Labor Force Participation and Area Under Rice

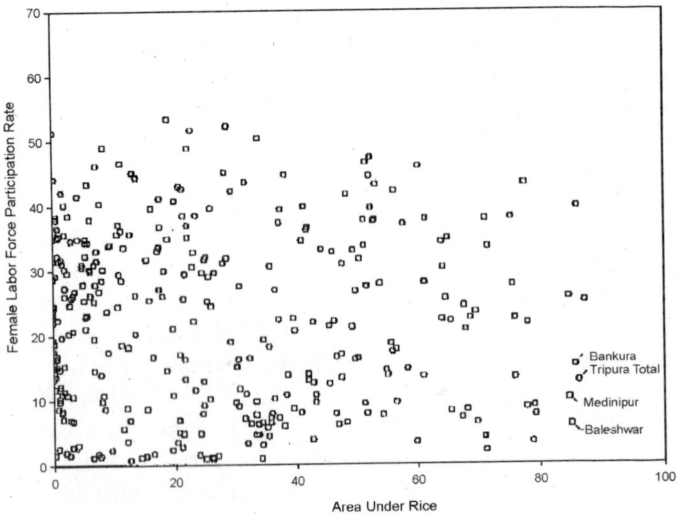

Source: 1981 Indian Development District Database (IDDD).

low female labor force participation rate. These outliers perhaps are influencing the relationship between the two.

After explicating the initial relationships among the variables, I proceed to explain female labor force participation rate by regions, and by separate examinations of the individual explanatory variables. Table 3.3 shows the results of least squares estimation technique, the method chosen for the analysis. The first row in Table 3.3 expresses FLFPR as a linear function of the dummy variables, North, South, and East. This is done to determine whether region is a useful predictor of female labor force participation rate. The result indicates that regional differences explain about 10 per cent of the variance in female labor force participation rates ($R^2 = 0.09487$). The value of the constant, 19.407, reports expected FLFPR for the Eastern Region (the reference group). As expected the predicted FLFPR for the North is lower than the East (19.407 – 0.0207 = 19.38), whereas, the South shows higher FLFPR than both the North and the East (b-coefficient = +9.138). These predicted values are the same as the subgroup means reported in Table 3.1. Among the other explanatory variables it is obvious that including the regional classification increases the predictive power of the model by explaining a larger proportion of the variance in female labor force participation rate (R^2 increases in all instances). Hence, it can be concluded that regional differentiation is an important variable.

A separate examination of the individual explanatory variables indicates that kinship structures have the largest impact on female labor force participation rates ($R^2 = 0.584$), followed closely by development levels ($R^2 = 0.539$), and then social differentiation ($R^2 = 0.357$). Agricultural practices, indicated by area devoted to rice cultivation, do not seem to have a significant effect on female participation in the economic activities ($R^2 = 0.101$).

It is important to understand the collective impact of these explanatory variables on female labor force participation. In order to do this, different combinations of the explanatory variables were considered, and finally four models were selected on the basis of R^2 values (measure of explained variance). Table 3.4 shows the parameters for the models that best predict female labor force participation rate. Region is controlled for in all the models.

Table 3.3

Regression Coefficients for the Effects of Each Explanatory Variable on Female Labor Force Participation in India: 1981

Indicator	*Constant*	*b Coeff.*	R^2	R^2 *before regions were included*
Case I				
Region	19.407		0.0948	
North		–0.0207		
South		+9.138*		
East		—		
Case II				
Agricultural Practices	22.61		0.101	0.003
Area under Rice		–0.053		
North		–2.217		
South		+7.353*		
Case III				
Patriarchy/Kinship	28.77		0.584 19	0.555
Marriage under 19		–0.130**		
Female Migration		–2.313***		
Females in High Paid Jobs		–1.940***		
Crime Against Women		0.121***		
North		5.045***		
South		8.240***		
Case IV				
Social Differentiation	18.12		0.357	0.275
Scheduled Castes		–0.325***		
Scheduled Tribes		0.294***		
Muslims		–0.068		
North		4.877*		
South		13.019***		
Case V				
Development	–56.88		0.539	0.512
Agricultural Product		–0.010***		
Urbanization Levels		–0.249***		
Male Labor Force Participation		1.518***		
Female Literacy		0.2148***		
North		4.744**		
South		8.248***		

*p<0.05, **p<0.01, ***p<0.001.

Table 3.4

Regression Coefficients for the Effects of Explanatory Variables on Female Labor Force Participation in India: 1981

Indicator	*Model 1*	*Model 2*	*Model 3*	*Model 4*
Constant	–13.996	26.67	–3.463	–1.929
Region				
North	6.211***	6.765***	6.831***	5.762***
South	8.683***	10.545***	9.978***	9.072***
East	—	—	—	—
Patriarchy/Kinship				
Marriage under 19	–0.130**	–0.076	–0.104*	–0.102*
Female Migration	–1.937***	–1.908***	–1.804***	–1.778***
Females in High Paid Jobs	–0.948***	–1.670***	–0.843***	–0.840***
Crime against women	0.133***	0.078	0.092**	0.085**
Development				
Agricultural Product	–0.006***		–0.005***	–0.005***
Urbanization Levels	–0.189***		–0.165***	–0.170***
Male Labor Force	0.840***		0.689***	0.690***
Female Literacy	0.066		0.007	0.013
Social Differentiation				
Scheduled Castes		–0.196**	–0.229**	–0.232**
Scheduled Tribes		0.163***	0.084**	0.086**
Muslims		–0.039	–0.074*	–0.069*
Agricultural Practices				
Area under Rice				–0.028
R^2	0.691	0.654	0.727	0.729

*p<0.05, **p<0.01, ***p<0.001.

Model 1 combines the variables of kinship structures and development. All the parameters show significant effects on FLFPR and 69 per cent of the variability in female labor force participation has been accounted for. Females married under the age of 19 years, female migration, and females employed in high paid jobs exhibit a negative association with FLFPR. In other words, female labor force participation is expected to be lower in regions where larger proportions of females are married under the age of 19 years, female migration is high, and more females are employed in high paid jobs. The rate of crime (CRIME) tends to increase with more females moving into the labor force (indicated by the positive b-coefficient).

Agricultural productivity and urbanization are negatively associated with FLFPR. Whereas, male labor force participation and female literacy show a positive influence, though female literacy ceases to be significant (compare it to Case V in Table 3.3). This is perhaps due to the fact that female literacy is closely associated with the kinship indicators and they are summarizing the effects of female literacy on female workforce participation rate. Southern India, as expected, has a higher female labor force participation rate than the East. Unlike the 'Region' case (Table 3.3, Case I), where FLFPR for North was lower than the East, here the parameter for North (b = 6.211) shows that with the indicators for kinship structures and development held constant, the predicted FLFPR in the North is about 6 per cent higher than the East. The negative value of the 'Constant' (–13.996) is not directly interpretable, since a negative percentage of female labor force participation is not possible. It does indicate, however, that female labor force participation is absent from the whole of India until the male labor force participation reaches nearly 40 per cent (see scatter plot, Figure 3.5). The areas with strong patriarchal

Figure 3.5

Male and Female Labor Force Participation Rates

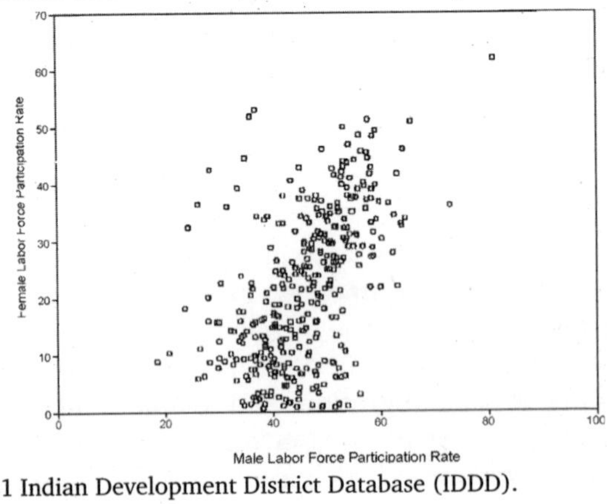

Source: 1981 Indian Development District Database (IDDD).

values will tend to have lower female labor force participation rates, and regions with high development levels are also likely to have fewer females in the labor force. But it is possible that less developed areas (largely rural areas with lower agricultural productivity) have lesser enforcement of patriarchal values, thus leading to larger proportions of women moving out into the paid workforce.

Model 2 includes variables for kinship structures and social differentiation and accounts for 65 per cent of the variability in female labor force participation rates, making it comparable to the previous model (Model 1 $R^2 = 0.649$). The presence of scheduled caste and Muslim population tends to suppress FLFPR, though the impact of Muslim population is not statistically significant. The scheduled tribe population has a positive association with FLFPR, and both North and South continue to show higher FLFPR than the East. The inclusion of social differentiation variables leads to reduction in size of almost all the coefficients for the kinship variables, with early marriage and crimes against women losing their significance. This may be due to the fact that most of the variables for kinship structures and social differentiation are closely related to each other.

The next model (Model 3) combines the variables of development and social differentiation with kinship structures and regions. There is an improvement in R^2 from the two previous models (R^2 in Model 3 = 0.727). All the indicators, except female literacy, show significant effects on female labor force participation rates, with nearly all the coefficients for social stratification larger in size. This indicates that the impact of social stratification on female labor force participation becomes more obvious when the effects of kinship structures and development levels are partitioned out of the equation.

The final model (Model 4) includes yet another variable, area under rice, to see whether agricultural practices in combination with the other factors leads to a better explanation of female labor force participation rates. The R^2 does not change significantly ($R^2 = 0.729$) with the inclusion of agricultural practices in the equation, but since this model contains all the relevant variables it will be considered the final model for explaining female labor force participation rates.

Before the results of this model can be accepted as reliable and valid, there is a need to test for hetroscedasticity and multicollinearity. To test for hetroscedasticity the residuals are plotted against the predicted values (Figure 3.6), and the results do show that the spread of the residuals increases with the magnitude of the predicted values suggesting that the equality-of-variance assumption is violated. The transformation of the data could be a solution to the problem of hetroscedasticity, but since this can produce interpretative problems, the results are accepted as they are.

Figure 3.6

Test for Heteroscedasticity—Dependent Variable: Female Labor Force Participation Rate

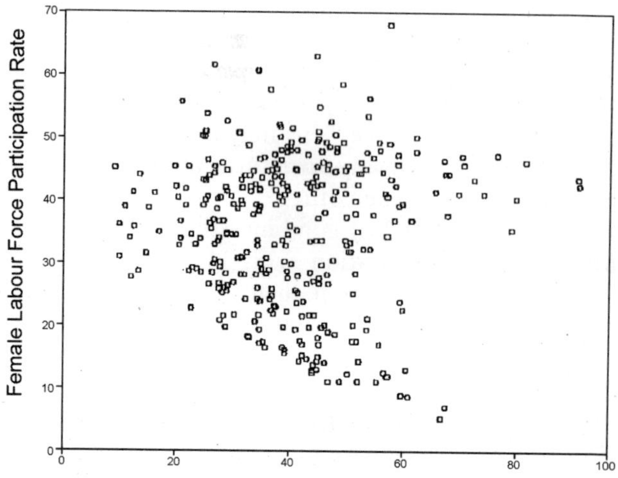

Source: 1981 Indian Development District Database (IDDD).

Next, the problem of high correlations between the independent variables is considered. The variance inflation factors (VIF) are calculated for each regression coefficient of the final model and the results are presented in Table 3.5. As the variance inflation factor increases, so does the variance of the regression coefficient. The results are not particularly disturbing. Except for the North and South variables, the VIFs are not very high. The high VIF for North and South is to be expected, since

Table 3.5

Collinearity Diagnostics

No.	Eigen value	Cond Index	Variance Proportions														
			Const	MAR19F	MIGR	HIGH	CRIME	PROD	URBZ	MLFPR	FLIT	SCP	STP	MUSL	RICE	NORTH	SOUTH
1.	9.61061	1	2E-05	0.00067	0.00126	0.0012	0.00175	0.0015	0.00135	3E-05	0.00051	0.00081	0.00065	0.00229	0.00175	0.00056	0.00044
2.	1.36053	2.658	0	0.00516	0.01462	0.01122	0.00229	0.00128	0.00753	0	0.00479	0.00084	0.00403	0.00085	0.00319	0.01159	0.0358
3.	1.1232	2.925	2E-05	0.00038	0.00307	0.04469	0.00681	0.01181	0.00113	4E-05	3E-05	0.00153	0.12379	0.00582	0.01313	0.00175	0.00866
4.	0.78733	3.494	0	0.00711	0.02368	0.06062	0.00038	0.01411	0.00624	0	0.00102	0.00146	0.08719	0.04337	0.00017	0.00278	0.03407
5.	0.61898	3.94	0	0.00192	0.00618	0.00334	0.08821	7E-05	0.01571	1E-05	6E-05	2E-05	0.00728	0.0735	0.22407	0.00165	0.1479
6.	0.41179	4.831	2E-05	1E-05	0.01255	0.00843	0.02188	0.0785	0.03461	5E-05	0.0007	0.01514	0.00994	0.47171	0.02605	0.00039	0.00782
7.	0.27946	5.864	1E-05	0.00308	0.02901	0.00265	0.07217	0.10447	0.08596	4E-05	0.00011	0.00464	0.13391	0.11584	0.29693	0.00026	0.03663
8.	0.23255	6.429	1E-05	5E-05	0.36242	0.12598	0.02023	0.1593	0.0294	8E-05	0.00072	0.02712	0.01891	0.13275	0.00178	3E-05	0.01398
9.	0.16698	7.587	0.0002	0.00836	0.05263	0.06437	0.6947	0.0571	0.16048	0.00037	0.00585	0.03681	0.00878	0.00516	0.0688	0.02111	0.00035
10.	0.14435	8.159	5E-05	0.07585	0.03495	0.30607	0.00412	0.00433	0	2E-05	0.1676	0.07454	0.05624	0.0051	0.00031	0.05106	0.02314
11.	0.10729	9.465	0.000150	0.01093	0.0361	0.18045	0.01673	0.44942	0.47599	8E-05	0.0875	0.14251	0	0.0002	0.03823	0.00247	3E-05
12.	0.0847	10.652	0	0.17925	0.22312	0.1222	0.04272	0.00239	0.13887	1E-05	2E-05	0.26321	0.07112	0.02843	0.10042	0.21869	0.11237
13.	0.0496	13.92	8E-05	0.62149	0.00132	0.00044	0.01327	0.04655	0.00973	0.00119	0.25699	0.03088	0.00634	0.0008	0.12753	0.3991	0.30423
14.	0.02135	21.219	0.02569	0.04424	0.01136	0.06154	0.00637	0.06577	0.03226	0.06151	0.06626	0.39827	0.46227	0.6187	0.09139	0.27623	0.37544
15.	0.0013	86.097	0.97374	0.0415	0.18773	0.00678	0.00838	0.00341	0.00075	0.93657	0.40786	0.00224	0.00955	0.05232	0.00624	0.01234	0.03224
	VIF			2.759	2.124	2.682	1.378	1.855	2.032	2.17	4.262	1.998	2.54	1.297	1.562	4.722	4.713

there is a strong relationship between the two (r = –0.7982, see Table 3.2). Further, the variance proportions are decomposed into a sum of components associated with each of the eigenvalues (see *Variance Proportions* under 'Collinearity Diagnostics' in Table 3.5). If a high proportion of two or more coefficients is associated with the same eigenvalue, there is evidence of near-dependency (SPSS, 1996: 355–357). In this table agricultural productivity (PROD) and urbanization levels (URBZ) have high proportions for the same eigenvalue. This indicates that these two variables are highly interdependent. Similarly, early marriage, patrilocal exogamy, and North, and scheduled caste and tribe and the 'Region' variables also have high proportions for the same eigenvalue. Hence, the problem of collinearity does exist, but as the intent here is to explore the relationships between the variables, and to test the conceptual theory, all the variables are retained in the equation.

After taking into account the results of the tests for hetroscedasticity and multicollinearity, Model 4 is accepted as the final model explaining female labor force participation rates. The R^2 value of 0.729 suggests a sizeable proportion of variance explained. Area under rice cultivation and female literacy are the only variables with regression parameter estimates that are not significantly different from zero. The parameters for all the other variables are significant at the 0.05 level, with half of them significant at 0.001 level. When all the variables are included, 'Region' appears to be very powerful in explaining variance in FLFPR. This is evident from the standardized regression estimate of South that has the largest z-score value (see Table 3.6). In other words, standard deviation change in the South variable produces larger z-score change in FLFPR than do the z-score changes in all of the other variables. Similarly, the standardized regression estimate of the North variables is also reasonably high. Other standardized parameter estimates reveal that female migration (MIGR) is the most important non-regional variable in explaining FLFPR, thus indicating the effects of patriarchal social structures on female labor force participation. Districts with a kinship structure that is characterized by exogamous systems will tend to have lower female participation in economic activities.

Table 3.6
Standardized Regression Coefficients: Model 4 (All India)

Variable	*Beta*
MAR19F	–0.14576
MIGR	–0.300904
HIGH	–0.243513
CRIME	0.060750
PROD	–0.205580
URBZ	–0.178929
MLFPR	0.126222
FLIT	0.006661
SCP	–0.084099
STP	0.180448
MUSL	–0.214113
RICE	–0.052383
NORTH	0.161894
SOUTH	0.364029

Despite the less than satisfactory data, the CRIME variable (violence against women) shows the expected relationship with FLFPR. Districts with higher female labor force participation will probably have higher levels of male domestic and non-domestic violence towards women. Participation of women in high paid jobs (HIGH) has a negative association with FLFPR. As discussed before, more women in high paid jobs should lead to a relatively more independent and unconventional life style, breaking down the patriarchal domination of men over women, leading to higher female participation in the labor force. But in this case the negative association is possibly due to the fact that a majority of the high paid jobs, essentially jobs in the non-agricultural sector, are concentrated in urbanized and industrialized regions of the country where the occupational structure is such that jobs for women are scarce. In such a job-scarce market, women with high educational level tend to be absorbed in the labor force, but a vast majority of women loose due to underdevelopment of contributory factors such as health and education, the prerequisites for entry of women in the non-agricultural sectors of the economy

(Jose, 1989). This is further reinforced by the negative association of FLFPR with the indicators of development. The higher the urbanization levels and agricultural productivity, the lower will be the FLFPR. Hence, the findings support the hypothesis that increased development levels may lower the economic status of women, at least initially. Male labor force participation rate and female literacy have a positive impact on female labor force participation, though the effect of female literacy is not significant.

The presence of scheduled castes and Muslim population suppresses FLFPR suggesting that scheduled castes conform broadly to the behavioral patterns of the dominant castes in the region (Das, 1976; Raju, 1994) and the tendency to seclude women from public domain in Muslim families coupled with the strict patriarchal controls leads to lower female participation in the labor force. The presence of a scheduled tribe population, on the other hand, has a positive association with FLFPR, maybe due to differences in kinship structures and status of women in tribal societies. Finally, when all the variables are controlled for, the regional effects remain strong with FLFPR being higher in South and North than the East. To judge whether FLFPR is different for the included categories of North and South a *t*-test for the difference in their regression coefficients was performed (not shown here). The *t*-value of 4.836 is significant at 0.05 level, indicating that North and South are significantly different from each other in terms of their female labor force participation rate.

Geographical Patterns of Female Labor Force Participation Rate

The observance of the ecological correlations among the dependent and the explanatory variables may help clarify the above described relationships further (see Maps[7] in Appendix 1). The whole belt extending from Punjab in the north-west to Bihar in the east have very low female labor force participation (Map 8). This region consists of all the districts in Punjab, Haryana, the *Terai* region and plains of Uttar Pradesh, adjoining districts on the Madhya Pradesh-Uttar Pradesh border, and Bihar. These districts have a strong patriarchal structure illustrated by their very high rate of patrilocal exogamy (marriages outside the village)

(Map 12), and sizeable proportion of females marrying before 19 years of age (Map 11). Most of these districts also have a wide male-female gap (compare Map 8 to Map 17) in the labor force participation providing further evidence of the strong hold of patriarchal kinship structures on women in this region. A cluster of few districts on the Uttar Pradesh-Bihar border (Ballia, Ghazipur Azamgarh, and Jaunpur in eastern Uttar Pradesh, and Siwan, Saran, Bhojpur, and Patna in western Bihar) shows a lesser gap in male-female labor force participation, i.e., both male and female labor force participation rates are low. These districts, on the east-Ganga plain, have been characterized as a 'problem region' having very high density of population, low growth rate, very low resource potential, and no possibility of immediate diversion of rural population into industrial and urban nuclei (Sengupta, 1968; Bose, 1994). A majority of the districts in the central Ganga plain (Uttar Pradesh and Bihar) also conform to this pattern along with having a large proportion of scheduled caste (Map 20) and some Muslim population (Map 22) which further suppresses female labor force participation. But Punjab and Haryana in northern India show very high levels of agricultural productivity (Map 15), a sizeable urban population (Map 16), and high levels of female literacy (Map 9). This area has been characterized as "one of the five dynamic regions in the country" (Sengupta, 1968; Bose, 1994: 71), though these states also have a sizeable scheduled caste presence. Thus, the whole belt extending from Punjab to Bihar can be divided into two groups: on the one hand are the economically developed regions of Punjab and Haryana where strong patriarchal structures have led to withdrawal of women from the labor force, supporting the hypothesis that increased affluence leads to fewer women moving out into the workforce, while on the other hand are the less developed regions of central and eastern Ganga plain (Uttar Pradesh and Bihar) where low levels of development, unfavorable patriarchal structures, a strong presence of scheduled castes and a sizeable Muslim population in a few districts, combine to produce low levels of female labor force participation.

The whole of West Bengal and the deltaic districts in the Utkal region of Orissa (Baleshwar, Cuttak, and Puri) also exhibit very low levels of female labor force participation. The strong presence of scheduled caste and Muslim population in West Bengal and some scheduled caste population in the deltaic region of Orissa could be the probable causes of lower female participation. All these districts also have a very large proportion of their cultivable area devoted to rice which actually should have pushed the participation rates up, but that does not seem to be the case here. Though the kinship patterns in these states are slightly different from the north, strict segregation of women especially among the upper classes is common and is probably leading to lower female participation in the economic activities. The female participation in the other districts of Orissa, especially in the south, is much higher than in the Utkal region. It is possible that moderate agricultural productivity in the deltaic region could have led to the withdrawal of women from the labor force. Similarly, increased affluence in the highly urbanized and industrialized region of West Bengal seems to have a negative effect on female labor force participation. Hence, the cultural patterns in these regions are overriding economic development to produce very low levels of female labor force participation.

The districts of Jaisalmer, Bikaner, and Ganganagar in the desert region of Rajasthan also have very low female labor force participation, though eastern Rajasthan has a slightly higher proportion of women workers in the labor force. The region west of the Aravalli range has a weak natural resource base (Sengupta, 1968; Bose, 1994: 73), hence the problems of economic underdevelopment coupled with the unfavorable kinship patterns seem to be affecting the female participation. The wide male-female gap in the labor force participation is further evidence of the strong patriarchal kinship structures in this region. The presence of scheduled caste population in all these districts and a sizeable proportion of Muslims in Jaisalmer have also depressed female labor force participation.

Kanniyakumari in Tamil Nadu, and Thiruvananthapuram, Kottayam, Mallapuram, and Kozikhode in Kerala also have very low female as well as male labor force participation. This indicates that it is not the cultural pattern, which is very different than the Hindu-Brahminic north, but low economic development that is responsible for overall lower participation rates. Recent studies (Issac and Tharakan, 1995) have shown that the employment opportunities in Kerala have stagnated due to the dismal performance in the industrial and agricultural sectors in the state since the 1970s.

All the metropolitan areas, Delhi, Bombay, Madras, and Calcutta, also show lower participation than expected, supporting the hypothesis that higher levels of urbanization do not encourage female labor force participation. Absorption of women in the urban sector is less due to the unavailability of employment opportunities (Raju, 1994).

High levels of female labor force participation are present in almost the whole of Kashmir region in Jammu & Kashmir state, two districts in northern Himachal Pradesh, the whole of Uttarakhand and Kumaon region in Uttar Pradesh, the southern parts of Madhya Pradesh and Orissa, the states of Maharashtra and Andhra Pradesh, and nearly all the northeastern states. The whole of Ladakh region and the Kashmir valley, except districts around the city of Srinagar, exhibit higher levels of female participation in the economic activity. Though this area has a Muslim majority the kinship structure is very different from the north Indian Hindu-dominated cultural pattern. Large numbers of men and women are involved in livestock-raising or other household industries making the proportion of economically active very high for both males and females. Moreover, the agricultural efficiency (yield per acre) in the Kashmir valley is very high (Bose, 1994) leading to higher absorption of workforce in the agricultural sector.

The districts of Lahul and Spiti and Kinnaur in Himachal Pradesh are largely tribal with a cultural pattern that does not restrict women from participating in the economic activities. Similarly, the hill districts of Uttarakhand (Uttar Kashi, Dehradun) and Kumaon (Chamoli, Tehri Garhwal, Pauri Garhwal, Almora, Pithoragarh) in Uttar Pradesh also have high female participation in the labor force. Though this region is not economically well developed, a cultural pattern that is favorable to women has encouraged the participation of females in the workforce. Berreman (1993: 372) describes the cultural pattern in these hill districts of Uttar Pradesh as being "a regionally distinct version of the major features found among most rural North Indians." He characterizes the women from this region as having "significantly more autonomy and social, economic, and political parity relative to men than is generally the case for plains women" (p. 372). Patrilocal exogamy practiced in the plains is absent in these mountainous districts (see Map 12) which means that women are in close contact with their natal family. This strengthens their position in the family. The division of labor in these districts is generally flexible with women participating fully in nearly every agricultural task along with men in this predominantly rice-growing area (Berreman, 1993).

The districts in southern Madhya Pradesh and Orissa also have very high female labor force participation rates. A majority of these districts have a sizeable scheduled tribe population with the districts of Bastar, Seoni, Mandla, Shahdol, Sarguja, and Raigarh in Madhya Pradesh and Koraput and Phulbani in Orissa being predominantly tribal. Similar to the hill districts of Uttar Pradesh, the region is less developed with hardly any industrial activity and low levels of urbanization, but a distinct cultural pattern, evident in the low patrilocal exogamy, leads to higher female labor force participation.

Nearly the whole of Maharashtra and Andhra Pradesh has high male and female labor force participation. High agricultural productivity, especially in the coastal districts, high degree of urbanization, high female literacy, and a favorable kinship pattern evidenced by fewer early marriages and low patrilocal exogamy, have combined to produce very high levels of female participation in the workforce.

The north-eastern region of India also exhibits high participation of women in the labor force. Though the development levels are not very high, a distinct Southeast Asian cultural pattern in these largely tribal states has led to high female literacy and participation in the workforce. Females have more autonomy and a better social status in the region. Moreover, a large Christian presence has influenced literacy levels in the region making economic advancement of women possible. Most of the agricultural area is devoted to rice and that too influences the female labor force participation positively. The reasons for lower participation in Tripura are not very clear. Despite having a similar cultural pattern and levels of economic development this state lags behind its neighbors. Perhaps there are other factors that need to be investigated.

Urban-Rural Differentials

The foregoing analysis explored the impact of structural factors on female labor force participation for the whole of India, but whether the same relationships hold true for the urban and rural India will be examined in this section. The rural-urban figures have been computed for all the variables except area under rice (RICE), females in high paid jobs (HIGH), crime rate (CRIME), and agricultural productivity (PROD) for which separate data were not available. The average female labor force participation in rural India is 25.03 per cent against the urban rate of 8.75 per cent. Table 3.7 shows that the bivariate relationships between rural female labor force participation and all the other explanatory variables exhibit a pattern similar to the one seen for the whole of India. But the correlations for urban female labor force participation and other variables are slightly different (Table 3.8). This is not surprising as the majority of India's population lives in rural areas and the statistics for the whole of India are expected to be very similar to the rural areas of the country.

A look at the zero-order correlations for the rural and urban areas (Table 3.7 and 3.8) shows a different relationship between female labor force participation and proportion of Muslim population and female literacy for urban and rural India. Though presence of Muslim population depresses female labor force participation in the rural areas, it is not the case in urban India. This finding is contrary to the widely held belief that presence of Muslims depresses female labor force participation in rural and urban areas alike (Raju, 1994). Perhaps the presence of upper class Muslims in the cities who "tend to give less weight to the strict observance of purdah" (Sopher, 1980: 186) leads to a higher participation in the workforce than would be generally expected for these groups. But a detailed investigation of this issue is needed.

Female labor force participation has a weak negative relationship to female literacy in the rural areas, whereas, this relationship is strong and significantly positive for the urban areas. This can be explained by the structural differences in the economy of rural and urban India. In the rural areas most females are engaged in the agricultural or other household based sectors where acquiring educational skills is not critical, in fact it may be

Table 3.7

Bivariate Correlations (Rural India)

	RFLFPR	RICE	RMAR19F	RMIGR	HIGH	CRIME	RSCP	RSTP	RMUSL	PROD	RMLFPR	FLITR	NORTH	SOUTH
RFLFPR	1													
RICE	–0.0756	1												
RMAR19F	–0.0746	–0.2175**	1											
RMIGR	–5260**	–0.0553	0.4082**	1										
HIGH	–5544**	–0.0318	–0.3020**	0.0463	1									
CRIME	0.2485**	–0.3133**	0.2809**	–0.1314*	–0.1117*	1								
RSCP	–0.4747**	–0.0663	0.2430**	0.2429**	0.2601**	–0.0887	1							
RSTP	0.4223**	0.1392**	–0.1220*	–0.3024**	–2156**	0.1187*	–0.4789**	1						
RMUSL	–0.0977	0.1484**	–0.0934	0.0093	0.0625	–0.2209**	–0.2312**	–0.1443**	1					
PROD	–0.4664**	–0.0435	–0.2971**	–0.0337	0.6417**	–0.1662**	0.3043**	–0.2610**	–0.0724	1				
RMLFPR	0.5280**	–0.0584	–0.0277	–0.4060**	–0.2358**	0.0965	–0.1193*	0.2638**	–0.07	–0.1285*	1			
FLITR	–0.0369	0.1815	–6358**	–0.3404**	0.3378**	–0.1929**	–0.1471**	–0.0489	–0.0703	0.2887**	–0.3124**	1		
NORTH	–0.2896**	–0.3366	0.4007**	0.4151**	0.0608	0.1808**	0.1824**	–0.0815	0.0554	0.0753	–0.2160**	–0.4580**	1	
SOUTH	0.3688**	0.0217	–0.2831**	–0.3416**	–0.0561	–0.064	–0.2195**	–0.0863	–0.0721	–0.0527	0.2355**	0.4472**	–0.7982**	1

* –Significance Level 0.05, ** –Significance Level .01 (2-tailed).

Table 3.8

Bivariate Correlations (Urban India)

	UFLFPR	RICE	UMAR19F	UMIGR	HIGH	CRIME	USCP	USTP	UMUSL	PROD	UMLFPR	FLITU	NORTH	SOUTH
UFLFPR	1													
RICE	0.0833	1												
UMAR19F	–0.1455**	–0.2001**	1											
UMIGR	–0.3256**	–0.2511**	0.4206**	1										
HIGH	–0.2909**	–0.0123	–0.3809**	–0.0564	1									
CRIME	0.0978	–0.2956**	0.2224**	0.0687	–0.1117*	1								
USCP	–0.3077**	–0.2388**	0.1906**	0.1898**	0.0757	0.0437	1							
USTP	0.2228**	0.1643**	–0.1069*	–0.2635**	–0.1006	–0.0165	–0.2791**	1						
UMUSL	0.1172*	–0.0518	0.2459**	0.2287**	–0.0199	–0.0455	–0.4552**	–0.0299	1					
PROD	–0.2707*	–0.0616	–0.3372**	0.0441	0.5591**	–0.1614**	0.2125**	–0.1946**	–0.1746**	1				
UMLFPR	0.3425**	0.0087	–0.3274**	–0.4311**	0.1433**	–0.0385	–0.0698	0.0119	–0.1201*	0.1869**	1			
FLITU	0.1304*	0.1660**	–0.7376**	–0.5164**	0.2788**	–0.0991	–0.1198*	0.1462**	–0.4151**	0.1551**	0.1436*	1		
NORTH	–0.3946**	–0.3337**	0.2974**	0.3371**	0.0608	0.1808**	0.2390**	–0.1766**	0.1007	0.0972	–0.0728	–0.3845**	1	
SOUTH	0.3981	0.0361	–0.1858**	–0.1977**	–0.0561	–0.064	–0.2634**	–0.0097	0.041	–0.0771	0.0333	0.3254**	–0.7982**	1

* –Significance Level 0.05, ** –Significance Level 0.01 (2-tailed).

considered detrimental in poor families who may have difficulty finding marriage partners for females who are educated and thus considered unsuitable for the exclusively domestic role that is considered 'ideal' for women. In the urban areas, on the other hand, most jobs are in the non-agricultural sector where education is an important determinant in the entry of women in the labor force (Jose, 1989).

Next, a comparison of the various models (Table 3.9 and Table 3.10) shows that there are some differences in the relationships between the dependent variable and the explanatory variables in rural and urban areas. The first model (Model 1)

Table 3.9

Regression Coefficients for the Effects of Explanatory Variables on Female Labor Force Participation in Rural India: 1981

Indicator	*Model 1*	*Model 2*	*Model 3*	*Model 4*
Constant	–9.128	28.324	–0.379	1.087
Region				
North	6.973***	6.955**	7.147***	6.021**
South	10.107***	12.862***	11.007***	10.030***
East	—	—	—	—
Patriarchy/Kinship				
Marriage under 19	–0.145**	–0.023	–0.088	–0.087
Female Migration	–1.289***	–1.409***	–1.232***	–1.211***
High Paid Jobs	–1.243***	–1.567***	–1.069***	–1.084***
Crime	0.126***	0.103**	0.079*	0.072*
Development				
Agricultural Product	–0.006***	—	–0.005***	–0.005***
Males in Labor force	0.762***	—	0.644***	0.644***
Female Literacy	0.024	—	–0.020	–0.012
Social Differentiation				
Scheduled Castes	—	–0.223**	–0.255***	–0.253**
Scheduled Tribes	—	0.140***	0.075*	0.078**
Muslims	—	–0.030	–0.067*	–0.061*
Agricultural Practices				
Area under Rice	—	—	—	–0.029
R^2	0.701	0.684	0.737	0.738

*p<0.05, **p<0.01, ***p<0.001.

Table 3.10
Regression Coefficients for the Effects of Explanatory Variables on Female Labor Force Participation in Urban India: 1981

Indicator	*Model 1*	*Model 2*	*Model 3*	*Model 4*
Constant	–5.043	12.215	–12.740	–13.302
Region				
North	–1.134	–1.078	–1.251	–1.097
South	3.300**	2.744**	2.901**	3.047**
East	—	—	—	—
Patriarchy/Kinship				
Marriage under 19	–0.144*	–0.127**	–0.106*	–0.106*
Female Migration	–1.066	–2.285***	–0.744	–0.717
High Paid Jobs	–0.307***	–0.407***	–0.359***	–0.360***
Crime	0.047**	0.060***	0.054***	0.005***
Development				
Agricultural Product	–0.007**	—	–0.001*	–0.001*
Males in Labor Force	0.446***	—	0.489***	0.492***
Female Literacy	–0.059	—	–0.005	–0.004
Social Differentiation				
Scheduled Castes	—	–0.003	0.013	0.019
Scheduled Tribes	—	0.064	0.078*	0.079**
Muslims	—	0.073***	0.067***	0.068**
Agricultural Practices				
Area under Rice	—	—	—	0.004
R^2	0.432	0.385	0.474	0.474

*p<0.05, **p<0.01, ***p<0.001.

includes variables for kinship structure and development in rural and urban India. When kinship structures and development levels are held constant the female labor force participation in the urban areas in the North is lower than the East and the South. But the rural female labor force participation rate in the North is higher than the East, but lower than the South. In other words, among the urban areas North has the lowest female labor force participation, whereas, for rural areas East has the lowest female labor force participation rate. Model 2 includes variables for kinship structures and social stratification. North continues to have the lowest female labor force participation for urban India but the North variable ceases to be statistically significant. This means that when kinship structures and social stratification are partitioned out of the equation the North is not significantly different from the East in terms of its impact on urban female labor force participation. Urban Muslims continue to have a positive association with female labor force participation, whereas, the presence of Muslims in rural areas depresses female labor force participation, though that is not statistically significant. Model 3 adds the development indicators to the kinship and social stratification variables. Once again urban female labor force participation is lowest in the North, though the difference from the East is not statistically significant. The final model (Model 4) includes all the relevant variables.

The beta values for the rural and urban (Model 4) (Table 3.11) indicate that in urban areas male labor force participation has the greatest impact on female labor force participation, followed by women in high paid jobs and southern region.

Table 3.11

Standardized Regression Coefficients: Model 4 (Rural and Urban India)

Variable	*Beta (Rural)*	*Variable*	*Beta (Urban)*
RMAR19F	–0.083547	UMAR19F	–0.149694
RMIGR	–0.305455	UMIGR	–0.069771
HIGH	–0.310523	HIGH	–0.282672
CRIME	0.070440	CRIME	0.148605
PROD	–0.192951	PROD	–0.110886
RMLFPR	0.211094	UMLFPR	0.339959
FLITR	–0.012405	FLITU	–0.011094
RSCP	–0.149409	USCP	0.017351
RSTP	0.104907	USTP	0.131105
RMUSL	–0.069286	UMUSL	0.200367
RICE	–0.046832	RICE	0.019356
NORTH	0.196928	NORTH	–0.098363
SOUTH	0.302990	SOUTH	0.252271

Whereas, in the rural areas the greatest influence is exercised by women in high paid jobs, followed closely by patrilocal exogamy and the North and South 'Region'. It is clear from the last model that 'Regions' accounts for a significant amount of variation in rural areas despite controlling for all the other explanatory variables. On the other hand, urbanization reduces the effect of 'Regions' as can be seen from the non-significance of the North variable in the urban model.

Geographical Variations (Urban and Rural)

There is a huge gap between the urban and rural female labor force participation in India. This is characteristic of dual economies like India, with large structural differences in the urban and rural economy. A majority of the women workers in India are engaged in the agricultural sector. The rural sector, characterized by low technology, makes it possible to absorb women, who by and large have very low educational or skill levels. On the other hand, there is a virtual absence of females in the urban sector. One reason for lesser number of females in the urban sector could be the problems of measurement and definition of what constitutes work. When a majority of females are own-account workers or family workers engaged in production of goods and services, that is not fully captured in the official statistics (Bennet, 1992; Acharya, 1996). Moreover, in a urban-industrial sector the lower education and skill levels make it harder for women to seek waged labor leading to withdrawal of women from the economic activities (Singh, 1984; Singh and Kelles-Viitanen, 1987; NIUA, 1991; Raju, 1994). Map 26 shows the difference between the urban and rural female labor force participation in India. The rural-urban gap in female labor force participation is the highest in the states that have a kinship pattern different from the Hindu-Brahminic north. On the one hand are the economically developed states of Maharashtra, Karnataka, and Andhra Pradesh, while on the other are the less developed regions of Himachal Pradesh, the hill districts of Uttar Pradesh, and the tribal belt on the Madhya Pradesh-Orissa border. Both the groups have a very high rural-urban gap indicating that women participate in large numbers in the rural areas but the urban participation rate is much lower. This indicates that irrespective of the development levels, favorable kinship patterns allow more women to move out into the workforce. Hence, it can be concluded that increased opportunities for women in the urban areas of these states will lead to a higher participation of women in the workforce.

Conversely, the situation is different in the belt extending from the highly developed Punjab in the north to the less developed Bihar in the east. The rural-urban gap is very low, with the rural participation almost equal to the urban rate in some of the districts. The strong patriarchal kinship structures have led to very low participation rates in urban and rural areas in these states. Uttar Pradesh and Bihar also have a sizeable scheduled caste population which perhaps is depressing the female labor force participation rate even further. Boserup (1970: 75) demonstrated that this was due to a very rigid patriarchal structure which enforces strict restrictions on movements of women outside the home. In such conditions the lower caste populations emulate the behavior of higher castes and even the 'poorest of the poor' keep their women home, leading to very low rates of participation in the labor force (Raju, 1994). Parts of West Bengal and coastal Orissa (the Utkal region) also exhibit a small rural-urban gap. Despite a slightly different kinship pattern, segregation of women, especially among the upper classes, is common and probably leads to lower female participation in the economic activities. Moderate to high affluence, as in the highly urbanized districts of West Bengal (around Calcutta), the agriculturally developed Punjab, and deltaic Orissa, has led to withdrawal of women from the labor force.

Surprisingly, despite a patriarchal structure that lowers the cultural worth of women, all the districts in Rajasthan, except for Jaisalmer and Ganganagar in the western part of the state, and most districts in central Madhya Pradesh have a high rural-urban gap in female labor force participation. This indicates that larger than expected proportions of women are engaged in economically productive work in rural areas of these states. Rural impoverishment in some of these districts may be the reason women are pushed into waged labor on farms. Moreover, this region has a significant scheduled caste population in the rural areas, who are among the poorest groups, which in this case is perhaps contributing to higher female participation rates. As studies (Rao, 1978; Raju, 1994; Sahoo and Mahanty, 1978) have suggested, the relaxation of social taboos against engaging in public activity for lower caste women, especially in conditions of extreme poverty, leads to higher participation by these groups, though this relationship does not hold always, as was demonstrated by Boserup (1970) in her study of Uttar Pradesh. This indicates that the presence of scheduled caste population affects female labor force participation differently in different regions.

Conclusion

The present analysis examines the combined effects of economic, cultural, and regional factors on female labor force participation rates. Kinship structures have the largest impact on female participation in wage labor even when development levels, social stratification, and agricultural practices are controlled for. Regions where females tend to move away after marriage are also characterized by lower educational levels, early marriage, and lower cultural valuation of women. This may reflect the family's perception of their daughter's economic worth (Rosenzweig and Shultz, 1982; Kishor, 1993). As the economic benefits from the earnings of a woman will accrue to her husband's family, this affects her parents' willingness to invest in educating their daughter to prepare her for the job market (Bennett, 1992). Hence, regions where patrilocal exogamy is practiced tend to have smaller proportions of females in the workforce. Conversely, FLFPR is higher in districts not practicing exogamy.

The analysis also indicates that development levels have a U-shaped relationship with FLFPR. Higher urbanization, female literacy, and agricultural productivity lead to lower female participation in the labor force, at least initially. Increasing urbanization levels initially lead to lower participation of women in the workforce as the traditional jobs which women perform in the agricultural sector are lost, whereas, the industrial and service sectors, in initial phases of development, are incapable of absorbing all the women who have been displaced. Similarly, increased literacy levels tend to lower female participation in waged labor due to low demand for less educated labor, but this relationship may change when females are educated beyond high school. Agricultural productivity too affects FLFPR negatively, as women are withdrawn from the labor force with increased affluence. The relationships between these factors of development and FLFPR could change with further increases in urbanization levels, education of women beyond high school and high levels of agricultural productivity. This conclusion may have some policy implications. Longitudinal analyses of these phenomena are required to further our understanding of their impact on female labor force participation.

Much of the variation in female labor force participation is attributed to the differing agricultural practices in various parts of India. It is widely believed that rice cultivation encourages female labor force participation due to its labor-intensive process. But the findings indicate that the relationship between area under rice and female labor force participation is far from conclusive and in fact a weak negative one. Most southern states and the hill districts of Uttar Pradesh have a high proportion of their cultivable area devoted to rice and also exhibit high female labor force participation rates, but other rice-producing areas, such as West Bengal or parts of Orissa do not show the same relationship. Here almost 100 per cent of the cultivable area is devoted to rice but the female labor force participation rate is very low. Moreover, many districts in central and western India do not produce rice but have a high female labor force participation rate. This indicates that it is not the ecological differences but rather the kinship patterns that influence female participation in the labor force. Regions with a favorable kinship pattern (most southern states, hill districts of Uttar Pradesh, the Kashmir region, and the tribal districts in southern Madhya Pradesh) which also happen to be rice-producing regions exhibit high participation of females, whereas, the parts of India that have an unfavorable kinship structure (parts of West Bengal, Bihar, Orissa) have lower participation rates despite being largely rice-producing states.

Thus, it can be concluded that it is important to include both cultural and economic factors in any analysis of female participation in the labor force. Though the differences in kinship structures, development levels, agricultural practices, and social differentiation do increase our understanding of the district level variations in female labor force participation rate, they do not fully explain the North-South, or North-East, or South-East differences. Perhaps there is more to the regional differences than the combination of these sociocultural and economic factors.

The ecological relationships between female labor force participation and the explanatory factors can be summarized as follows:

1. *Districts with reasonably high level of economic development and a kinship structure that is favorable to women*: Most southern states, especially Maharashtra and Andhra Pradesh fall into this category.
2. *Districts with high levels of economic development but a kinship structure that lowers the cultural worth of women*: despite high levels of development female labor force participation is very low in Punjab and Haryana in the North. The situation is not very different in parts of West Bengal and Orissa in the East, where patriarchal kinship structures override moderate levels of development to produce very low rate of female participation in the workforce.
3. *Districts with less economic development, but a favorable kinship structure*: in some cases despite a favorable kinship structure low levels of development depress female labor force participation. For instance, Kerala has a lower female participation rate than expected despite a favorable kinship structure. But in other cases having a cultural system that is favorable to women can lead to higher participation by women in the economic activities overriding the impacts of less economic development. The prime examples are the Northeastern states, the Kumaon region of Uttar Pradesh, and the tribal districts of Himachal Pradesh and Madhya Pradesh.
4. *Districts with low economic development and an unfavorable kinship structure*: such districts have the most restrictive attitude to women's work. Low development levels and a strong patriarchal structure combine to produce very little participation by women in the economic activities. Most of Uttar Pradesh plains, northern Bihar, and the desert region of Rajasthan are prime examples of this category.

Notes

1. A total of 366 districts, an administrative unit below the State level, have been included in the study. There is no data for the state of Assam as the 1981 Census was not conducted in the state. Moreover, the small states and union territories of Arunachal Pradesh, Delhi, Goa, Daman and Diu, Manipur, Nagaland, and Pondicherry are treated as districts. A list of the districts included in the study along with a map is attached in Appendix 1.
2. Those who work for at least 183 days (six months) preceding the date of survey are treated as Main Workers and those who work for fewer days are treated as Marginal Workers.
3. The list of 37 major crops for which area was available is given in the IDDD codebook.
4. Articles 341 and 342 of the Indian Constitution refer to certain special groups of people as 'Scheduled Castes' and 'Scheduled Tribes'. These groups are given special consideration under the constitution.
5. Price data are available only for 37 crops. Agricultural Product is the average over three years 1979–80, 1980–81, and 1981–82 (see the India Development District Database Codebook for further details).
6. Following Kishor (1993) North includes all the districts of Bihar, Delhi, Gujarat, Haryana, Himachal Pradesh, Jammu and Kashmir, Madhya Pradesh, Punjab, Rajasthan, and Uttar Pradesh. South includes Andhra Pradesh, Goa, Daman and Diu, Karnataka, Kerala, Maharashtra, Pondicherry, and Tamil Nadu. East comprises of all the districts of Arunachal Pradesh, Manipur, Nagaland, Orissa, and West Bengal.
7. The indicators under each explanatory factor are grouped together and the maps pertaining to each group are placed together. For instance, all the maps pertaining to kinship structures are placed together, while the ones showing development indicators follow in a group and so on.

4

The Social Status of Women

Despite concerted efforts to improve the position of women in the Indian society, the overall social status of women continues to be low. There are inequitable gaps between men and women in nutrition and health care, in literacy and education, in life expectancy and in most other aspects of their lives, indicating a low cultural evaluation of women in the Indian setting. As observed in the extant literature, low level of literacy among women is often seen as an indicator of the humble social status assigned to women (Sopher, 1980; Bradley and Khor, 1993; Cipolla, 1969). Based on the review of the literature and on the results of Principal Component Analysis in a previous chapter (see Chapter 2), literacy is taken as a surrogate measure of the broader social condition of women in India.

Increasing literacy levels has often been regarded as a prerequisite for social and economic development in India (Schuth, 1980). Literacy is considered both as an agent of socioeconomic progress and as a reflection of the social, cultural and economic system (Government of India, Education Commission Report, 1966; Raza, 1990; Freebody and Welch,

1993). For instance, studies have shown that many development processes are feasible only when the population achieves a relatively high level of literacy (Schuth, 1980). And by the same token, higher development levels lead to higher literacy levels. The former view, of literacy being the agent of development and social change, has promoted the idea that literacy alone can solve the technological, social and economic problems of the country. The literacy/human capital rationale has led planners, policy-makers and educators to focus their attention and resources on achieving universal literacy.

The other view, that literacy is a reflection of the social, cultural and economic system of a country, has also received considerable attention, and it is with this view that this chapter is primarily concerned. In order to understand the reasons for low overall literacy levels of females as well as wide regional variations in female literacy rates, it is important to recognize that "women are situated in an unequal social structure with their identities circumscribed by categories such as class and caste" (Poonacha, 1993: 2192). Due to the social and economic problems women face, their options often remain limited. Hence, it is illusory to talk of affiliation of literacy with a range of social and economic effects independent of the materiality of women's lives (Freebody and Welch, 1993).

This chapter explores the economic, cultural, and social circumstances in which women are situated and how these circumstances condition their prospects of being literate or illiterate. In other words, what are the social processes and factors that influence female literacy in India? Do kinship structures affect women differently in different parts of India? Are these structures related to regional variations in levels of development? What are the effects of these factors, individual and combined, on female literacy rates? This chapter deals with these questions and tries to explain the combined effects of kinship structures, economic development, agricultural activity, social stratification, and religion on patterns of female literacy rates in India.

Background

India's progress towards its goal of achieving mass literacy can be characterized as far from satisfactory. The crude literacy rate in

1981 was only 36 per cent, and nearly half of the males and three-fourth of the females were illiterates (Registrar General of India, 1981). The huge difference between the male and female literacy levels is often attributed to difference in the cultural evaluation of females versus that of males in India.

A number of scholars (Sharma and Rutherford, 1987; Howes, 1992) have attempted to study the origins and patterns of regional variations in overall literacy levels in India on a macro scale using the state as a unit of analysis. Others (Gosal, 1964; Raza, 1990; Gustafsson, 1991) have examined the relationships between overall literacy and urbanization, agricultural prosperity, economic development, caste, and religion on a micro scale using district as the unit of analysis. But these studies did not specifically focus on female literacy as a component of overall literacy. Krishan and Shyam (1974) described the pattern of urban literacy in India, but again the focus of the study was not on female literacy.

Numerous other studies have attempted to describe the deplorable state of female literacy in India (Kurrien, 1990; Bennet, 1992; UNESCO, 1984, 1986, 1987; Krishan and Shyam, 1973). But these studies usually have been undertaken on an all-India level and have done little to identify the regional variations in literacy rates. Sharma and Rutherford (1990) explored the links between female literacy and fertility levels in India. A study by Patel (1984) focused only on literacy among tribal women in Gujarat. Sopher (1980) examined regional variations in overall literacy on a micro scale (district level) but his study was focused on measuring and explaining the sex-disparity in literacy. He proposed an index to measure the male/female disparity in literacy and then mapped the results to reveal the regional variations. Sopher was not very convinced that variations in literacy in India can be completely explained by the "level of economic development" (p. 141) and thus pointed towards cultural factors as a possible residual explanation. But he did not attempt to quantify the observed cultural patterns, rather he just mapped the residuals from regression equation offering that as an explanation of the effect of 'non-developmental' factors on literacy (Sopher, 1980: 143).

Most of the studies mentioned above have some gaps that the present chapter attempts to fill. For instance, the studies undertaken on an all-India level are too aggregated, while the ones focused on a sub-region of only one state are too specific with conclusions which cannot be applied to the whole of India. The present chapter is based on a district-level analysis for the whole of India. Moreover, as mentioned before, I will be including both economic and non-economic factors in an attempt to identify and explain the regional variations in female literacy in India.

Data and Methodology

The attempt here is to explore the relationships between certain economic and non-economic factors and female literacy. In other words, how much variation in female literacy can be accounted for by patriarchal kinship structures, levels of development, agricultural practices, demographic characteristics, or religion, caste and class differentiation? It is pertinent to mention here that there exists a problem of circularity, because most of these indicators themselves are influenced by levels of literacy to some extent. For instance, fertility levels or the indicators of economic development are greatly affected by literacy levels, especially female literacy (Sopher, 1980). Nevertheless, measures of each of the hypothesized explanatory variables have been identified. The chapter uses district as the unit of analysis and is based primarily on the 1981 census data obtained from the IDDD.

The *female literacy rate* (FLIT) is measured as the share of female literates out of the female population above the age of 5 years. The Census of India defines a literate as an individual who can read and write with understanding in any of the languages in India.

$$\text{FLIT} = \frac{\text{Female Literates}}{\text{Female Population (over 5 year of age)}} \times 100$$

Patriarchal Kinship Organization: Total Fertility Rate (TFR), Juvenile Sex Ratio (SR09), females married under the age of 20 years (MAR19F), Patrilocal Exogamy (MIGR), and female labor force participation rate (FLFPR)[1] are included as the indicators of kinship structure. High fertility levels and early marriage, which tend to be regarded as characteristic of those regions where patriarchal control over women is strong, are expected to be associated with lower literacy levels. In most cases migration of women outside their village after marriage, patrilocal exogamy, is expected to terminate their schooling. Hence, literacy levels are expected to be lower in regions where patrilocal exogamy is practiced. Female labor force participation rate is expected to be positively correlated with literacy levels. Participation in wage labor is expected to increase a woman's economic worth and make it possible for her to assert her views and choices in the family. This should positively affect the education of girl children in the family. But in the Indian context this may not always be the case. As discussed previously (see Chapter 3), increased literacy does not always translate into higher labor force participation for women and vice versa. Thus, literacy levels may not be positively influenced by larger proportions of women in the workforce.

$$\text{Juvenile Sex Ratio} = \frac{\text{Females (age group 0–9)}}{\text{Males (age group 0–9)}} \times 1000$$

Finally, the imbalance in the sex ratio of children in the age group of 0–9 years is considered to be an indicator of gender discrimination in Indian society. From an early age daughters are discriminated against, which affects their access to resources and in turn their chances of survival (Kishor, 1993; Malhotra et al., 1995). This discrimination manifests itself in the preference given to educating a son versus a daughter in the family, as investing in the education of a son is perceived to be economically beneficial for the family. Also, as the extant literature shows (Gosal, 1964; Krishan and Shyam, 1973; Sopher, 1980; Malhotra et al., 1995), education among women is discouraged as it threatens to break down the patriarchal control of male members over women. Their contact with the outside world in the form of education and, subsequently, employment allows social mobility for women and may make them 'unsuitable' for the exclusively domestic role propounded as the 'ideal' for women in the Indian social system. Hence, it is expected that in the regions where gender discrimination is prevalent, literacy levels are likely to be low.

Social Stratification: Several studies have shown a strong positive correlation between the social class and educational attainment of individuals (Patel, 1984; Sopher, 1980). Studies point out that scheduled caste (SC) and scheduled tribe (ST) populations in India are situated at the bottom of the social hierarchy and are thus not only disadvantaged economically but also have been deliberately excluded from the possibility of getting education (Sopher, 1980: 168). Thus, the SC and ST females face additional constraints over and above the general prejudice against educating females in India. Their literacy levels are expected to be low, affecting the overall female literacy negatively. Similarly, the presence of Muslim population, with their tendency to seclude women from public domains and to maintain strict patriarchal controls over women, are expected to depress Muslim women's literacy levels. These three proportion of SC, ST, and Muslim populations are included as indicators of social differentiation in India.

Economic Development: The level of economic development is likely to have a considerable bearing on the literacy levels, just as literacy tends to play an important role in economic development of a region (Raza, 1990; Sopher, 1980). Many studies have used the levels of economic development as an indicator to explain variations in literacy levels on a national scale (Golden, 1955). Other studies, however, point to a more complex relationship between the two (Sopher, 1980; Galtung, 1972; Cameron, 1975). In this chapter economic development is measured by per cent males in non-agricultural sector, levels of urbanization, agricultural productivity, and male literacy.

Agricultural Practices: Area under rice cultivation is taken as an indicator of agricultural practices in India. Literacy levels are expected to be higher in areas where wet-rice cultivation is practiced due to its positive impact on female labor force participation (Malhotra et al., 1995; Bardhan, 1974; Moore, 1973). But the findings in the previous chapter (see Chapter 3) suggest that the often hypothesized relationship between rice-cultivation and female labor force participation may not be a straight-forward one. The reason for including area under rice as a variable is not only to test the relationship between female labor force participation and literacy, that is already being done (FLFPR is an independent variable), but because varying land use patterns by themselves may also have a differential effect on female literacy. For instance, it is possible that regions with similar levels of female labor force participation may have different levels of female literacy because of the differences in the land-use practices.

Regional Variables: As mentioned in the previous chapter, dummy variables are used to estimate differences between regions and to evaluate whether region moderates the effects of other explanatory variables. The three dummy variables are North, South, and East.

Findings

The mean values (Table 4.1) reveal the following pattern: female literacy is the highest in the South, followed by the East, and lowest in North India. Unlike in the previous chapter where the economic participation rate of women in the North and East was nearly the same, in the case of female literacy there is considerable difference between the East and North (over 8%). This difference is generally explained in terms of the prolonged impact of Christian missionaries among the tribal groups of the East (Sopher, 1980; Gosal, 1964).

Table 4.1

Average Female Literacy by Regions: 1981

Region	*Average Female Literacy (in per cent)*
East	28.81
North	20.47
South	37.31

A preliminary look at the female literacy map (Map 9) confirms the above findings. The map when compared to some literacy maps pertaining to earlier periods (see Sopher, 1980) reveals that though the female literacy levels have increased appreciably over time the geographical pattern remains much the same as what it was about 50 years ago (Gosal, 1964; Krishan and Shyam, 1973; Sopher, 1980). This indicates that regions that had an initial advantage in terms of educational attainment continue to show higher levels of female literacy. Generally speaking, the coastal areas exhibit higher female literacy compared to the inland regions of India, with the state of Kerala in the South and Mizoram in the North East exhibiting the highest female literacy levels. Pockets of high female literacy are also found around the large metropolitan areas of Bombay, Madras, Calcutta, and Delhi.

On the other hand, majority of the districts in the states of Uttar Pradesh, Madhya Pradesh, Bihar, Rajasthan and Orissa have low levels of female literacy. A detailed district-wise analysis is presented later.

In order to understand the reasons behind the regional variations in female literacy I begin by analyzing the zero-order correlation coefficients and the scatter plots (Table 4.2) for the female literacy and the various explanatory variables. The correlations indicate some interesting relationships: female literacy (FLIT) shows a strong negative relationship with all of the kinship indicators except juvenile sex ratio (JSR) which shows the expected positive relationship. Total fertility rate (TFR), early marriage (MAR19F), and patrilocal exogamy (MIGR) have a very strong negative relationship with female literacy, whereas, the relationship with female labor force participation rate (FLFPR), though significant at 0.05 level, is slightly weaker than the three mentioned above. This is probably due to the fact that female literacy does not always translate into higher participation of females in the workforce due to the existing economic structure in India. The only indicator of kinship patterns showing a positive relationship with female literacy (FLIT) is juvenile sex ratio (SR09), but the correlation is weak and insignificant ($r = 0.0427$).

Female literacy also exhibits a negative relationship to all the indicators of social stratification, though the correlations with scheduled tribe (STP) and Muslim population (MUSL) are not statistically significant. A look at the scatter diagrams indicates (Figures 4.1 and 4.2) that the outlying districts are probably influencing the relationship making the correlations insignificant. All the indicators of development show a strong, positive, significant relationship with female literacy, indicating that regions with higher proportions of males in the non-agricultural sector (MNAG), high levels of urbanization (URBZ), high agricultural productivity (PROD), and high male literacy (MLIT) are expected to have high female literacy. Finally, the agricultural practice of wet-rice cultivation (RICE) seems to have a positive impact on female literacy, though it is not clear at this stage whether this effect is due to the increased economic status of women in statistically those regions, or because of the distinct land-use practice in the rice-growing regions of India.

Table 4.2

Bivariate Correlations (All India)

	FLIT	TFR	SR09	MAR19F	MIGR	FLFPR	SCP	STP	MUSL	MNAG	URBZ	PROD	MLIT	RICE	NORTH	SOUTH
FLIT	1															
TFR	–0.6314**	1														
SR09	0.0427	–0.4159**	1													
MAR19F	–0.6156**	0.5190**	–0.1410**	1												
MIGR	–0.4181	0.3397**	–0.4104**	0.4659**	1											
FLFPR	–0.1203*	–0.2372	0.5866**	–0.0649	–0.4190**	1										
SCP	–0.1823**	0.1849**	–0.3272**	0.3117**	0.2620**	–0.4177**	1									
STP	–0.0868	–0.0072	0.4095**	–0.0863	0.2668**	0.4442**	–0.4479**	1								
MUSL	–0.0851	0.1281*	–0.0151	–0.1665**	0.0214	–0.1	–0.2666**	–0.1505**	1							
MNAG	0.6655**	–0.3360**	–0.0745	–0.4490**	–0.4745**	–0.0705	–0.1836**	–0.0688	0.0247	1						
URBZ	0.5240**	–0.0775	–0.1592**	–0.2574**	–0.3184**	–0.2600**	–0.083	–0.1484**	0.0322	0.8505**	1					
PROD	0.2796**	–0.1019	–0.4368**	–0.2746**	–0.0432	–0.4510**	0.2753**	–0.2543**	–0.0889	0.1859**	0.1563**	1				
MLIT	0.9115**	–0.5871**	–0.0004	–0.5148**	–0.3772**	–0.0621	–0.1414**	–0.1544**	–0.1612**	0.6152**	0.4720**	0.1712**	1			
RICE	0.1325*	–0.3629**	0.3690**	–0.1879**	–0.0504	–0.0582	–0.0858	0.1330*	0.1104*	–0.004	–0.0767	–0.0536	0.0622	1		
NORTH	–0.4457	0.6030**	–0.4765**	0.3628**	0.3886**	–0.2461**	0.2098**	–0.075	0.0502	–0.2317**	–0.1376**	0.0868	–0.3913**	–0.3366**	1	
SOUTH	0.4427	–0.5495**	0.3391**	–0.2562**	–0.3102	0.3080**	–0.2445**	–0.0943	–0.0372	.2524**	0.1843**	–0.0674	0.4013**	0.0403	–0.7982**	1

–Significance Level 0.05, ** –Significance Level 0.01 (2-tailed)

Figure 4.1
Female Literacy and Scheduled Tribe Population

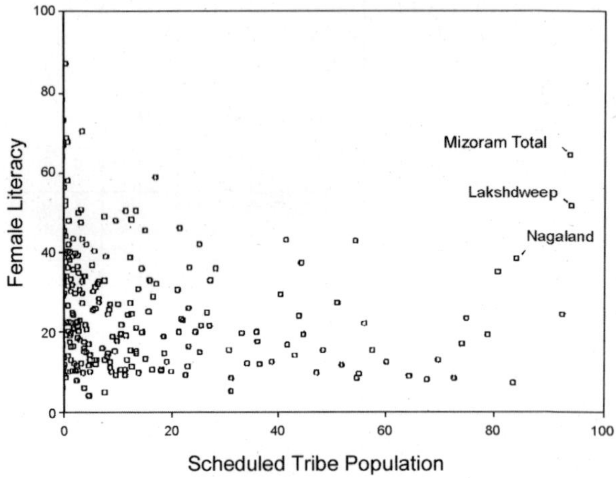

Source: 1981 Indian Development District Database (IDDD).

Figure 4.2
Female Literacy and Muslim Population

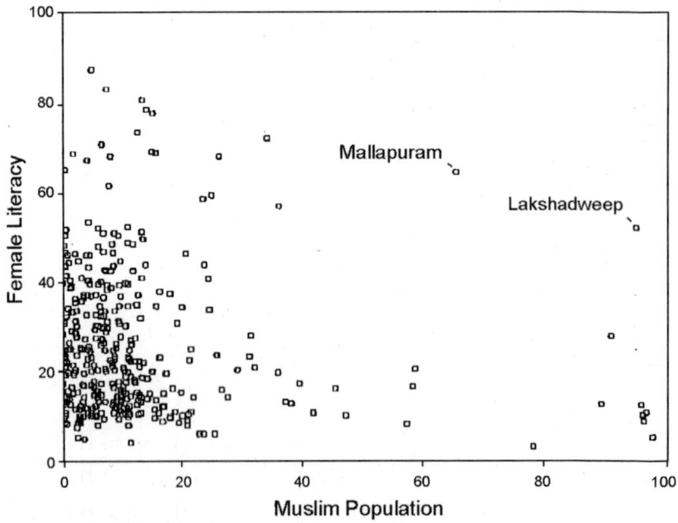

Source: 1981 Indian Development District Database (IDDD).

After explicating the initial relationships among the variables, I proceed to explain female literacy rate by regions, and by separate examinations of the individual variables. Table 4.3 shows the results of the least squares regression estimation technique. The first row expresses female literacy (FLIT) as a linear function of the region variables, North, South, and East. The R^2 indicates that regional differences explain about 22 per cent of the district level variation in female literacy. This shows that region is a very important explanatory variable and a predictor of female literacy. The value of the constant, 28.81, reports expected female literacy for the reference group, the Eastern region, with the North being lower than the East (b-coefficient for North = –8.34) and South being considerably higher than both the East and the North (b-coefficient = +8.50). These predicted values are the same as the subgroup means reported in Table 4.1. Among the other explanatory variables, the inclusion of the regional variables increases the predictive power of the model by explaining a larger proportion of the variance in female literacy (R^2 increases in all instances). Hence, it can be concluded that regional differentiation is an important variable.

A separate examination of the individual explanatory variables (see Table 4.3) indicates that levels of economic development have the largest impact on female literacy ($R^2 = 0.876$), followed by Kinship Structures ($R^2 = 0.678$), and Social Differentiation ($R^2 = 0.266$). Agricultural practices and Regional classification follow closely behind ($R^2 < 0.23$).

Next, I explore the collective impact of these explanatory variables on female literacy. The regression analysis is used here as a device for exploring the relationships between the variables, rather than as a tool for building predictive models. Hence, all the variables enter the equation at once and the full model is then interpreted. In order to see the impact of these explanatory variables on female literacy different combinations of the explanatory variables were considered, and finally four models were selected. Region is controlled for in all the models (Table 4.4).

Table 4.3

Regression Coefficients for the Effects of Each Explanatory Variable on Female Literacy in India: 1981

Indicator	*Constant*	*b-Coeff.*	R^2	R^2 *before regions were included*
Case I				
Region	28.813		0.219	
North		–8.344***		
South		+8.500**		
East		—		
Case II				
Agricultural Practices	26.804		0.221	0.017
Area under Rice		0.033		
North		–6.969*		
South		+9.616**		
Case III				
Patriarchy/Kinship	139.54		0.678	0.648
Total Fertility Rate		–8.97***		
Juvenile Sex Ratio		–0.05***		
Marriage under 19		–0.29***		
Female Migration		–2.25***		
Female labor force participation		–0.40***		
North		2.98		
South		9.40***		
Case IV				
Social Differentiation	43.38		0.266	0.112
Scheduled Castes		–0.489***		
Scheduled Tribes		–0.205***		
Muslims		–0.162**		
North		–10.915***		
South		3.195***		
Case V				
Development	–23.60		0.876	0.861
Agricultural Product		0.003***		
Urbanization levels		0.012		
Male Literacy		0.855***		
Male Non-agricultural workers		0.275***		
North		–3.629***		
South		1.003		

*$p<0.05$, **$p<0.01$, ***$p<0.001$.

Table 4.4

Regression Coefficients for the Effects of Explanatory Variables on Female Literacy in India: 1981

	Models with Male literacy				Model without Mlit
Indicator	*Model 1*	*Model 2*	*Model 3*	*Model 4*	*Model 4a*
Constant	–23.875	143.905	–12.683	–12.375	101.93
Region					
North	1.514	2.841	2.269*	2.399*	1.573
South	4.046***	8.767***	5.383***	5.522***	6.580**
East	—	—	—	—	—
Patriarchy/Kinship					
Total Fertility Rate	–2.028***	–8.436***	–2.492***	–2.436***	–7.922***
Juvenile Sex Ratio	0.024*	–0.056***	–0.013	0.012	–0.028
Marriage under 19	–0.135***	–0.282***	–0.098***	–0.099***	–0.270***
Female Migration	–0.758***	–2.253***	–0.763***	–0.768***	–1.157***
Female labor force	–0.214***	–0.496***	–0.262***	–0.259***	–0.422***
Development					
Male Non-agricultural	0.137	—	0.103	0.102	0.459***
Agricultural Product	0.001*	—	0.001	0.001**	–0.001
Urbanization levels	0.024	—	0.029	0.030	0.053
Male Literacy	0.757***	—	0.774***	0.775***	—
Social Differentiation					
Scheduled Castes	—	–0.363***	–0.048	–0.047	–0.223*
Scheduled Tribes	—	–0.018	0.088***	0.087***	0.003
Muslims	—	–0.151***	0.020	0.019	–0.134***
Agricultural Practices					
Area under Rice	—	—	—	0.004	–0.027
R^2	0.905	0.706	0.912	0.912	0.755

*p<0.05, **p<0.01, ***p<0.001.

Model 1 combines the variables of kinship structure and development. Approximately 91 per cent of the variability in female literacy has been accounted for. But these results have to be interpreted with caution as some of the independent variables are collinear. This also is the reason for some of the variables being statistically insignificant despite the high overall multiple correlation. For instance, juvenile sex ratio (SR09) is barely significant at 0.05 level. This is due to the fact that juvenile sex ratio is closely associated with the 'region' variables, and from a statistical sense these variables are essentially doing the same thing, i.e., virtually all the variance in female literacy accounted for by 'region' variables is shared with juvenile sex ratio and there is very little of female literacy accounted for by sex ratio alone. Similarly, proportion of male workers in the non-agricultural sector (MNAG) and urbanization (URBZ) are not statistically significant, and agricultural productivity (PROD) is barely so. This is due to the fact that these variables are very closely associated with male literacy (MLIT), and MLIT is summarizing the effects of other variables on female literacy. Despite the collinearity among these variables, all these are included in the equation as the purpose here is to explore the relationships between them.

All the kinship variables, except juvenile sex ratio, have a negative association with female literacy, indicating that regions with strong patriarchal control over women will have lower female literacy levels. As expected juvenile sex ratio has a positive relationship with female literacy. In other words, regions where the juvenile sex ratio is more balanced are the regions where females are valued more, thus their access to resources like education increases, affecting the literacy levels positively. All the economic development indicators have a positive impact on female literacy. Unlike the 'Region' case (Table 4.3, Case I), where literacy levels in the North were about 8 per cent lower than the East, here the parameter for North (b = 1.514) shows that with patriarchal values and development levels held constant, the predicted female literacy in the North is higher than the East. The negative value of the Constant (–23.87) is not directly interpretable, since a negative percentage of female literacy is not possible. It does indicate, however, that female literacy is absent from the whole of India until the male literacy reaches a certain level. This is evident from the scatterplot (Figure 4.3) where female literacy emerges only after 20 per cent of the males are literate. Furthermore, the comparison between Model 1 and the individual Case III (see Table 4.3) shows that when economic development variables are controlled the coefficients for kinship variables reduce substantially in size, but continue to be significant. This is due to the fact that fertility rate (TFR), early marriage (MAR19F), and patrilocal exogamy (MIGR) are strongly related to male literacy and so male literacy is summarizing the effects of these variables on female literacy.

Figure 4.3
Male and Female Literacy

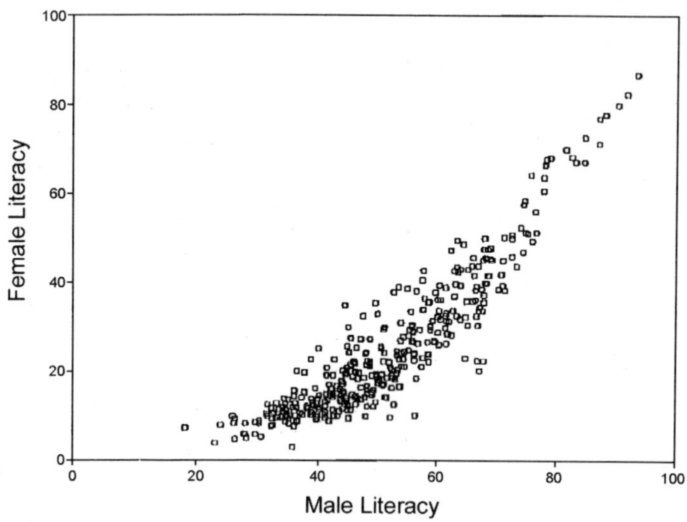

Source: 1981 Indian Development District Database (IDDD).

Model 2 includes variables for kinship structures and social stratification. This model accounts for 70 per cent of the variability in female literacy, thus indicating that development factors have a greater impact on female literacy than the social stratification factors (R^2 of 0.90 in Model 1 versus 0.70 in Model 2). All the variables of patriarchy continue to have more or less the same b-coefficients as in case III (Table 4.3), indicating that social stratification variables do not have much impact on patriarchal structures. The scheduled caste, scheduled tribe, and Muslim population has a dampening effect on female literacy. But scheduled tribe coefficient is not statistically significant. North and South continue to have higher female literacy than the East.

Model 3 combines the variables of development, social stratification, and kinship structures. The R^2 increases appreciably (0.91) but many of the indicators lose their significance. As explained before, this probably is due to multicollinearity. The final model (Model 4) includes area under rice cultivation in addition to all the variables mentioned before. This is done to see whether agricultural practices, in combination with other factors, lead to a better explanation of female literacy. The R^2 does not change significantly with the inclusion of area under rice, but since this model contains all the relevant variables it will be considered the final model for explaining female literacy rates.

Before the results of this model can be accepted as reliable and valid, a test for hetroscadasticity and multicollinearity is conducted. The hetroscadasticity test (Figure 4.4) indicates that

Figure 4.4

Test of Hetroscadasticity—Dependent Variable: Female Literacy

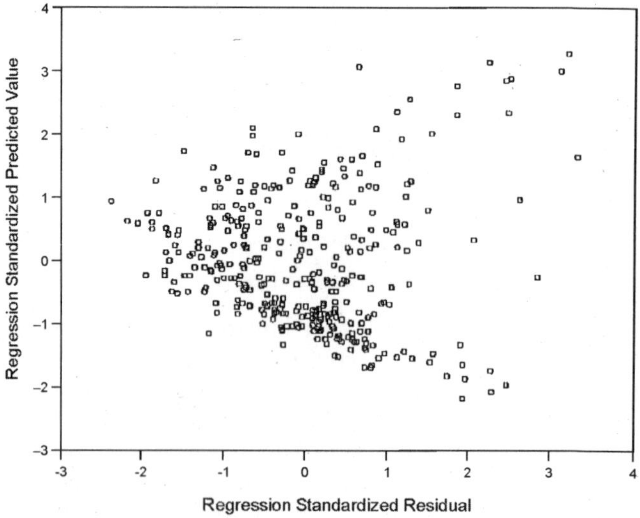

Source: 1981 Indian Development District Database (IDDD).

the spread of the residuals increases with the magnitude of the predicted values suggesting that the equality-of-variance assumption is violated. As mentioned before, the transformation of the data could solve this problem, but since this can give rise to interpretative problems, the results are accepted as they are. Finally the test for collinearity among the independent variables indicates high Variance Inflation Factors (VIF) for male non-agricultural workers and urbanization, and North and South. These high VIFs are expected as there is a strong relationship between the males employed in non-agricultural sector and urbanization levels on the one hand ($r = 0.85$), and the regional variables on the other ($r = -0.79$). Moreover, the decomposition of the variance proportions shows that the very same variables are associated with the same eigenvalues, which is evidence of near-dependency.

In this table (see Table 4.5) male non-agricultural workers (MNAG), urbanization (URBZ), and male literacy (MLIT) all have high proportions associated with the same eigenvalue. This indicates that these three variables are highly interdependent. Similarly, juvenile sex ratio and the East (constant) are the other two variables with high proportions for the same eigenvalue. Hence, it can be said that some problem of multicollinearity does exist. However, as the intent here is to explore the relationships between the variables all the variables are retained in the equation.

The final model (Table 4.4, Model 4) explains about 91 per cent of the district level variation in female literacy. As expected many variables in the models have regression parameter estimates that are not significantly different from zero. For instance, juvenile sex ratio (SR09) is not significant in the model because it is closely associated with the North, South, and East variables, and the regional variables have already accounted for the variance. This is evident when SR09 is regressed on the region variables (not shown): the region variables explain 23 per cent of the variance in SR09. Similarly, male non-agricultural workers and urbanization are insignificant as male literacy (MLIT) continues to summarize the effects of other variables on female literacy. A regression of female literacy on male literacy shows that male literacy explains nearly 84 per cent of the variation in

Table 4.5

Colllinearity Diagnostics

No.	Eigen value	Cond Index	Const	TFR	SR09	MAR19 F	MIGR	FLFPR	MNAG	URBZ	PROD	MLIT	SCP	STP	MUSL	RICE	NORTH	SOUTH
1.	10.903	1	0	7E-05	0	0.00068	0.00082	0.00008 4	0.0002	0.00037	0.00101	0.00018	0.00066	0.0007	0.00124	0.00119	0.00044	0.00037
2.	1.3223	2.872	0	6E-05	0	0.00393	0.01714	0.00289	0.00075	0.00158	0.00055	0.00023	0.00241	0.01185	0.00019	0.00394	0.01244	0.04569
3.	1.0104	3.285	0	2E-05	0	0.00097	0.00025	0.00697	0.00057	0.00429	0.01166	0.00012	0.00181	0.22362	0.00866	0.00261	0.00086	0.00956
4.	0.7123	3.912	0	0	0	0.00271	0	8E-05	7E-05	0.00042	0.00878	0.00018	0.00669	0	0.45456	0.02632	1E-05	0.00252
5.	0.6193	4.196	0	0	0	0.01574	0.04315	0.00378	0.00499	0.02266	0.02529	0.00010	0.00171	0.03072	0.00047	0.00784	0.00513	0.04924
6.	0.4960	4.688	0	0.00017	0	0.00573	0.00132	0.01287	0.00018	0.00193	0.03164	2E-05	0.00322	0.0007	0.03770	0.34115	0.00628	0.00939
7.	0.3110	5.921	0	0	0	0.01749	0.00741	0.00546	0.00408	0.05205	0.30014	1E-05	0.00086	0.0128	0.03884	0.05316	0.00029	0.01058
8.	0.2365	6.789	0	1E-05	1E-05	0.00106	0.26749	0.071136	1E-05	0.01005	0.02043	4E-05	0.03209	0.23386	0.00272	0.4292	0.00639	0.03286
9.	0.1441	8.696	0	0.00062	1E-05	0.19494	0.14053	0.06771	0.00465	0.00598	0.00714	0.01182	0.12620	0.12787	0.10327	0.0.1053	0.0477	0.00254
10.	0.0964	10.631	2E-05	4E-05	3E-05	0.30176	0.04161	0.00302	0.0006	0.00429	0.17810	0.00993	0.42057	0.07212	0.002520	0.11478	0.04664	0.02122
11.	0.0507	14.657	2E-05	0.00063	2E-05	0.03168	0.22999	0.37685	0.013	0.02829	0.17579	0.01927	0.00252	0.05029	0.01337	0.03883	0.57998	0.50442
12.	0.0439	15.756	0.00027	0.00275	0.00036	0.14887	0.07278	0.12522	0.00651	0.1395	0.00558	0.21374	0.18715	0.02554	2E-05	0.10706	0.2095	0.20765
13.	0.0304	18.935	0.00054	0.09444	0.00091	0.19436	0.01855	0.0013	0.33061	0.21241	0.00031	0.00416	0.09348	0.11672	0.11037	0.00073	0.0508	0.02365
14.	0.0170	25.259	0.0006	0.11193	0.00057	0.07959	0.00274	0.13912	0.51168	0.42818	0.05321	0.34525	0.5251	0.05927	0.18702	0.00011	0.01397	0.1551
15.	0.0049	47.023	0.01557	0.53855	0.04714	0	0.0187	0.16962	0.02313	0.03645	0.02900	0.31405	0.06221	0.02474	0.01622	0.23028	0.00037	0.05713
16.	0.0002	214.131	0.98296	0.25072	0.95093	0.00049	0.13752	0.01329	0.09898	0.05156	0.15137	0.08089	0.00591	0.00918	0.00017	0.01854	0.01921	0.00766
VIF				3.704	3.124	2.320	2.508	3.301	6.821	5.742	2.006	2.864	2.060	2.112	1.624	1.806	4.577	4.511

the female literacy. Though the removal of male literacy from the model would make some of the variables significant, it is not advisable to exclude an important predictor variable from the equation.

With all the variables in the model, male literacy (MLIT) followed by female labor force participation (FLFPR) and 'Region' appear to be very powerful in explaining variance in female literacy. This is evident from the standardized regression estimates of these variables (Table 4.6): male literacy has the highest z-score value among all the variables, which means that a standard deviation change in the MLIT produces the largest z-score change in female literacy. This indicates that with increased development levels in India, female literacy is expected to improve, loosening the strong patriarchal hold over females. Female labor force participation is the second most important predictor of female literacy, but, as expected, the relationship is negative. Districts with higher female labor force participation

Table 4.6

Standardized Regression Coefficients: Model 4 (All India)

Variable	*Beta*
TFR	–0.123072
SR09	0.032039
MAR19F	–0.083444
MIGR	–0.105470
FLFPR	–0.217360
MNAG	0.052292
URBZ	0.030726
PROD	0.064232
MLIT	0.671792
SCP	–0.023147
STP	0.100409
MUSL	0.019719
Rice	0.007428
North	0.073195
South	0.155603

rate may not have high female literacy levels. The link between female labor force participation and female literacy has been explored in the previous chapter too.

Kinship structures continue to be important in determining female literacy levels. All the kinship variables, except juvenile sex ratio (JSR), show a negative relationship to female literacy, thus indicating that districts with higher total fertility rate (TFR), early marriage (MAR19F), and patrilocal exogamy (MIGR) will tend to have lower female literacy.

All the development indicators have a positive relationship with female literacy. Districts with larger proportion of males in non-agricultural sector (MNAG), higher urbanization levels (URBZ), greater agricultural productivity (PROD), and higher male literacy (MLIT) will tend to have higher female literacy.

The presence of scheduled castes (SCP) suppresses the female literacy, but the regression coefficient is not significant. The scheduled tribe (STP) and Muslim population (MUSL) show a positive relationship to female literacy. The work of Christian missionaries among the scheduled tribe populations in India has considerably affected their literacy levels. But the positive b-coefficient for the Muslim population needs some consideration. On comparing Model 4, that includes MLIT, with Model 4a, that is without MLIT, (see Table 4.4) it can be seen that when male literacy is not included in the equation both scheduled caste (SCP) and Muslim population (MUSL) show a negative impact on female literacy. The change in signs for the Muslim population after the inclusion of male literacy (MLIT) indicates that literacy in general is lower where there is concentration of Muslim population. However, when female literacy is compared to male literacy, which is essentially what is being done by including MLIT in the equation, then after controlling for differences in male literacy, female literacy rates are higher where Muslims are in larger proportions. This suggests that the overall literacy levels for Muslim population are low and the sex disparity in literacy is less among them as compared to the total population of India.

Area under rice has a positive impact on female literacy, but the relationship is not very strong. Female literacy is expected to be higher in regions where wet-rice cultivation is practiced mostly due to the increased labor force participation rate of women. But a comparison of the maps showing area under rice (Map 23), female labor force participation rate (Map 8), and female literacy (Map 9) show that this is not always the case. For instance, most districts on the Ganga delta in West Bengal have more than 75 per cent of their area devoted to rice but the female labor force participation rate is very low, and female literacy is reasonably high. The districts of West Godavari, East Godavari, and Krishna in Andhra Pradesh, Thanjavur in Tamil Nadu, and Uttar Kannada in Karnataka also fall into the same category. On the other hand, in all the districts of Arunachal Pradesh the area devoted to rice is high, female labor force participation is also high, but female literacy is extremely low. What factors other than female participation in workforce are influencing the relationship between the land-use practices and female literacy need to be investigated further.

Finally, when all the variables are controlled for, the regional effect remains strong, with North and South having higher literacy levels than the East. In order to assess whether FLIT is significantly different for the included categories of North and South, a *t*-test for the difference in their regression coefficients is performed. The result (*t* value of 3.822) is significant at 0.05 level, indicating that North and South are significantly different from each other in terms of their female literacy.

Geographical Patterns of Female Literacy

The relationships explored above become clearer when we look at the geographical pattern of female literacy (Map 9) and compare it to the pattern of these explanatory variables (see Maps). Starting from the extreme north, the state of Jammu & Kashmir has one of the lowest literacy levels. The only exceptions are the districts of Jammu and Udhampur to the northwest, where female literacy levels are above 15 per cent. The state is predominantly Muslim (Map 22), especially the Kashmir region, and this is probably depressing the female literacy level in these districts. The Jammu-Udhampur-Kathua region, on the other hand, is predominantly Hindu and has higher female literacy. The other reason for low literacy level in this state could be the low level of economic development. The maps pertaining to the development indicators show that this region is one of the least urbanized (except for the region around the city of Srinagar) (Map 16), has low agricultural productivity (Map 15), less than 25 per cent of male population in non-agricultural occupations (Map 18), and low male literacy levels (Map 19). The conspicuous factor to notice here is that the indicators that measure the kinship structure do not seem to have the expected relationship to female literacy in this region. This is evident from the fact that though most of these districts have low patrilocal exogamy (Map 12), lesser proportions of females who marry early (Map 11), higher female labor force participation (Map 8) and a juvenile sex ratio in favor of females (Map 14) (all the ingredients that should put these districts in the 'high female literacy' category), but the literacy levels are very low. This indicates that the region is culturally different from the Hindu-Brahminic culture prevalent in most of northern India, and it is not so much the patriarchal kinship structures but the presence of a distinct Muslim culture and the low level of economic development that are playing the biggest role in influencing female literacy in the state of Jammu and Kashmir.

The next distinct cluster of districts having low female literacy is present in the Terai region extending from Pilbhit in Uttar Pradesh to Purnia in Bihar and the adjoining plains' districts of Uttar Pradesh. These districts are characterized by strong patriarchal kinship structures evidenced in their low female labor force participation rate, low juvenile sex ratio, large proportion of females who marry early, high rate of female migration associated with marriage (patrilocal exogamy), and very high fertility rate. These factors, combined with low development levels, a sizeable proportion of scheduled castes in Lakhimpur, Hardoi, Unnao, Rai Bareli, Barabanki, and Sitapur, and Muslims in Moradabad, Bijnor, and Rampur, have arrested the growth of female literacy. The northern districts of Bihar are very similar to the Terai region of Uttar Pradesh, but a few districts south of river Ganga that are close to Patna and a few around the urban center of Ranchi are doing better. Though the Chotta Nagpur plateau is the resource-rich region of India with vast potential mineral reserves, the process of industrialization has been slow (Bose, 1994), dragging the literacy levels down for both males and females in the districts of Palamu, Hazaribagh, Giridih, Nawadah, and Dumka.

On the other hand, the hill districts in Kumaon region (districts of Chamoli, Tehri Garhwal, Pauri Garhwal, Almora) have a moderately high female literacy compared to the other districts in Uttar Pradesh. These districts have traditionally had high male literacy (Sopher, 1980), probably due to the practice of males entering the military services in large numbers (Gosal, 1964) which seems to have positively influenced the female literacy in the region. These districts are not economically very well developed, with low agricultural productivity and urbanization levels, but the juvenile sex ratio indicates that gender discrimination is not so prevalent in the region. As mentioned before (see Chapter 3) these hill districts have a kinship pattern that is different from the plains' districts in Uttar Pradesh. Higher proportions of females are engaged in productive work, with some of these districts having almost 25 per cent of their agricultural land devoted to rice. Moreover, patrilocal exogamy is less, and the fertility rate and incidence of early marriage are less in comparison to the Terai region discussed above and the plains' districts in Uttar Pradesh. This indicates that it is the favorable kinship structure which probably affects the female literacy levels positively in this part of the country.

The plains of Uttar Pradesh extending between the rivers Ganga and Yamuna (districts of Saharanpur, Muzaffarnagar, Meerut, Agra, Kanpur, and Lucknow) have moderate levels of female literacy. The proximity of these districts to Delhi metropolitan area and the pockets of urbanization created by the large cities of Kanpur and Lucknow seem to have a positive influence on the female literacy rate. But a strong patriarchal control over women, evident from low juvenile sex ratios, low proportions of females in the workforce, high rates of female migration associated with marriage, and very high fertility levels, keeps the female literacy levels to below 35 per cent. Surprisingly despite sizeable Muslim populations, Meerut and Lucknow have reasonable rates of female literacy. Here probably the economic development plays a greater role in influencing literacy levels than the social stratification.

Another problem area in central India is in the Bundelkhand region on the Uttar Pradesh-Madhya Pradesh border. Female literacy levels are very low in districts such as Lalitpur, Hamirpur,

Banda, Fatehpur, and Mirzapur in Uttar Pradesh, and Shivpuri and Tikamgarh in Madhya Pradesh. This region was described as having a moderately high agricultural efficiency in a quantitative study of agricultural regionalization in India in 1968 (Sengupta, 1968), but over the years water scarcity has made this land unproductive and with the absence of any industrial development the region has turned into one of the least developed regions in India. This is also evident from the maps (10–14) indicating low agricultural productivity, fewer males in non-agricultural sector, and less urbanization. This region recently has been witnessing a spate of poverty-driven suicides by the villagers in these districts (Mishra, 1998). With no jobs in the region rural migration rates are as high as nearly 40 per cent against the national average of 11 per cent (Mishra, 1998: 28), and the efforts made by the state governments to revive the region have been half-hearted and so unsuccessful. In such circumstances it is impossible to expect any social development in the region.

Another cluster of districts having low literacy levels is located in the western half of Madhya Pradesh on the Malwa Plateau, and the region along the eastern side of the Aravalli range in Rajasthan. The districts stretching from Guna to West Nimar on the Madhya Pradesh-Rajasthan border and along the Aravalli hills from Alwar to Dungarpur and Banswara bordering Gujarat, all have very low female literacy. Dungarpur, Banswara, and Jhabua also have a very large scheduled tribe population (>60%) that is non-Christian. High incidence of early marriage and patrilocal exogamy and high fertility in the region indicate that the tribal population has completely assimilated into the Hindu-Brahminical culture. This coupled with the industrial backwardness (Sengupta, 1968) and low development levels have led to very low female literacy rates in the region. But as Bose (1994) pointed out there is a possibility of developing this region industrially, especially by exploiting the vast reserves of metallic and non-metallic minerals, and diverting the rural populations to the industrial and urban nuclei. This could then positively impact the literacy levels in the region. Closely associated with this low literacy area are the districts along the western side of Aravallis in the Great Indian Desert (Thar Desert). Here too the problem of economic underdevelopment and a kinship system that lowers the cultural worth of women lead to very low literacy levels for females. Unlike the districts east of Aravalli range these districts extending from Jaisalmer to Churu have a weak natural resource base (Sengupta, 1968) which makes the task of social development harder but much more important.

A distinct cluster of low-female-literacy-districts also appears on the Madhya Pradesh-Andhra Pradesh-Orissa border. A combination of factors are operating in the region leading to low female literacy in these eight districts in northern Andhra Pradesh (Adilabad, Karimnagar, Nizamabad, Medak, Mahbubnagar, Nalgonda, Srikakulam, and Vizianagaram), one in southern Madhya Pradesh (Bastar), and four in southern Orissa (Koraput, Kalahandi, Balangir, and Phulbani). Some of these districts, such as Bastar, Koraput and Phulbani, have a sizeable scheduled tribe population who are non-Christians which is probably depressing the literacy levels not only for females but also for males. The reason for overall low levels of literacy in these tribal districts is the lack of economic development in the region. Though a large proportion of agricultural land is devoted to rice, oilseeds, and millet (Sengupta, 1968), the agricultural productivity, as shown in the map, is very low. With no industries in the region there is no incentive for the population to acquire education. On the other hand, the kinship structure here is different from the North, which is evident in the very high juvenile sex ratio, very low patrilocal exogamy, and a fertility rate less than the Indian average of 4.9. Hence, it can be concluded that it is not the active discrimination against women, as in the Malwa Plateau, that is driving the female literacy down, but the lower levels of economic development. Thus, any efforts to develop this tribal region economically by attracting industries and other businesses and services will lead to a higher literacy level for both males and females. The other districts in the Telangana region of Andhra Pradesh have a sizeable proportion of scheduled caste population which probably is depressing both male and female literacy. Thus, as explained before, it is probably not so much the discrimination against women but the lack of development that is playing a big role in keeping the literacy levels low in the region.

Starting from Rajkot-Amreli in Gujarat down the western coast to Kanniyakumari in Tamil Nadu all the coastal districts have very high female literacy. As the literature indicates (Gosal, 1964; Sopher, 1980), this is probably due to a headstart in education by these districts as a result of the early contact with Britishers and exposure to western ideas. Kerala, Mizoram and Punjab stand out as the three states having very high female literacy in nearly all their districts. The matrilineal society of Kerala and the strong Christian influence are cited as the two most important factors for high level of female literacy in this part of India (Sopher, 1980; Rao, 1957). This is evident from the maps pertaining to the indicators of kinship structure. The juvenile sex ratio is quite high, whereas the rate of early marriage, patrilocal exogamy, and fertility levels are low. Though the indicators of development show that the state is not highly urbanized or industrialized (the proportion of males in non-agricultural workforce is mostly below 25%, except for the districts of Ernakulam and Kozikhode), and agricultural productivity too is moderate, the female literacy levels are the highest in the country. Also the state has a sizeable Muslim population in districts like Mallapuram (above 60% population is Muslim), and some scheduled castes in Idukki and Palghat districts, which according to conventional belief should have led to a lowered female literacy rate. But the fact that these districts too have an equally high female literacy indicates that the existence of the cultural/social institutions in Kerala that fostered female literacy even before the advent of Christianity (Sopher, 1980) have played a larger role in influencing literacy than either the developmental levels or the social stratification.

Another region that stands out because of very high female literacy rate is the Northeast. All the states, except Arunachal Pradesh and Manipur, exhibit high female literacy. As mentioned before, the kinship structures of this largely tribal region are significantly different from the rest of India. Females have more autonomy and a better social status in this region. Moreover, a large Christian presence has also influenced the literacy levels in these states. Most of the agricultural area is devoted to rice-cultivation and, as expected, female labor force participation is very high. Again, as in the case of Kerala, the region is not highly urbanized and industrialized, but female literacy levels seem to be influenced greatly by the cultural patterns of the region. The proportion of tribal population in Manipur is less compared to its neighboring states, indicating a large degree of intermixing with other cultural groups, especially Hindus, and that has probably led to the female literacy levels here lower than the surrounding states (Sopher, 1980). The reasons for low literacy levels in Arunachal Pradesh are not so clear. The state has a cultural pattern and development level almost similar to the neighboring states, but has the lowest male and female literacy levels in the region. Very low level of urbanization could be one reason but Tripura with a similar urbanization level has a much higher literacy level in the same region. Perhaps there are other factors which need to be investigated.

A cluster of districts having high female literacy also appear in the northern states of Punjab and the adjoining districts of Himachal Pradesh (Kangra, Una, Hamirpur). High level of development seems to influence the female literacy in the region, despite very strong patriarchal values evident in very low female labor force participation rate in the region, and low juvenile sex ratio. Very high agricultural productivity, high levels of urbanization, and a large proportion of males in the non-agricultural sector, have led to very high literacy levels for both males and females. Surprisingly the per cent of females who marry early is unexpectedly low in these districts, perhaps contributing to the higher female literacy levels. The probable explanation of this pattern is that educating a daughter could be a means of a rapid upward social mobility for the family (Sopher, 1980), as a marriage alliance with a family of higher status could enhance the status of the woman as well as her family.

Some other regions of high female literacy levels appear along the Nasik-Nagpur line in Maharashtra, the West Godavari and Guntur districts on the mouths of rivers Krishna and Godavari in Andhra Pradesh, Cuttak and Puri on the Mahanadi delta in Orissa, and the North and South 24 Parganas, Howrah, Hugli, and Barddhaman on the Ganga delta in West Bengal. Almost all these districts have been defined as being highly developed (Mitra, 1961) based on their ecology, agricultural infrastructure, workforce participation rates, potential of human resource, trade, manufacturing and infrastructure, and organized industry in the modern sector (Bose, 1994). The high levels of development in these regions have pushed the literacy rates up both for males and females. The cultural pattern too in most of these districts is conducive to growth of literacy among women. This is evident from the reasonably high juvenile sex ratios, fewer early marriages, and almost no patrilocal exogamy. But not many females are engaged in the workforce, except in the districts falling on the Nasik-Nagpur line. West Bengal and Orissa conform more to the northern cultural pattern where there is a strict segregation of women especially among the upper classes and hence not many women enter the workforce. Education of females is obviously not for the purposes of employment in these regions. A probable explanation for this could be the same as the one given for the northern state of Punjab, that female education is a means of gaining upward social mobility through marriage.

Urban-Rural Differentials

Though the foregoing analysis explained the impact of the social structures, institutions, and development levels on female literacy for the country as a whole, it is important to see whether similar relationships hold true for the urban and rural India. All the variables have been computed for the rural and urban areas separately, except for the Total Fertility Rate (TFR), Agricultural Productivity (PROD), and Area under Rice (RICE) for which separate data were not available. Rural India has an average female literacy of 19.85 per cent compared to 49.56 per cent in the urban areas. A look at Table 4.7 indicates that the 'rural correlations' are very similar to the All-India correlations (see Table 4.2). But the bivariate relationships for the urban female literacy and other variables is slightly different (Table 4.8). This is not surprising as the majority of India's population lives in rural areas and the statistics for the whole of India are expected to be very similar to the rural areas of the country.

A comparison between the zero-order correlations for the rural and urban areas (see Tables 4.7 and 4.8) shows a significant difference in the correlations between female literacy and female labor force participation rate, proportion of scheduled tribe population, and proportion of Muslim population in rural and urban areas. Female literacy has a weak negative relationship to females in the workforce in the rural areas, whereas, this

Table 4.7

Bivariate Correlations (Rural India)

	FLITR	TFR	SR09R	RMAR19F	RMIGR	RFLFPR	RSCP	RSTP	RMUSL	RMNAG	PROD	RMLIT	RICE	NORTH	SOUTH
FLITR	1														
TFR	–0.6810**	1													
SR09R	0.0963	–0.4250**	1												
RMAR19F	–0.6358**	0.5676**	–0.1734**	1											
RMIGR	–0.3404**	0.3652**	–0.4727**	0.4082**	1										
RFLFPR	–0.0369	–0.2483**	0.5744**	–0.0746	–0.5260**	1									
RSCP	–0.1471**	0.1721**	–0.3454**	0.2430**	0.2429**	–0.4747**	1								
RSTP	–0.0489	–0.0136	0.4039**	–0.1220*	–0.3024**	0.4223**	–0.4789**	1							
RMUSL	–0.0703	0.1017	0.0105	–0.0934	0.0093	–0.0977	–0.2312**	–0.1443**	1						
RMNAG	0.5610**	–0.4703**	0.0211	–0.4498**	–0.3971**	0.1474**	–0.1766**	0.0515	0.0786	1					
PROD	0.2887**	–0.1019	–0.4305**	–0.2971**	–0.0337	–0.4664**	0.3043**	–0.2610**	–0.0724	0.1549**	1				
RMLIT	0.8892**	–0.6100**	0.0093	–0.5256**	–0.2127**	–0.0108	–0.1022	–0.1415**	–0.1457**	0.5300**	0.1875**	1			
RICE	0.1815**	–0.3629**	0.3996**	–0.2175**	–0.0553	–0.0756	–0.0663	0.1392**	0.1484**	0.0714	–0.0435	0.0937	1		
NORTH	–0.4580**	0.6030**	–0.4720**	0.4007	0.4151**	–0.2896**	0.1824**	–0.0815	0.0554	–0.2623**	0.0753	–0.3777**	–0.3366**	1	
SOUTH	0.4472**	–0.5495**	0.3275**	–0.2831**	–0.3416**	0.3688**	–0.2195**	–0.0863	–0.0721	–0.2757**	–0.0527	0.3790**	0.0217	–0.7995**	1

* –Significance Level 0.05, ** –Significance Level 0.01 (2-tailed)

Table 4.8

Bivariate Correlations (Urban India)

	FLITU	TFR	SR09U	UMAR19F	UMIGR	UFLFPR	USCP	USTP	UMUSL	UMNAG	PROD	UMLIT	RICE	NORTH	SOUTH
FLITR	1														
TFR	–0.5865**	1													
SR09R	0.0326	–0.2062**	1												
UMAR19F	–0.7376**	0.4887**	0.0684	1											
UMIGR	–0.5164**	0.3771**	–0.2053**	0.4206**	1										
UFLFPR	0.1304*	–0.3364**	0.2640**	–0.1455**	–0.3256**	1									
USCP	–0.1198*	0.1648**	–0.2152**	0.1906**	0.1898**	–0.3077**	1								
USTP	0.1462**	0.0019	0.2029	–0.1069*	–0.2635**	0.2228**	–0.2791**	1							
UMUSL	–0.4151*	0.2281**	0.0486	0.2459**	0.2287**	0.1172*	–0.4552**	–0.0299	1						
UMNAG	0.4519**	–0.2014**	–0.0998	–0.4020**	–0.4842**	0.0729	0.0158	–0.0266	–0.2589**	1					
PROD	0.1551**	–0.1037	–0.3483**	–0.3372**	0.0441	–0.2707**	0.2125**	–0.1946**	–0.1746**	0.2020**	1				
UMLIT	0.8802**	–0.5493**	0.1363**	–0.5050**	–0.4912**	0.2350**	–0.0772	0.1618**	–0.4826**	0.3594**	–0.0808	1			
RICE	0.1660**	–0.3706**	0.2216**	–0.2001**	–0.2511**	0.0833	–0.2388**	0.1643**	–0.0518	–0.0188	–0.0616	0.0712	1		
NORTH	–0.3845**	0.6064**	–0.3595**	0.2974**	0.3371**	–0.3946**	0.2390**	–0.1766*	0.1007	–0.0847	0.0972	–0.3727	–0.3337**	1	
SOUTH	0.3254**	–0.5505**	0.3048**	–0.1858**	–0.1977**	0.3981**	–0.2634**	–0.0097	0.041	0.0305	–0.0771	0.3410	0.0361	–0.7964**	1

* –Significance Level 0.05, ** –Significance Level 0.01 (2-tailed)

relationship is strong and significantly positive for the urban areas. As discussed before, this can be explained by the structural differences in the economy of rural and urban India.

The relationship between female literacy and proportion of scheduled tribe population also varies between urban and rural India. It is weakly negative for the rural areas in India, but positive and significant for the urban India. This shows that in the rural areas the presence of scheduled tribe population depresses female literacy, but this is not the case in the urban areas of the country. In the rural areas scheduled tribe populations are at the bottom of the social hierarchy, not very different from the scheduled castes.

These tribal groups, especially the non-Christian tribes, are primarily engaged in agricultural activities and are culturally not very different from the Hindu Brahminic culture. However, in the urban areas the long contact with Christian missionaries, and special government programs to encourage literacy among these special groups has led to higher literacy levels among them.

The relationship with Muslim population also varies between rural and urban areas. Though it is negative in both, in urban areas the presence of Muslim population depresses female literacy more than in rural areas. The rural female literacy is low as a whole, so the effect of Muslim population, though negative, does not stand out as a reason for low female literacy. Whereas, in the urban areas there is a huge gap between female literacy among Muslim and non-Muslim groups. Sopher (1980: 173) explains this association of increased Muslim presence with a reduction in literacy levels in Indian cities as a result of "particular historical social environment that is the more pervasive in Indian cities the larger the Muslim minority".

A look at the various models (see Table 4.9 and 4.10) indicates that the rural models are very similar to the all-India models (see Table 4.4), whereas the urban models have some differences. A comparison between the first model (Model 1) in rural and urban India shows that when kinship structures and development levels are held constant the female literacy in the urban areas in the North is lower than the East and the South. But rural female literacy in the North is higher than the East, but lower than the South. Also, the juvenile sex ratio is significant in the rural model but ceases to be significant in the urban areas.

Table 4.9
Regression Coefficients for the Effects of Explanatory Variables on Female Literacy in Rural India: 1981

Indicator	*Model 1*	*Model 2*	*Model 3*	*Model 4*
Constant	–23.736	127.148	–12.169	–10.726
Region				
North	2.152	2.259	2.826*	3.244**
South	5.015***	7.431***	6.435***	6.872***
East	—	—	—	—
Patriarchy/Kinship				
Total Fertility Rate	–1.966**	–8.991***	–2.534***	–2.389***
Juvenile Sex Ratio	0.025*	–0.048**	0.014	0.011
Marriage under 19	–0.127***	–0.266***	–0.084**	–0.085**
Female Migration	–0.546***	–0.933***	–0.559***	–0.575***
Female labor force	–0.203***	–0.356***	–0.245***	–0.239***
Development				
Male non-agricultural	0.139	—	0.072	0.069
Agricultural Product	0.001*	—	0.001*	0.001*
Male Literacy	0.717***	—	0.740***	0.742***
Social Differentiation				
Scheduled Castes	—	–0.270***	–0.051	–0.050
Scheduled Tribes	—	–0.010	0.081***	0.080***
Muslims	—	–0.091**	0.029	0.026
Agricultural Practices				
Area under Rice	—	—	—	0.014
R^2	0.877	0.669	0.886	0.887

*p<0.05, **p<0.01, ***p<0.001.

Moreover, it changes its sign from a positive in the rural model to a negative in the urban one. This shows that high sex ratio in favor of females in the rural areas significantly impacts literacy levels but the relationship does not hold true in the urban areas. This probably is due to the fact that active gender discrimination is prevalent more in the rural areas in India and hence, lessening of

Table 4.10

Regression Coefficients for the Effects of Explanatory Variables on Female Literacy in Urban India: 1981

Indicator	*Model 1*	*Model 2*	*Model 3*	*Model 4*
Constant	–2.879	92.936	–6.595	–12.735
Region				
North	–0.409	3.732*	–0.511	0.551
South	1.392	6.892***	1.112	2.412**
East	—	—	—	—
Patriarchy/Kinship				
Total Fertility Rate	–0.448	–3.239***	–0.643	–0.154***
Juvenile Sex Ratio	–0.006	--0.008	–0.007	–0.009
Marriage under 19	–0.542***	–0.810***	–0.522***	–0.518**
Female Migration	–1.00	–4.459***	–0.848	–0.597
Female labor force	–0.247***	–0.261**	–0.282***	–0.263***
Development				
Male non-agricultural	0.086*	—	0.106**	0.123**
Agricultural Product	0.001**	—	0.001**	0.001**
Male Literacy	0.955***	—	1.002***	1.028***
Social Differentiation				
Scheduled Castes	—	–0.122	0.020	0.062
Scheduled Tribes	—	0.114	0.052*	0.054*
Muslims	—	–0.182***	0.052*	0.057**
Agricultural Practices				
Area under Rice	—	—	—	0.036**
R^2	0.909	0.706	0.912	0.915

*p<0.05, **p<0.01, ***p<0.001.

the patriarchal values will lead to a more balanced sex ratio and in turn positively impact the position of women. Whereas in the urban areas the sex ratio, though not completely balanced, is more favorable to women and any further improvement does not translate into substantial change in women's access to social resources.

Model 2, which includes kinship and social stratification variables, shows that all but one of the variables exhibit a negative relationship with female literacy both in urban and rural areas. As mentioned before, the presence of scheduled tribes in the rural India affects female literacy negatively but this is not so for the urban areas. When kinship/patriarchal structures and social stratification are held constant, South India has the highest female literacy followed by the North and finally the East. Model 3 adds the development indicators to the kinship and social stratification variables. Once again the urban areas in Northern India have the lowest female literacy, and the juvenile sex ratio continues to have a negative relationship with female literacy in urban areas. The lowest female literacy rates in urban India, as shown in Model 1 and 3, clearly indicate that when development levels are controlled, north India has the lowest female literacy.

The final model (Model 4) for rural and urban areas shows that almost all of the kinship variables continue to have a negative association with female literacy, except for the juvenile sex ratio that has a positive impact on female literacy in the rural areas, but not so in the urban India. Another variable that has a different impact on female literacy between urban and rural areas is the proportion of scheduled caste population. While the presence of scheduled castes has a negative impact on female literacy in the rural areas, it is just the opposite in the urban areas. As the b-coefficient suggests, female literacy is positively impacted by scheduled caste population in urban areas when all the other explanatory variables are held constant. The scheduled caste population is primarily concentrated in the rural areas in India. Low economic status and a lower position in the Indian social hierarchy has led this group to be primarily engaged in the agricultural sector where acquiring literacy is not critical. Hence, the literacy levels among them are very low, depressing the overall literacy levels in rural areas. On the other hand, acquiring literacy is necessary for employment purposes in the urban areas. Moreover, the more aware and economically better off sections among the scheduled castes in cities have managed to increase their literacy levels by availing themselves of various government benefits and development programs. This perhaps is indicated in the statistical analysis, where the presence of scheduled caste population ceases to have a negative impact on female literacy in urban areas. A detailed investigation of this issue may yield a better explanation. The South continues to have higher female literacy, both in urban and rural areas, followed by the North and the East.

A look at the beta values (standardized b-coefficients) (Table 4.11) shows that while in urban areas male literacy (UMLIT) has the greatest impact on female literacy followed by the early marriage (UMAR19F), in the rural areas, the greatest influence is exercised by male literacy, female labor force participation rate, the region, female migration, and fertility rate, in that order. This indicates that to some extent urbanization operates uniformly in reducing the impact of kinship factors or social stratification factors on female literacy in various parts of India. This is evident by the fact that North versus East ceases to have a significant impact on female literacy in the urban areas though South versus East remains significant (see Urban Model 4). However, in rural India 'Region' is significantly important in terms of its impact on female literacy.

Table 4.11

Standardized Regression Coefficients: Model 4 (Rural and Urban India)

Variable	*Beta (Rural)*	*Variable*	*Beta (Urban)*
TFR	–0.129087	TFR	–0.009930
SR09R	0.034184	SR09U	–0.028442
RMAR19F	–0.081953	UMAR19F	–0.315605
RMIGR	–0.144763	UMIGR	–0.025198
RFLFPR	–0.239070	UFLFPR	–0.114331
RMNAG	0.023804	UMNAG	0.062054
PROD	0.060368	PROD	0.077997
RMLIT	0.685789	UMLIT	0.722399
RSCP	–0.029868	USCP	0.024798
RSTP	0.107304	USTP	0.039202
RMUSL	0.029314	UMUSL	0.073985
RICE	0.023487	RICE	0.070513
NORTH	0.105443	NORTH	0.021465
SOUTH	0.205880	SOUTH	0.086650

Geographical Variations (Urban and Rural)

There is a large degree of spatial covariation between the urban and rural female literacy patterns despite differences in urban and rural conditions. Nevertheless, Map 29 shows a fairly large difference in rural and urban female literacy rates in almost all the districts of India. A few clusters of very high urban-rural gap emerge on the map, more so in northern India. A close look at this pattern of high urban-rural gap in female literacy indicates two features: firstly, the pattern is closely associated with the presence of urban centers, thus indicating that urbanization has a strong positive impact on female literacy more so in the low literacy regions of northern India; and secondly, the presence of scheduled caste/tribes negatively impacts female literacy levels, especially in the rural areas.

A near contiguous line of districts extending from Punch in Jammu and Kashmir to Pithoragarh in Kumaon region of Uttar Pradesh have a high rural-urban gap in female literacy. Overall female literacy levels are low in these regions but the presence of urban centers like Srinagar, Shimla, and Dehradun have pushed up the literacy levels thus increasing the urban-rural gap. As discussed before it is not so much the strong patriarchal structures that are having a negative impact on female literacy but the lack of development and poverty that are dragging down the female literacy levels in rural areas in these states.

Similarly the cities of Jodhpur, Jaipur, and Udaipur in Rajasthan, and Bhopal, Indore, and Jabalpur in Madhya Pradesh have created islands of high female literacy among these largely low female literacy states. The districts with high proportion of scheduled tribe population on the Rajasthan-Madhya Pradesh-Gujarat border, such as Dungarpur, Banswara, Jhabua, and Panchmahal, also have very high urban-rural gap in female literacy. This is probably due to the fact that these non-Christian scheduled tribe populations are concentrated in the rural areas leading to very low levels of literacy in the rural areas, whereas the population in the urban areas is much more mixed, leading to higher literacy levels for urban females.

Another cluster of districts having high rural-urban difference appears on the Bihar-West Bengal-Orissa border. Some of these districts have very high proportions of non-Christian scheduled tribe population in rural areas, whereas others have a large proportion of scheduled caste population in rural areas. This leads to lower literacy levels among females in rural areas, confirming the statistical result that presence of scheduled tribe and scheduled caste populations has a negative impact on female literacy in the rural areas, but not so in the urban areas. This indicates that urbanization significantly reduces the impact of social stratification factors on female literacy.

Conclusion

This analysis examines the combined effects of economic, cultural, and regional factors on female literacy in India. Development level has the largest impact on female literacy when all the other explanatory variables are controlled for. Kinship structures too have a significant impact on literacy levels but their impact is felt more in the rural areas, and not so much in the urban areas. Similarly, 'Region' appears to be very important in explaining variations in female literacy in the rural areas but less in the case in urban India. These findings should have some policy implications, which should be designed differently for rural and urban India.

The geographical association of female literacy with the other explanatory variables can be summarized as follows:

1. *Districts with high level of economic development and a kinship structure that is favorable to women*: broadly speaking a majority of the coastal districts, especially on the west coast (in the states of Maharashtra and Gujarat) fall into this category.
2. *Districts with high levels of economic development but a kinship structure that lowers the cultural worth of women*: high development levels override the unfavorable kinship pattern to produce high female literacy levels in a few districts in West Bengal and Orissa, and most districts of Punjab.
3. *Districts with less economic development, but a favorable kinship structure*: in some cases very low levels of development weigh much more heavily compared to a favorable kinship structure in influencing female literacy levels. For instance, in the districts of northern Andhra Pradesh female literacy is very low despite a favorable kinship structure. But

in other cases having a cultural system that is favorable to women can lead to higher literacy levels despite less economic development. Kerala, the north-eastern states and the Kumaon region of Uttar Pradesh are a case in point.

4. *Districts with low economic development and an unfavorable kinship structure*: this is the worst case of all where the female literacy levels are among the lowest. The Terai region of Uttar Pradesh, the Bundelkhand region on Uttar Pradesh-Madhya Pradesh border, and the Malwa Plateau region on Madhya Pradesh-Rajasthan border are prime examples of this category.

Other factors that influence female literacy are the presence of scheduled castes and tribes, especially in the rural areas. These groups occupy the lowest position in the social hierarchy and are thus disadvantaged economically and socially. Christian influence has led to higher literacy levels for a few but overall literacy levels among these groups are low. The relationship between the agricultural practices and female literacy did not come out very clearly in this analysis and needs further investigation.

The future of India's female literacy hinges on the continued focus on the social, cultural, political and economic lives of the women of India (Freebody and Welch, 1993: 4). It is futile to talk about improving literacy levels among females in India without paying attention to the larger socioeconomic structure in which women exist.

Note

1. MAR19F, MIGR, and FLFPR are defined in Chapter 3.

5

The Political Status of Women

Political activism by women in India has its roots reaching far back into the colonial era. The women's movement gained momentum during the freedom struggle and continues to grow, widening its base at the grass-roots level (Kannabiran and Kannabiran, 1997; Agnihotri and Mazumdar, 1995; Kumar, 1995). But women's representation in the formal political process has lagged behind that of men. Women are not only a minority in the Parliament and the state legislative assemblies in India (Desai and Bhagwati, 1973; Varma, 1997; Kumar, 1995) but fewer women than men exercise their right to vote (Shukla, 1988). Though the importance of social action in effectively questioning and perhaps even challenging the existing political structure is not to be minimized, it is by direct political participation that any meaningful transformation towards gender equality and justice can be achieved. Hence, by keeping away from formally participating in the political system women forfeit a voice in politics (Kannabiran and Kannabiran, 1997; Jones, 1993).

The role of women in the political process can be assessed either by the proportion of females contesting elections or by their participation in the electoral process through voting. Though the former indicator has been used in many studies as a measure of women's political status (Desai and Bhagwati, 1973; Kumar, 1995; Baig, 1976; Kumari and Dubey, 1994), it is hard to draw a link between women's representation in elected offices and the political status of women in general, as women are grossly underrepresented in both the state legislatures and the Parliament in India. Moreover, it has also been seen that female members of the parliament or state assemblies have fewer resources to work with, are given 'less important' portfolios, and do not necessarily uphold the interests of women and work for their empowerment (Weiner, 1975). Thus, the link between females in public offices to women's political status as a whole remains tenuous.

In this chapter proportion of women who voted in an election is taken as a surrogate measure of women's political status in India (see Chapter 3: Principal Components Analysis results). This is not to say that the connection between enfranchisement and women's status is a straight-forward one. The right to vote or even to exercise that right does not guarantee a higher status, political or social (Varma, 1997; Kumar, 1995; Misra, 1997). For instance, it has been pointed out that in patriarchal structures more often than not the choice of whether to vote or who to vote for lies not with the woman but other family members (Varma, 1997), thus leading to a mere token participation by women (Kumari and Kidwai, 1994). But the above mentioned studies do point to the fact that in a democratic setting participation in elections could enhance women's political awareness and provide them with a political voice and a means of transforming the social system.

The success of any democratic system rests on the participation by the electorate. In India the female voter turnout has always been much lower than the male voter turnout in nearly all the elections in the last 60 years. In order to understand the low levels of female participation in the Indian electoral process, it is important to see the sociocultural environment in which women exist. Low levels of literacy, economic dependence on the male members of the family, strong patriarchal values, poor health conditions, caste and community affiliations—all combine together to influence and restrict women's role in the political process. Do these factors affect women's capacity to participate differently in different parts of India? Does economic development play a role in conditioning women's response to the electoral process? This chapter will try to answer these questions and explore the combined effects of kinship structures, economic development, social stratification, physical accessibility, and religion on female political participation in India.

Background

India is one of the few countries in the democratic world to go through numerous consecutive elections in recent years. Every election is followed by an analysis of how the electorate voted, what the level of participation was, and what were the factors that led to the electorate voting in a certain pattern (Weiner, 1980; Butler, Lahiri and Roy, 1991; Mcmillan and Chandra, 1998). Most of these studies are on an all-India level, with some mention of states, but there is no special focus on women's role and participation. Some other studies on the state level (Richter, 1975; Weiner and Field, 1975, 1977) have attempted to identify the economic and social determinants of political behavior in the erstwhile princely states, the tribal constituencies, and the urban constituencies in India. Richter (1975) found that the nature of the political regime under which people lived conditioned their response to the electoral participation, while Weiner and Field (1975) found a distinctive regional pattern in tribal voting patterns based on the local characteristics of the area in which they were located and the differences among them in terms of their demographic distribution, levels of modernization, intensity of self-awareness, and relationship with state and central authority. Weiner and Field (1977) in their study of electoral participation in urban constituencies observed an interesting pattern indicating no major difference between the urban and rural areas but rather a major difference between states and regions of states in India. Similarly, Dikshit (1995) related the voter turnout in the state assembly elections to the development levels of various states. He pointed to the growing convergence in turnout rates among urban and rural regions of the country, and attributed the higher voter participation in the scheduled caste and scheduled tribe constituencies to the increased politicization of these populations. Chandidas (1972) compared the voter participation in the 1967 and 1971 parliamentary elections in India and concluded that the major reason for the drop in voter turnout is the de-linking of the assembly elections from the parliamentary elections in India. He also emphasized the easy accessibility of polling stations as a major factor in influencing voter turnout positively. These state-level analyses are too gross to bring out the minute regional variations in voting patterns in India.

Several other studies on a micro-scale utilizing district as a unit of analysis have tried to explain voter participation in India. For instance, Dasgupta and Morris Jones (1975) explored the influence of developmental and cultural factors on political participation for the whole country. Another study for the state of Uttar Pradesh (Frankel, 1977) related economic variables to the electoral data and found that economic development leads to higher participation by the electorate. Dikshit and Sharma (1982) analyzed the trends in voter participation in state legislative assembly elections for Punjab. They related voter turnout to the development levels, social pluralism (measured by scheduled caste population, Sikhs, Hindus, Punjabi speakers and Hindi Speakers), and agricultural development in the constituencies. Similarly, Benjamin, Blue and Coleman (1971) related voter participation in India to modernization, and participation in trade union and other religio-welfare organizations. But in all these studies no attention is given to the gender gap in voter participation.

Some attempts have been made to understand the participation of women in the electorate process in India on a macro-level with the states as the unit. Varma (1997) delineated the factors influencing voting decisions for men and women and then went on to discuss the factors that prevent access of women to the polling stations. He discussed the gender gap in voting on a state-level for the 1996 Lok Sabha (House of Parliament) elections. Similarly, Mazumdar (1979) analyzed women's role in the electoral process on a state level relating it to the levels of urbanization and industrialization in different states. Though she did mention the impact of cultural patterns on women's voting no special attention was given to analyzing the cultural-political connection in detail. Several other studies have tried to analyze women's role in Indian politics on a micro-scale. Kumari and Kidwai (1994) analyzed the voter participation by women in the legislative assembly elections of Delhi. The authors looked at the relationship between the women voters, the electoral process, and the social system in which women exist, and suggested that participation in elections is an important source of political socialization for women (p. 31). Similarly, Shukla (1988) explored the impact of education, family, mass-media, and political parties on women's participation in the electoral process in Kodarma sub-division in Bihar. According to him education is the most important factor in influencing women's participation in politics and voter participation is based on the interest in politics, political knowledge, exposure to election campaigns, and faith in the efficacy of elections.

The studies mentioned above are either too aggregated, such as the ones on state-level, or too specific, focusing on a particular region or part of the state. The present study is based on the district as the unit of study and combines both economic and non-economic factors that may help in understanding the regional variations in turnout of women voters.

Data and Methodology

In this study the relationships between certain economic and non-economic factors and female voter turnout are explored. The analysis is done by aggregating the constituency-level election data pertaining to state legislative assembly elections for the years 1977, 1978 and 1980[1] to the district-level[2] and then correlating it to the socioeconomic variables derived from the 1981 census.[3]

Female voter turnout is considered a measure of political status of women and measured as the share of female voters out of the female electors for the respective election years.

$$\text{FVOTE} = \frac{\text{Female Voters}}{\text{Female Electors}} \times 100$$

Political Socialization: The involvement of the population in the political process is referred to as the political socialization and is measured by the proportion of male voters out of total male electors in a district. It is expected that regions where the population is more active in the political process will also have a higher female participation.

$$MVOTE = \frac{\text{Male Voters}}{\text{Male Electors}} \times 100$$

Patriarchal Kinship Organization: Early Marriage (MAR19F), Patrilocal Exogamy (MIGR), Female labor Force Participation (FLFPR), Total Fertility Rate (TFR), and Female literacy (FLIT) are included as indicators of patriarchal kinship structures. It is expected that kinship structures that are characterized by patrilocal exogamy and early marriage will depress female voter turnout. While high female labor force participation and literacy levels are likely to have a positive impact on female participation in the political process, a high fertility rate, on the other hand, is symbolic of a stranglehold of traditional values and institutions on women, and thus is expected to lower female participation in political process.

Social Stratification: Several studies point to the general political marginalization of Scheduled Caste (SC) and Scheduled Tribe (ST) populations due to their lower social and economic status in India (Dikshit, 1995; Weiner and Field, 1975). Despite many efforts by the government to encourage political participation by these groups, such as reserving constituency seats for schedule caste and tribal candidates, the voter turnout remains lower than the non-scheduled caste and non-tribal populations. But other studies have indicated that social mobilization along caste lines can lead to higher participation by these groups in the electoral process (Benjamin, Blue and Coleman, 1971; Rudolph and Rudolph, 1967). The caste-based political groups compete for power through the expansion of their activities among their populations, thus leading to greater participation by the members of their group. Thus, it is expected that there will be higher voter turnout in those regions of India where there is considerable political mobilization among scheduled caste/tribal populations, whereas, the regions that have sizeable SC and ST populations but less political mobilization will tend to have lower voter turnout. The female voting turnout is expected to be closely associated with the pattern discussed above.

The presence of Muslim population, with their tendency to seclude women from public sphere, is expected to depress Muslim women's participation, thus affecting the overall female participation rate negatively in regions of Muslim dominance.

Economic Development: Nearly all the studies on voter turnout rates have indicated a positive relationship between levels of development and voter participation rates, though some (Benjamin, Blue and Coleman, 1971) have pointed out that the relationship between urbanization levels and participation in the electoral process is far from straightforward. The study shows that very low or very high levels of urbanization have almost no effect on the voter turnout rates, and in fact political participation may decrease in very highly urbanized areas such as the metropolitan areas (also see Weiner and Field, 1977: 17). It is in the regions that are at the middle level of urbanization that the voter turnout is high. The reason for a lower voter turnout in highly urbanized areas of India could be the "loss of generalized support for the political system" (Benjamin, Blue and Coleman, 1971: 234).

In this chapter, percentage of males in non-agricultural sector (MNAG), urbanization (URBZ), and Agricultural Productivity (PROD) are included as indicators of economic development.

Physical Accessibility: The selection of this measure is based on the fact that the election commission in India generally establishes polling booths in villages with a population of approximately 800 to a 1000 voters (Weiner, 1980; Chandidas, 1972). The smaller villages are then clubbed together and attached to the polling stations that are within the prescribed limit of two kilometers, i.e., no voter has to travel more than 2 km to reach the polling station (Chandidas, 1972: 1366; Election Commission, 1969). Despite the stipulations of one polling station located within the radius of 2 kilometers and serving approximately 1000 persons, those regions of India where the proportion of smaller villages is large and each village does not have an independent polling station show a lower voter turnout. Several studies (Chandidas, 1972; Dikshit, 1995) have indicated a strong positive relationship between accessibility to the polling booths and voter turnout in India. Using the number of villages having less than 1000 population as a measure of physical accessibility, Chandidas (1972) concluded that there is a strong negative correlation between the number of villages with less than 1000 population and the voter turnout in parliamentary elections in India.[4] He found that almost 72 to 85 per cent of the variation in voter turnout on a state-level can be explained by this variable alone (Dikshit, 1995). The relationship between physical accessibility and female voter turnout is expected to be strong as women in India are more restricted in their movements outside the home. Social and familial pressure against traveling long distances for the fear of anti-social elements or anticipated violence, and lack of time from household chores (Varma, 1997) could be some of the reasons for low female voter turnout in villages that do not have a polling booth in close vicinity.

In this study physical accessibility is measured by the ratio between the number of polling booths and villages in a district.

$$\text{Accessibility} = \frac{\text{Number of Polling Station}}{\text{Number of Village}}$$

It is expected that higher the ratio more will be the participation of women in the polls.

Regional Variables: As done in the previous chapters, dummy variables are used to estimate differences between the North, South and the East and to estimate whether region moderates the effects of other explanatory variables.

Findings

The mean values (Table 5.1) suggest that the female voter turnout is the highest in the South, followed by the East, and then the North. There is considerable difference between the voter turnout in the South and the other regions of India.

Table 5.1

Average Female Voter Participation by Regions: 1977–80

Region	*Average Female Vote (in per cent)*
East	48.54
North	44.82
South	66.48

The geographical distribution of female voter participation (Map 10) confirms this pattern with most southern states having a high female voter participation (above 50%), whereas, all the northern states exhibit a much lower turnout. Kerala, Karnataka, Andhra Pradesh, and parts of Maharashtra have a female voter participation of over 65 per cent, while Uttar Pradesh, Madhya

Pradesh, Rajasthan, Bihar, and Orissa lag behind with less than 35 per cent of women exercising their franchise. A detailed district-wise analysis is presented later.

The zero-order correlations (Table 5.2) reveal the nature of relationships between the dependent variable (FVOTE) and the various independent variables. Female voter turnout as expected has a very strong positive relationship to male voter participation, indicating that regions with a high degree of political awareness will have a high participation rate for females. Three indicators of patriarchal kinship structures—early marriage (MAR19F), patrilocal exogamy (MIGR), and total fertility rate (TFR)—have a negative impact on female voter turnout, whereas female labor force participation (FLFPR) and female literacy show the expected positive relationship. The relationships with the social stratification variables are not that straightforward. Both scheduled castes (SCP) and scheduled tribes (STP) exhibit a negative influence on female voter participation but the correlation with scheduled caste population is not statistically significant. Surprisingly the presence of Muslim population does not exert a negative influence on female voters, as measured by a positive correlation that is very weak and insignificant (0.0292). The scatter plot (Figure 5.1) indicates the districts of Srinagar, Anantnag, Baramulla, and Punch in Jammu & Kashmir, and Malappuram in Kerala, have a very large Muslim population and also reasonably high female voter participation. These outlying districts are probably influencing the correlation, making it a weak positive relationship to the dependent variable. One explanation for the high voter participation despite presence of Muslim population in Jammu & Kashmir could be the revival of religio-ethnic feelings among these populations, leading to the expansion of political activities and greater participation by the members of the group. This region has been witnessing a strong separatist movement in recent years. On the other hand, in Kerala, as explained in the previous chapter, the existence of cultural/social institutions proffering a higher status to women have led to higher participation for women in all spheres, cutting across caste and religious lines. A more substantive investigation of these outlying districts, done later, may yield a more satisfactory explanation.

Table 5.2

Bivariate Correlations

	FVOTE	MVOTE	MAR19F	MIGR	FLFPR	TFR	FLIT	SCP	STP	MUSL	MNAG	URBZ	PROD	ACCES	NORTH	SOUTH
FVOTE	1															
MVOTE	0.8250**	1														
MAR19F	–0.3468**	–0.1225*	1													
MIGR	–0.2740**	–0.1659**	0.4659**	1												
FLFPR	0.1250*	0.1973**	–0.0649	–0.4190**	1											
TFR	–0.4092**	–0.2849**	0.5190**	0.3397**	–0.2372**	1										
FLIT	0.4953**	0.2401**	–0.6156**	–0.4181**	–0.1203*	–0.6314**	1									
SCP	–0.0999	–0.0975	0.3117**	0.2620**	–0.4177**	0.1849**	–0.1823**	1								
STP	–0.1875**	–0.1641**	–0.0863	–0.2668**	0.4442**	–0.0072	–0.0868	–0.4479**	1							
MUSL	0.0292	0.0742	–0.1665**	0.0214	–0.1	0.1281*	–0.0851	–0.2666**	–0.1505**	1						
MNAG	0.3486**	0.0775	–0.4490**	–0.4745**	–0.0705	–0.3360**	0.6655**	–0.1836**	–0.0688	0.0247	1					
URBZ	0.2213**	0.0253	–0.2574**	–0.3184**	-2600**	–0.0775	0.5240**	–0.083	–0.1484**	0.0322	0.8505**	1				
PROD	0.2365**	0.086	–0.2746**	–0.0432	–0.4510**	–0.1019	0.2796**	.2753**	–0.2543**	–0.0889	0.1859**	0.1563**	1			
ACCES	0.3297**	0.2273**	–0.2941**	–0.1344*	–0.1111*	–0.4368**	0.6331**	–0.1242*	–0.1683**	0.1484**	0.3255**	0.1983**	0.1399*	1		
NORTH	–0.5549**	–0.4663**	0.3628**	0.3886*	–0.2461**	0.6030	–0.4457**	0.2098**	–0.075	0.0502	–0.2317**	–0.1376**	0.0868	–0.3026**	1	
SOUTH	0.6399**	0.5694**	–0.2526**	–0.3102**	0.3080**	–0.5495**	0.4427**	–0.2445**	–0.0943	–0.0372	0.2524**	0.1843**	–0.0674	0.3994	–0.7982**	1

* – Significance Level 0.05 ** – Significance Level 0.01 (2-tailed)

Figure 5.1

Female Voter Participation and Muslim Population

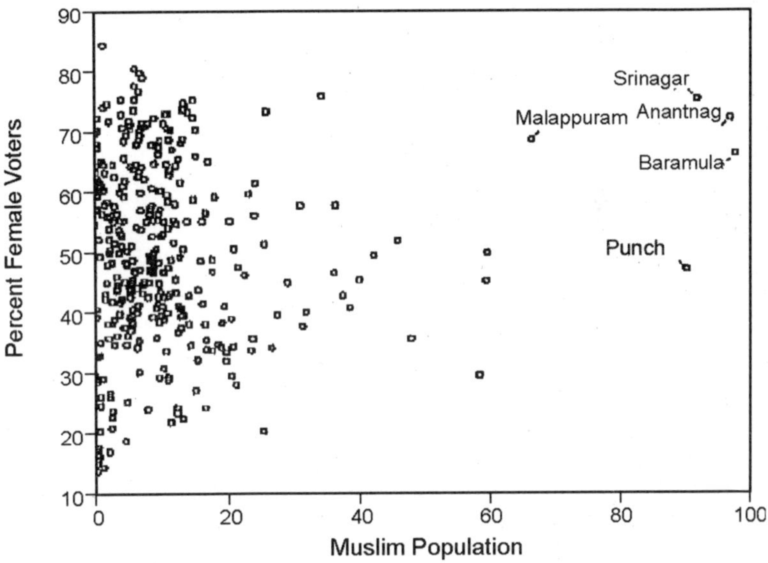

Source: 1981 India Development District Database (IDDD)

All the indicators of development and physical accessibility, as expected, are positively correlated with female voter turnout, indicating that districts with higher proportions of males in non-agricultural sector (MNAG), higher levels of urbanization (URBZ), higher agricultural productivity (PROD), and higher polling station-to-village ratio (ACCES) will have more females participating in the electoral process. Though the scatter diagram (Figure 5.2) indicates the relationship of female voters to urbanization may be a tenuous one, with the outlier districts of Bombay, Hyderabad, Delhi, Madras, and Calcutta metro areas influencing the correlations to be positive (r = 0.22). Similarly, the moderately positive correlation (r = 0.32) between accessibility and female voter turnout may be influenced by the densely populated districts of Kerala and Delhi that appear as outliers on the scatter diagram (Figure 5.3).

The next step is to separately examine the individual determinant groups and see their impact on female participation. Table

Figure 5.2

Female Voter Participation and Urban Population

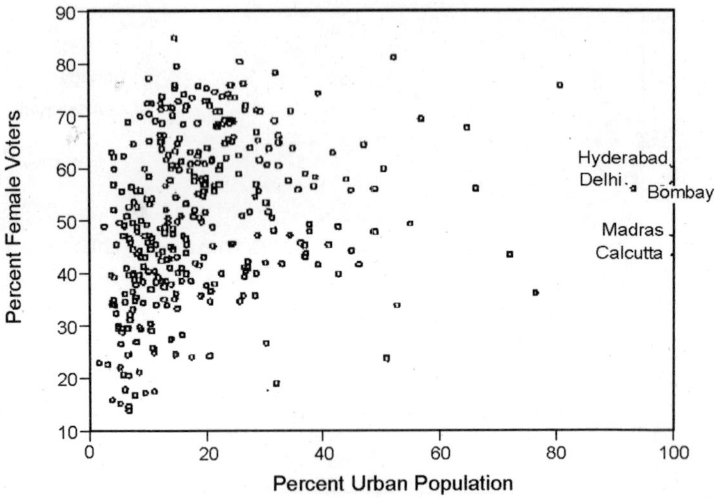

Source: 1981 India Development District Database (IDDD)

Figure 5.3

Female Voter Participation and Physical Accessibility

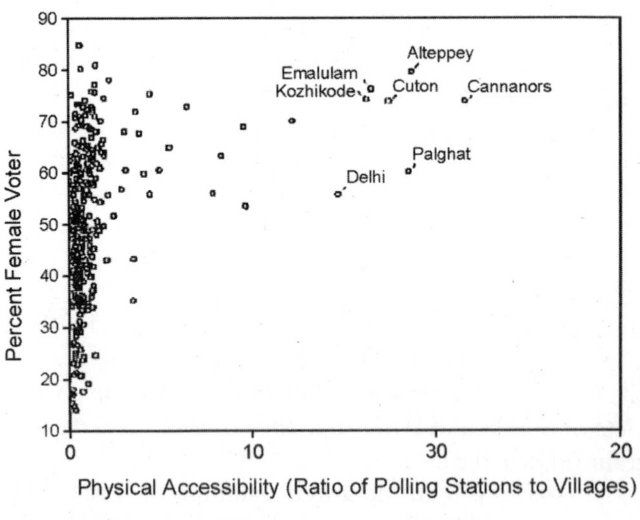

Source: 1981 India Development District Database (IDDD)

5.3 shows the results of the least squares estimation technique. Case I expresses female voter turnout (FVOTE) as a linear function of the region variables, North, South, and East. The R^2 indicates that regional differences explain about 41 per cent of the variation in women's political participation, indicating the importance of this explanatory variable as a predictor of female participation. The value of the constant, 48.54, is the average female participation for the reference group, Eastern India. The North has a lower participation rate (b-coefficient = –3.719), whereas the South is considerably higher than both the East and the North (b-coefficient = +17.944). A look at all the other explanatory variables (Table 5.3: Cases II to VI) reveals that the inclusion of the regional variables substantially increases the predictive power of the models (the R^2 increases in all the instances). This is a strong indicator of the importance of the 'Region' variable in assessing variations in female political participation in India.

The examination of the other explanatory variables (Cases II to VI) in Table 5.3 shows that political socialization (measured by per cent male voters) has the largest impact on female voter turnout ($R^2 = 0.727$), followed by the development levels ($R^2 = 0.522$), and patriarchal kinship structures ($R^2 = 0.478$). Social Differentiation and Physical Accessibility follow closely with R^2 of 0.438 and 0.421 respectively. Contrary to the expectations, physical accessibility does not turn out to be a great predictor of female voter participation. Previous studies on a state level (see Dikshit, 1995, and Chandidas, 1972) had indicated the importance of this variable by suggesting that nearly 72 to 85 per cent of the variation in voter turnout on a state-level can be explained by this variable alone. But this does not seem to be the case at the district-level. Perhaps the disaggregation by the district-level renders this relationship ineffective or large states that have evenly distributed polling stations and not much variation in turnout are depressing the explanatory power of this variable (Dikshit, 1995: 91).

Table 5.3

Regression Coefficients for the Effects of Each Explanatory Variable on Female Voter Participation in India: 1977–80

Indicator	*Constant*	*b Coeff*	R^2	R^2 *before regions were included*
Case I				
Region	48.545		0.414	
North		–3.719		
South		+17.944***		
East		—		
Case II				
Political Socialization	–9.128		0.727	0.681
Male Voter Turnout		0.961***		
North		–3.042*		
South		+5.728**		
Case III				
Kinship Structures	30.902		0.478	0.284
Marriage under 19		–0.119*		
Female Migration		0.322		
Female labor force participation		0.033		
Total Fertility Rate		2.672*		
Female Literacy		0.263***		
North		–2.651		
South		16.633***		
Case IV				
Social Differentiation	51.46		0.438	0.084
Scheduled Castes		–0.008		
Scheduled Tribes		–0.125**		
Muslims		0.029		
North		–5.714**		
South		15.741***		
Case V				
Development	38.226		0.522	0.172
Male non-agricultural workers		0.552***		
Urbanization levels		–0.172**		
Agricultural Product		0.006***		
North		–3.508		
South		17.317***		
Class VI				
Physical Accessibility	48.289		0.421	0.108
Access		0.479		
North		–3.842		
South		16.642***		

*p<0.05, **p<0.01, ***p<0.001.

After a series of separate examinations, I proceed to explore the collective impact of these explanatory variables on female voter turnout. Several combinations of the explanatory variables were considered before selecting the final four models presented in Table 5.4. 'Region' is controlled for in all the models.

Model 1 combines the variables of kinship structure and development. The R^2 shows that nearly 56 per cent of the variability in female political participation has been accounted for by these variables. All the variables, except early marriage (MAR19F), are statistically significant. MAR19F does not come out significant due to its close association with patrilocal exogamy (MIGR). From a statistical standpoint virtually all the variance in female voter turnout accounted for by the patrilocal exogamy (MIGR) is shared with early marriage (MAR19F) and there is very little variance in female voter turnout being accounted for by early marriage (MAR19F) alone. The three patriarchy variables—early marriage, female labor force participation, and female literacy—show the expected relationship with female voter turnout. But patrilocal exogamy and total fertility rate indicate an unexpected positive relationship to FVOTE. A look at the simple correlations (Table 5.2) of patrilocal exogamy (MIGR) and total fertility rate (TFR) with the other indicators shows that both these indicators have a stronger relationship to the 'Region' variables than to female voter participation (FVOTE). Hence, it appears that 'Region' is moderating the effect of these two variables on female voter participation. For instance, the simple correlation between fertility rate (TFR) and North is 0.6030 and between North and FVOTE is –0.5549. In other words, Northern districts tend to have higher fertility and as these very districts have lower female voter participation we assume that regions with higher fertility have fewer women participating in the electoral process. But the multiple regression analysis disentangles these relationships to indicate that when the 'Region' is held constant both these variables, patrilocal exogamy and fertility levels, exhibit a positive relationship with the female voter participation. This result castes doubt on the validity of the expectations that higher fertility levels or patrilocal exogamy lead to lower voter participation for women.

Table 5.4

Regression Coefficients for the Effects of Explanatory Variables on Female Voter Participation in India: 1977–80

Indicator	*Model 1*	*Model 2*	*Model 3*	*Model 4*
Constant	6.679	0.708	–18.299	–38.506
Region				
North	–6.617**	–8.569***	–2.540*	–3.580*
South	15.428***	12.270***	4.843***	5.254**
East	—	—	—	—
Political Socialization				
Male voters	—	—	0.943***	0.914***
Patriarchy/Kinship				
Total Fertility Rate	4.815***	5.088***	—	3.220***
Marriage under 19	–0.019	0.0008	—	–0.082*
Female Migration	0.967**	0.983**	—	0.773**
Female labor force	0.194**	0.338***	—	0.108*
Female Literacy	.239***	0.304***	—	0.232***
Development				
Male non-agricultural	0.578***	0.517**	0.602***	0.618***
Agricultural Product	0.007***	0.008***	0.004***	0.003***
Urbanization	–0.218**	–0.197**	–0.127**	–0.190***
Social Differentiation				
Scheduled Castes	—	0.126	—	0.126*
Scheduled Tribes	—	–0.105**	—	–0.020
Muslims	—	0.094*	—	0.021
Physical Accessibility				
Access	—	—	—	–0.432*
R^2	0.556	0.583	0.811	0.835

*p<0.05, **p<0.01, ***p<0.001.

Further, a comparison between Model 1 and Case III (Table 5.3) shows that when the development variables are controlled the coefficients for kinship variables increase in size. Similarly, partitioning out the kinship variables increases the effect of the development variables on female voter turnout (see Case V in

Table 5.3). This indicates that the full impact of patriarchal values or development levels on female political participation can only be seen when the effects of the other are partitioned out of the equation. Two of the development variables, males in non-agricultural occupations and agricultural productivity, have the expected association with female voter participation, indicating that districts with a larger proportion of males in non-agricultural occupations and higher agricultural productivity will tend to have higher participation of females in the electoral process. The association with urbanization, on the other hand, is negative, indicating that higher the level of urbanization, lower is the female participation in the political process. This result corroborates the Benjamin, Blue and Coleman's findings (1971) of lower voter turnout in highly urbanized regions of the country, possibly due to disillusionment with the political system among the urban masses. Also the simple correlation between urbanization and female voter participation is not a particularly strong one ($r = 0.22$), whereas, the relationships between urbanization and female literacy (FLIT) and males in non-agricultural workforce (MNAG) are very strong. These two (MNAG and FLIT) in turn have a strong correlation with female voter turnout. Hence, holding FLIT and MNAG constant, urbanization shows a negative effect on female electoral participation. In other words, if literacy levels and proportion of males working in non-agricultural sector are held constant, then women tend to vote less in urban areas.

Model 2 combines the variables of development, social stratification, and kinship structures. The R^2 increases slightly from 0.556 to 0.583, improving the predictive power of the model somewhat. Almost all the kinship and development indicators still remain significant. Among the social stratification indicators, scheduled caste and Muslim population show a positive, though insignificant, relationship with female voter turnout.

Whereas, scheduled tribe population continues to show a negative association despite controlling for these other explanatory variables. Partitioning of social stratification variables increases the b-coefficients of the development indicators, suggesting that when social stratification variables are accounted for, the effect of development levels on female voter participation is more evident. The South continues to have a higher participation rate than the East, but the North still lags behind.

Model 3 combines the indicators of development with male voter participation. The R^2 indicates that almost 82 per cent of the variability in female voter participation is accounted for by these variables. The negative constant indicates that female voter participation is absent from the whole of India until the male participation reaches a certain level. The scatter diagram (Figure 5.4) shows that female voter participation emerges only after the

Figure 5.4

Female and Male Voter Participation

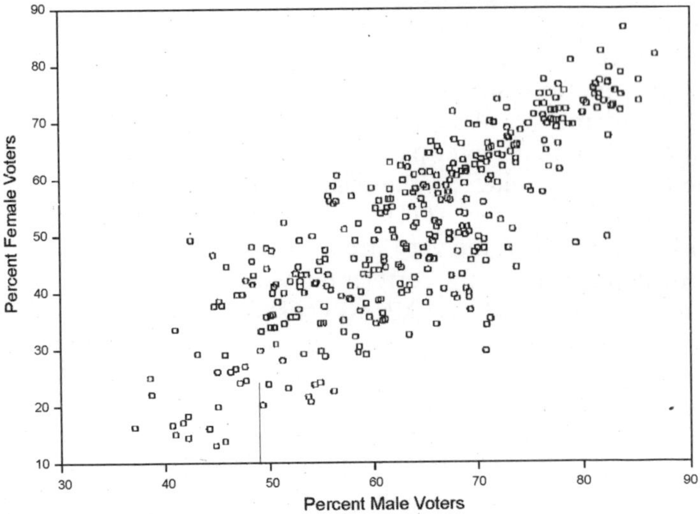

Source: 1981 Indian Development District Database (IDDD)

male voter turnout approaches 40 per cent. This itself is an evidence of the strong patriarchal hold on women in Indian society. Moreover, there is a very weak positive correlation between male voters and the indicators of development (see correlations Table 5.2). This suggests that male voter participation is not affected by development levels as much as the female participation is. In other words, less developed regions in India tend to have lower female voter turnout but the patriarchal hold can be eased with increasing economic development, leading to higher participation by women. Despite holding male participation and development levels constant, 'Region' still accounts for significant variation in female voter turnout.

Finally Model 4 includes all the relevant variables in an effort to explain the variation in female voter participation. As in the previous chapters tests for hetroscadasticity and multicollinearity were conducted, but despite unsatisfactory results (not presented here) all the variables are retained in the equation, as the intent here is to test the conceptual theory and explore the relationships between all these variables, rather than build predictive models.

Model 4 (Table 5.4) explains about 84 per cent of the variability in the female voter participation. Surprisingly, nearly all the variables, except scheduled tribe and Muslim population, have parameters that are significantly different from zero. A regression analysis of all the variables without 'Region' renders many of these parameters insignificant (results not shown here) indicating that their relationships to 'Region' are important in defining their effect on female voter turnout. The standardized regression estimates (Table 5.5) of all the variables in the model indicate that male voter participation (MVOTE) is the most

Table 5.5

Standardized Regression Estimates: Model 4

Variable	*Beta*
MVOTE	0.646616
MAR19F	–0.074883
MIGR	0.114022
FLFPR	0.097638
TFR	0.174572
FLIT	0.249871
MNAG	0.338564
URBZ	–0.207494
PROD	0.136497
SCP	0.066342
STP	–0.025083
MUSL	0.023248
ACCES	–0.081655
NORTH	–0.117225
SOUTH	0.158910

powerful variable in explaining female participation in elections. This is followed by male non-agricultural workforce, female literacy, and 'Region'. This shows that as the political socialization or awareness among the population increases both male and female participation in the political process will increase. Males in non-agricultural workforce is the second most important predictor of female participation in the electoral process stressing the importance of increased development levels in increasing women's role in the political arena in India. Female literacy follows close behind indicating that loosening of patriarchal values will lead to higher participation of women in the political process.

Among the kinship variables early marriage (MAR19F) has a negative impact on female voters but is barely significant. Districts with higher female literacy (FLIT) and labor force participation (FLFPR) will tend to have higher female voter participation, but the positive impact of patrilocal exogamy (MIGR) and fertility rate (TFR) continues. All the development indicators are significant and districts with larger proportions of male non-agricultural workforce (MNAG) and agricultural productivity (PROD) will tend to have higher political participation by females. Urbanization (URBZ) continues to show a negative association with female voters.

Indicators of social stratification do not show a significant effect on female political participation. Both scheduled castes and Muslims have a positive impact on female participation, but the scheduled caste population is barely significant, whereas, Muslim population is not significant at all. The scheduled tribe population depresses female participation in the electoral process, but again the coefficient is not significant. When all the variables are controlled, accessibility has a negative impact on female participation. This is perhaps due to the fact that physical accessibility, measured by the ratio of polling stations-to-villages, is the highest in the big metropolitan areas, but as discussed before the female voter turnout is not very high in those highly urbanized areas.

The regional effect remains strong even after controlling for all the other variables. The participation of females in the elections is significantly higher in the South than the East, but North continues to show lower participation levels than the East.

The *t*-test for the difference in regression coefficients of the included categories of North and South shows that FVOTE is significantly different for these. The result (*t* value of 6.95) is significant at 0.05 level, indicating that the North and South are significantly different from each other in terms of their female voter participation.

Geographical Patterns of Female Voting

The relationships explored between female electoral participation and the other explanatory variables become clearer on analyzing the geographical patterns created by all these variables (see Maps: Appendix 1). The whole of Uttarakhand and Kumaon region consisting of the districts of Uttar Kashi, Tehri Garhwal, Chamoli, Pithoragarh, Almora, and Garhwal in northern Uttar Pradesh have very low female electoral participation (Map 10). These districts also have very low male voter participation (Map 24) indicating that the region as a whole has little voter turnout. As described in the previous chapter (Chapter 3), these hill districts have a cultural pattern that is different from the patriarchal kinship pattern prevalent in most of the northern states in India. This is evident from their very low patrilocal exogamy, their tendency of females not marrying early, a moderate female literacy, and fertility rates below the national average (Maps 9, 11–13). Female labor force participation is also very high in this region (Map 8), indicating that gender discrimination is not the reason for lower female voter turnout in this part of Uttar Pradesh. But a very low agricultural productivity (Map 15) in this largely rural area (urban population is very small in all these districts; Map 16), coupled with some proportion of scheduled caste population (Map 20), and very low physical accessibility (Map 25) (measured by ratio of polling stations to villages), have lowered the voter participation rates both for males and females in this region.

The Terai region and the plains of Uttar Pradesh, and the adjoining Maithila region in northern Bihar also have lower participation of females in the elections. The districts of Pilibhit, and Bharaich in Terai, and Barabanki, Lucknow, Hardoi, Sultanpur, Unnao, Rae Bareli, and Pratapgarh in the plains of Uttar Pradesh, and Pashchim and Purba Champaran, Gopalganj, and Siwan in Bihar particularly stand out with their very low female voter turnout. On the other hand, the male voter participation is reasonably high in all these districts, except Bharaich and Lucknow. Lucknow, despite being a significantly large urban center, has lower male and female voter turnouts. This could be due to the aforementioned reason of high levels of urbanization having a dampening effect on the voter participation. Moreover, the presence of a distinct Muslim culture in Lucknow is pushing down the female voter turnout even further. The large gender gap in voting indicates the presence of a strong patriarchal hold on women in the region as can be seen by a large proportion of early marriages, high levels of patrilocal exogamy, very low female literacy, and low levels of economic participation. The problem is compounded by low levels of development in the region and low accessibility to the polling stations. The presence of scheduled castes and Muslims in sizeable proportion do nothing to ease the situation.

The third region having low female turnout is in East-central India extending from southern Bihar, to the whole of inland Orissa, to four districts in eastern and one in southern Madhya Pradesh. This region stands out as the largest single block of nearly contiguous districts having very low female voter participation in India. This single block can be divided into two distinct groups: one, the districts of Sarguja, Siddhi, and Shadol in Madhya Pradesh, and Palamu, Hazaribagh, and Dhanbad districts in Bihar where the gender gap in voter turnout is high, and second, the districts in Orissa (except Kalahandi and Balangir) and Bastar in southern Madhya Pradesh which do not show a large difference between male and female voter participation. The patriarchal kinship structure in eastern Madhya Pradesh and southern Bihar (the first group) is more in line with the northern pattern evidenced by low literacy levels, high fertility, and larger proportions of females married under 19 years of age. On the other hand, most districts in Orissa, and Bastar in southern Madhya Pradesh (the second group) have a different cultural pattern than the North. Hence, in these districts it is not the active discrimination against women, as in the first group described above, but other factors that are responsible for their low female voter participation. Most of these districts have a sizeable scheduled tribe and some scheduled caste population, and very low development levels indicated by fewer males in non-agricultural workforce, low levels of urbanization, and less agricultural productivity. Moreover, accessibility to the polling stations in these sparsely populated areas also affects female voting negatively. Hence, it can be concluded that in the first group low levels of development coupled with a cultural pattern that lowers the cultural worth of women play a role in lowering female voter turnout, whereas in the second group it is the low level of development, presence of tribal populations, and physical constraints that are negatively affecting female participation in the electoral process.

Most districts in southern Rajasthan and, unexpectedly, Gujarat also have lower participation of females in the elections, with the districts of Jaisalmer in western Rajasthan, and Panch Mahals and the Dangs in western and southern Gujarat standing out conspicuously. The male-female gap is very high in Jaisalmer as well as nearly all the other districts of Rajasthan, though this is not the case with the low-female-participation—districts of the Dangs and Panch Mahals in Gujarat. The other districts in Gujarat do show a sizeable gender gap in voter participation. There is a considerable difference in kinship structures of these two states as indicated by the 'kinship' maps. A strong patriarchal structure that affects women's status negatively, presence of scheduled caste and even a sizeable Muslim population in Jaisalmer district, and low levels of development and accessibility to polling stations (Varma, 1997) seem to be the reasons for lower participation in Rajasthan. Whereas, a high proportion of non-Christian tribals, and low levels of development are depressing the female voter turnout in the Dangs and Panch Mahals districts of Gujarat. But the reasons for lower participation in other districts of Gujarat are not very clear. This part of India is reasonably well developed with high levels of urbanization, high agricultural productivity, and reasonably high proportions of males in the non-agricultural workforce. Moreover, the patriarchal kinship structures are different from the North, indicated by low proportion of early marriages, lower patrilocal exogamy, reasonably high female labor force participation and literacy, and below the national average fertility levels. The physical accessibility also does not seem to be hindering the participation of women (the ratio of polling stations to villages is quite high). Perhaps the urbanization-voting link discussed before is responsible for lower female participation in districts having a large urban population in Gujarat. But a more detailed investigation may yield a better explanation of the situation in Gujarat.

A very high female participation occurs in the southern states of Andhra Pradesh, Karnataka, Tamil Nadu, and Kerala, the eastern states of Manipur, Mizoram, and Tripura, and Punjab in the north. The districts extending from Jalgaon to the Vidarbha region of Maharashtra (Akola, Amravati, Nagpur, Bhandara, Wardha, Yavatmal, and Chandarpur), and the prosperous sugar-cane belt comprising of the districts of Ahmadnagar, Satara, Sangli, and Kolhapur in the southern part of the state have female voter turnout almost equal to the male voter participation, indicating that there is no active discrimination against women in political participation. This region also has a very high proportion of females engaged in economic activities and a reasonably high female literacy. Except for pockets of highly industrialized centers, around Bombay, Pune, and Nagpur, the development levels are not exceptionally high (Joshi, 1968). But a strong tradition of social movements by the reformists have had an enduring impact on the population of this region, leading to the break down of the caste and gender barriers, and encouraging female literacy and female participation in the political process (Joshi, 1968).

All the districts in Karnataka, except Bidar, Gulbarga, Bijapur, Raichur, and Bellary in the north, and the whole of Andhra Pradesh also show very high female voter turnout. These regions also have very high male voter participation, indicating a high level of political awareness and socialization among the masses. A cultural pattern that is conducive to women's involvement in social, political, and economic activities accompanied by moderately high levels of development have led to a higher participation by women in these states. All the districts of Kerala, except Palakkad and Idduki, have a high female voter turnout. Although Kerala is not a highly industrialized or urbanized state high levels of literacy and cultural/social institutions that have fostered political consciousness among almost all the classes have led to consistently high voter turnout in the state both for males and females (Hardgrave, 1975). The two districts that lag behind in female voter turnout have a sizeable scheduled caste population and are predominantly rural, with the lowest levels of industrialization and urbanization in Kerala. But despite these conditions the voter turnout, though not as high as the other districts of the state, is still much higher than many parts of northern India. As discussed in the last chapter, this indicates that cultural factors in this region play a larger role in influencing participation of women in the political arena than either the development levels or the social stratification.

The state of Tamil Nadu has a high voter turnout with over 50 per cent of women electors participating in the elections. The participation is the highest in the districts of Thanjavur and Pudukkottai in the eastern part of the state. The existence of a kinship system different from the North Indian Hindu-Brahminic one is illustrated in the kinship pattern maps. Fewer early marriages, negligible patrilocal exogamy, lower fertility levels, reasonably high female labor force participation, and high female literacy have contributed to larger proportions of women participating in the political process. Another important feature associated with political participation in this state has been the mass mobilization and politicization of the "backward" castes in the state. Tamil Nadu has a sizeable scheduled caste population, but mobilization of these lower castes by a nationalist political party (Dravida Munnetra Kazhagam—DMK) has led to a higher participation by these sections of the society[5] (Barnett, 1975). Those districts where the DMK was well established, for instance, Thanjavur (that now has been divided into Thanjavur and Pudukkottai districts) show a very high turnout for both men and women voters. This indicates that the mobilization of the large sections of these previously unmobilized populations, a kinship structure that does not lower the cultural worth of the women, and reasonably high levels of development (see Maps) are some of the reasons for high participation in this southern state.

Another cluster of high female participation emerges in the Northeastern region of India. Almost all the states have high female voter turnout. Most of these states have witnessed political agitations of some sort over the past decade and that may be the reason for increased politicization among these largely tribal lands. This coupled with a distinct cultural pattern has led more women to participate in the political process. The female voter participation in the states of Meghalaya and Arunachal Pradesh, though high, lags behind their neighbors, probably due to the difficulty in accessing the polling stations (see Map 25).

A cluster of four districts in northern India (Bhatinda, Sangrur, and Patiala in Punjab, and Ambala in Haryana) also exhibits higher female participation. High levels of development, largely fueled by very high agricultural productivity, has masked the ill-effects of a traditional Hindu-Brahminic culture leading to high literacy levels and political participation among women. The physical accessibility to the polling booths is also very high in this densely populated region of the country, aiding in the participation by women. Finally, the northern-most part of India, the state of Jammu & Kashmir, also shows very high political participation by women. A long separatist movement in this Muslim-dominated state has probably led to increased politicization of this ethnically distinct group, leading to a greater participation by their members. Thus, in this case political mobilization has reversed the expected relationship between Muslim population and participation of women in public arena.

Conclusion

This analysis examines the combined effects of economic, cultural, and regional factors on women's political participation in India. Political socialization has the largest impact on female voter turnout when all the other factors are accounted for. Patriarchal structures and development levels play a stronger role than social stratification in influencing female voter turnout. The regional variations persist despite controlling for measures of patriarchal kinship structures, economic development, and social stratification. This suggests that factors other than the ones considered here continue to influence the North-South-East differential in female voter turnout in India.

As done in the previous chapter, the geographical pattern of the association of female voter participation with the explanatory factors can be summarized as follows:

1. *Districts with high levels of economic development and a kinship structure that is favorable to women*: the states of Andhra Pradesh and Karnataka fall into this category.
2. *Districts with high levels of economic development but a kinship structure that lowers the cultural worth of women*: high development levels override the unfavorable kinship pattern to produce high female participation in Punjab and parts of Haryana.
3. *Districts with less economic development, but a favorable kinship structure*: in some cases very low levels of development weigh much more heavily compared to a favorable kinship structure and curtail female participation in the political process. For instance, in the Uttarakhand and Kumaon region of Uttar Pradesh female voter turnout is very low despite a favorable kinship structure. But in other cases, such as Kerala, having a cultural system that is favorable to women can lead to higher participation despite less economic development.
4. *Districts with low economic development and an unfavorable kinship structure*: this is the worst case of all where the female participation is among the lowest. The Terai and the plains of Uttar Pradesh, Madhya Pradesh, Bihar, and Rajasthan are prime examples of this category.

Over and above this classification based on kinship structures and development levels there is another category of states in India where levels of development, kinship structures, and social stratification have been overridden to show greater participation of women in the political process. These are the states of Maharashtra, Tamil Nadu, the Northeastern states, and the Kashmir portion of the Jammu & Kashmir state. The major reason for high levels of political participation in this disparate group of states is political mobilization either by the nationalist political parties as in the case of Tamil Nadu, or by the social reformist movements, as in Maharashtra, or by separatist movements, as in Kashmir and the Northeast. The political mobilization of the masses has successfully altered the expected relationships between development levels and political participation, for instance in the Northeast there is a high female voter turnout despite lower levels of development. Similarly, it is expected that scheduled castes and Muslim population could lead to lower participation levels, but in the cases of Kashmir, which is predominantly Muslim, and Tamil Nadu, that has a large scheduled caste population, these relationships have been reversed by politicization of the population. This suggests that increased mobilization could lead to higher participation by the people making the democracy more responsive and vibrant. But all the states mentioned above have a kinship structure different from the core-Hindu-Brahminic pattern of the North. Micro-level studies focusing on social or political movements in the heartland Hindi belt of India could show whether the effects of mass mobilization can override the patriarchal stronghold on women in those parts of India.

Women's political status can be assessed by the role women play in the political institutions and the extent of their participation in the formal processes of political system. Though it is clear that achieving "numerically impressive participation in the political process" is not the end goal in itself (Kumari and Kidwai, 1994: 24), it definitely is a step towards altering the structures of power. As this study demonstrates, any effort to analyze the political status of women should include both cultural and economic factors influencing the lives of women in India.

Notes

1. Data for State Assembly elections pertains to various years. Assembly elections in 1980: Arunachal Pradesh, Goa, Daman and Diu, Gujarat, Kerala, Manipur, Mizoram, Orissa, Punjab, Sikkim, Pondicherry; 1978: Andhra Pradesh, Karnataka, Meghalaya, Maharashtra, 1977: Bihar, Haryana, Himachal Pradesh, Jammu & Kashmir, Nagaland, Tripura, West Bengal, Madhya Pradesh, Rajasthan, Tamil Nadu, Uttar Pradesh.
2. Election data was not available for eleven districts (total Andaman & Nicobar Islands; Chandigarh; Dadra & Nagar Haveli; Faridabad in Haryana; Pulwama, Badgam, Kupwara, and Kargil in J&K; Wayanad in Kerala; total Lakshadweep; and Ghaziabad in UP). Hence, this analysis is based on 355 districts.

3. It was not possible to include the Urban-Rural analysis in this chapter due to the unavailability of the electoral data for the urban and rural constituencies.
4. Dikshit (1995) tested the relationship between voter turnout in the 1962 and 1967 state legislative assembly elections and the ratio of polling stations to villages for all the states and came up with similar results (higher the ratio, greater is the voter turnout).
5. In the 1940s DMK (translated into English it stands for 'Dravidian Progressive Federation') emerged as a major nationalist political party championing the cause of the under-represented non-Brahmin castes in Tamil Nadu (The Brahmins occupy the highest place in the Indian social system, which is hierarchically organized into endogamous groups) (Bhatt, 1980). Using cultural nationalist symbols, like the Tamil language, they were instrumental in the politicization of these backward groups which led to higher participation of these castes in the political process of the state. For a complete description of the emergence of the non-Brahmin movement in Tamil Nadu see Barnett (1975), and Rudolph and Rudolph (1967).

6

Conclusion

A considerable body of literature has emerged outlining the status of women in India. Starting from the earliest historical accounts of women in the early nineteenth century, two distinct facets of Indian women emerge in the writings: on the one hand is the image of women as a source of power (*Shakti*), while on the other hand, females are dependent, exploited, and oppressed and considered subordinate to males (Berreman, 1993; Forbes, 1996). The truth lies somewhere in between. Women in India live under powerful social and cultural structures that constrain their lives, but they also "use social arrangements creatively to carve out spaces for themselves" (Jeffery and Jeffery, 1996: 2). This study was not focused on women's agency, but rather, was an attempt to understand the diversities and variations in women's lives in different parts of the country. Tremendous improvements can be seen in the health and well-being of women over the years. Studies indicate an increase in literacy levels, life expectancy, and workforce participation for women in almost all parts of India. But women's status relative to men is still far from equal. Though gender differentiation is present throughout India, there are wide spatial inequalities in terms of women's status. This study, thus, was an effort to describe and explain these spatial variations.

Most early studies on women's status focused on *status* as a unitary construct and tried to search for a universal explanation of the low status of women. Recognizing the inadequacies of such research the present study focused on the multidimensionality of the concept and argued that the complexity of the phenomenon makes it necessary to see how women are represented in the various dimensions of status. Also in many studies the interrelationship between the various economic and non-economic structural factors is carried on at the abstract level without the actual demonstration of these relationships on the ground, but the present research has demonstrated the variety and specificity of these interrelationships and their effect on women's status in India by using the available census data.

Summary of Findings and Policy Implications

To understand the complex multidimensional concept of *status of women* and to explore the causes behind the regional variations in women's position in India, a wide range of different variables were chosen. Based on the results of Principal Components Analysis, three independent dimensions (economic, social, and political) emerged, indicating that the dynamic and variable nature of women's status cannot be captured by any single dimension. The first dimension was labeled as the economic status of women as it includes women's participation in the economic activities. The second dimension has to do with social well-being of women measured by literacy. Finally, the third dimension represents issues and activities concerning power and control over women. The independence of these three dimensions is highlighted by the contrasting performance of specific states on each dimension. Once the multidimensionality of the concept was established the position of women in each dimension was examined by exploring the underlying causes for the low status of women.

The persistence of the female-male gaps in human development in India is definitely indicative of the low status assigned to women in the Indian social system. This is obvious from the findings which suggest that fewer females than males are involved in waged labor, are literate, and participate in the electoral process in India. Further, a significant finding of the study is that the structural processes of kinship structures, development, and social stratification interact with each other to affect women's status differently in different parts of India. Thus, 'place' does play a significant role in the constitution of gender differences in India.

Kinship structure appears to be the most powerful factor affecting women's participation in the workforce (the economic dimension), in most cases overriding the development factors. Development levels, in fact, affect female participation negatively. This is due to the fact that the majority of jobs in the highly industrialized and urbanized regions are not suited to women because of their lower skill and educational levels. A very strong patriarchal kinship structure inhibits women's participation in the labor force in almost the whole of North India, except the culturally distinct regions of Jammu & Kashmir, Himachal Pradesh, and hill districts of Uttar Pradesh. On the one hand are the less developed regions such as the plains' districts of Uttar Pradesh, and most of Bihar and Madhya Pradesh, where a twofold or double oppression of patriarchal kinship structures and low levels of development produce low participation rates for women. On the other hand are the two most developed states in northern India, Punjab and Haryana, which also exhibit very low levels of female labor force participation due to a strong patriarchal structure. This shows that the kinship structures have a very strong effect on women's participation in the workforce, irrespective of the development levels in northern India.

The culturally distinct regions in northern India mentioned above—Kashmir, which is predominantly Muslim, parts of Himachal Pradesh that are largely tribal, and the hill districts of Uttar Pradesh—all have kinship structures that are different from the north-Indian Brahminical pattern and thus, exhibit a higher participation of women in the workforce. Similarly, a favorable kinship pattern in southern India has led to very high levels of participation of women in the economic sector. These examples clearly suggest that the social processes, reflected in the kinship structures, have a very strong impact on female labor force participation rate and that subordination of women in the economic realm is clearly a product of the kinship structures. In terms of policy implications it means that increasing development levels will not make much of a difference in women's economic status in these parts of India, rather as Rubin (1976, rpt. 1990: 102) suggests reorganization of the gender system is necessary to improve women's economic status. And this, she feels, can be achieved through sustained political action.

The only state that stands out as an anomaly to this 'kinship structure-economic status' link is Kerala in the southern part of the country. Here one would expect that favorable kinship patterns would lead to a higher participation by women in the waged labor, but it is just the opposite. Despite a favorable kinship pattern the female labor force participation rate is low in Kerala due to a sluggish economy which is unable to generate jobs for both men and women. In this case, then, the development factors are weighing more heavily than kinship patterns in influencing female labor force participation rate. Hence, in order to bring about a change in the economic position of women strategies to improve the economic structure will have to be employed in Kerala.

Kinship structures prevalent among the dominant groups continue to hold their sway despite caste and class differences in the Indian society. In other words, social stratification does not have a significant independent effect on the economic status of women. It was found that the scheduled castes in India conform broadly to the behavioral patterns of the dominant castes in the region. If scheduled caste population was concentrated in a region having an unfavorable kinship pattern, such as in Uttar Pradesh or Bihar, then their presence further reduces women's participation in the workforce. In such situations, despite very low levels of development (where women's labor is essential for the maintenance of the household), very few scheduled caste women venture out into the labor force, reducing the overall participation rate of women. Another evidence of this conformity with the dominant group can be seen in most southern states which have a high proportion of scheduled castes; here the kinship patterns are favorable, which leads to a higher participation by women belonging to these castes, increasing the overall female workforce participation rate.

An anomaly to this relationship can be seen in the case of Rajasthan where, despite unfavorable kinship structures, the scheduled caste presence does not hinder the participation of women in the workforce in the rural areas. This perhaps is due to conditions of extreme poverty that is bringing more scheduled caste women into the labor force in some of the districts in eastern Rajasthan. Poverty in Uttar Pradesh and Bihar, however, does not seem to have the same effect, which suggests that the relationship between gender and social hierarchy is far from straightforward. In Uttar Pradesh or Bihar, contrary to the often proposed relationship between caste and gender[1] (see Srinivas, 1977; Liddle and Joshi, 1986), women's position is not tied to the caste it belongs, but rather it depends on the historical development of gender relations in specific regions. In other cases, like Rajasthan, the lower caste women do seem to have more autonomy, supporting the caste-gender thesis, i.e., the subordination of women increases with increasing caste status. This underlines the importance of recognizing the significance of spatial unevenness and geographic variations in these structural processes (in this case kinship structures and social stratification) and their varying impacts on female status.

As sometimes is the case with the scheduled castes, Muslims also behave in a pattern similar to the dominant group of the region. In the Muslim-dominated districts of Kerala and Jammu and Kashmir female labor force participation is high, perhaps due to the impact of kinship structures that are favorable to women's participation in the 'outside' activities. But the presence of Muslims in the plains of Uttar Pradesh and parts of Bihar suppresses female labor force participation. Muslim women in these parts, unlike in Kerala and Kashmir, observe strict 'purdah' (veiling) and their movements outside the home are restricted, keeping with the larger environment in these regions.

The tribal populations in India usually have a kinship pattern that differs significantly from the traditional Hindu-Brahminical culture and this leads to higher labor force participation rates for these groups even though they are almost at the bottom of the social hierarchy, along with the scheduled castes. For instance, where large proportions of scheduled tribes are present in southern Madhya Pradesh and Orissa the workforce participation rate for women is very high, suggesting that a large number of tribal women are engaged in economic activities. Here again the impact of kinship structures seems to be overriding development and social stratification factors.

Thus, kinship structure is decidedly the most influential factor in determining women's participation in the economic activity. According to McDowell (1991: 128):

> 'Familial' relations and culturally-specific attributes of femininity shape women's availability for and access to waged labor as well as playing a key role in producing and maintaining gender ideologies.

Nevertheless, as clearly demonstrated in this study, the interaction of these varied kinship structures with the varying development levels and the different social hierarchies produces a complex picture of women's economic status in India.

The exploration of the second dimension of women's status (the social status) suggests a different picture from the one presented above. Here development levels seem to be playing a more significant role than the kinship structures or social stratification in defining regional variations in female literacy levels in India. Again this is not the case universally. Urbanization operates uniformly to reduce the effects of kinship structure and social stratification on female literacy. This can be seen by the fact that the effects of kinship structures on female literacy are stronger in the rural areas than in urban India. Despite a strong patriarchal structure in Punjab and West Bengal, female literacy is high, indicating that high levels of development are overriding the constraints created by the kinship factors. For most of Rajasthan, Uttar Pradesh, Bihar, and Madhya Pradesh, low levels of development and unfavorable kinship structures combine to produce very low levels of literacy, with pockets of high female literacy around the urban centers. The policy implications of such a finding are that increasing urbanization could perhaps lead to higher literacy levels in these states. Contrastingly, in Kerala and the hill districts of Uttar Pradesh a favorable kinship structure leads to very high levels of female literacy despite low levels of development. Here kinship structures seem to be more influential in affecting women's social status.

The presence of scheduled castes, especially in the rural areas, generally depresses female literacy as can be seen in Uttar Pradesh plains and Bihar. Low levels of development coupled with patriarchal kinship structures and a low position in the social hierarchy leads to what has been referred to as the 'triple oppression' of scheduled caste women (see McDowell's (1991) reference to Black women in capitalist societies). The presence of scheduled castes also seems to depress female literacy levels in Andhra Pradesh, despite a favorable kinship structure. Low levels of urbanization could be the primary factor that is influencing literacy levels in most districts of the state. Increased urbanization may lead to a rise in their social status, as is observed in the cases of Punjab and West Bengal which have sizeable scheduled caste populations. It should be noted that the female labor force participation in these same districts of Andhra Pradesh is high, indicating that women from this strata of society are involved in economic activities but as most of these are working in the agricultural sector there is no impetus to be literate.

The presence of scheduled tribe population has a variable effect on female literacy. The districts with tribal population that is largely Christian have very high literacy levels, as in the case of most Northeastern states. But the presence of non-Christian tribal population, for instance, in southern Madhya Pradesh and Orissa, depresses female literacy largely due to very low levels of development. Here again increased urbanization may help increase the literacy levels of both males and females.

The presence of Muslims is usually associated with lower female literacy, but this is not always the case. For example, urbanization seems to override the effects of Muslim presence in the cities of Meerut and Lucknow in Uttar Pradesh. In Kerala, it is the kinship structures that have a stronger impact than either development or social stratification. This is evident in the case of Malappuram district where there is a sizeable Muslim population, but the existence of social institutions that have encouraged literacy levels override the effects of social stratification.

Again this analysis brings to light that, though development levels may be strongly influencing female literacy in general, there is a need to see how these structural aspects vary over space individually and in interaction with each other. It is this variation that leads to differences in female literacy from one region of India to another.

Finally, the analysis of the political status of women (the third dimension) shows that political socialization has the largest impact on women's voter participation in India, followed by development levels and the kinship structures. This is evidenced well in Maharashtra, Tamil Nadu, and the Northeast where sustained political or social movements have led to a higher participation of women in the political process. But this is not always the case. For instance, development seems to be the most important factor in producing high levels of political participation by women in Punjab and Haryana. Here there is no strong history of sustained political or social movements, except for the recent brief separatist movement in Punjab. These states also have a strong patriarchal kinship structure, but high levels of development seem to override all other factors leading to very high female voter turnout. Low levels of development appears to be the reason behind lower participation of women in the political process in the Kumaon and Uttarakhand regions despite a favorable kinship structure. The double oppression of low levels of development and an unfavorable kinship structure depress women's participation in the political process in plains of Uttar Pradesh and Bihar. So in all the above cases 'development' seems to be a significant factor affecting female voter participation and it is possible that increased development levels may lead to higher participation of females in these regions.

But in contrast to the situation in Uttar Pradesh and Bihar, Kerala shows a very strong female participation despite low levels of development. Here a favorable kinship structure and, more importantly, the presence of social institutions that have fostered political consciousness among all the classes seem to be playing a significant role in positively affecting female participation in the political process.

Social stratification does not have a very strong effect on female participation in the electoral process. In fact, the politicization of these marginal groups leads to very high levels of voter participation in some parts of the country. Though a majority of the scheduled castes again adhere to the behavior pattern of the dominant castes in terms of voter participation, increasing politicization of these groups, especially in regions where kinship structures are favorable, leads to higher participation rate in the political process. For instance, in Tamil Nadu the mobilization and politicization of the backward castes has led to a very high rate of female voter turnout.

Similarly, the participation of the scheduled tribes and Muslims depends largely on the political socialization of the group. In the tribal districts in Madhya Pradesh and Gujarat female participation in the political process is very low. The absence of any mass political or social movements combined with low levels of development and less accessibility depress female voter turnout in these districts. On the other hand, the primarily tribal northeast has witnessed political agitations over the past years which has led to a high female voter turnout. Similarly, the presence of Muslim population in the plains' districts of Uttar Pradesh lowers the participation rate of women in the political arena in the absence of any sustained political movements in this less developed part of the state. But increased politicization of the group in the Muslim-dominated state of Jammu & Kashmir has led to a high female voter turnout.

Bringing all these different facets of women's status together, it can be concluded that women's economic, social, and political status are influenced by different factors. Spatial variations in 'sex/gender systems', uneven development, and social stratification combine to influence women's status differently in different places. This indicates that particularity of the place affects the status of women in India. In other words, the effect of 'Region' is strong in influencing women's status. In this study 'Region' is considered as the unique historical combination of social and economic processes and the major divisions considered are the North, South and East.

But, despite controlling for all the cultural and economic variables included in this study the North-South-East differences in women's status are not fully accounted for. This indicates that there is much more that makes a 'Region' unique and that perhaps other factors than the ones included in this study could lead to a greater understanding of the variations in women's status in India. This is task for future studies.

Conclusion

In conclusion, the multidimensionality of the concept of status of women is obvious and, in fact, further reinforced by the fact that each dimension seems to be influenced by a particular structural factor. But going beyond that, it is important to recognize the mutual interdependence of gender relations, development levels, and social stratification without underestimating the full significance of each in Indian society. In some cases economic development interacts with kinship patterns to produce the major spatial variations in women's status in India, and in others, it is development levels and social stratification that has the greatest influence.

This study has raised significant questions about the universality of gender inequality in India. In spite of the limitations of the data, the results outlined above seem meaningful in the context of the social/historical realities of women's lives in different parts of India. Moreover, one positive aspect of such a detailed empirical analysis for the whole of India is its wide spatial sweep, which documents the spatial and social patterns of gender inequality for the whole country and can be very useful in designing general policies on a state or an all-India level. At the same time the exploration of the relationships at the district level make it possible to design locally appropriate policies for districts that have been identified as 'problem areas'. Utilizing the results of this study, individual case studies using different tools, such as interviewing techniques, and at a different scale of analysis can be taken up which may illuminate women's lives in specific contexts. This would be more sensitive to and closer to the experiences of women being studied and could complement the present work, a task that can be taken up in subsequent research efforts.

Notes

1. The extant literature on the position of Indian women suggests that there is a negative relationship between class and patriarchy. Women from the lower socioeconomic strata (such as the scheduled castes) exhibit greater sexual freedom and higher labor force participation than the upper class women from the affluent sections of the society (Srinivas, 1977; Liddle and Joshi, 1986).

Appendix 1
Maps

Map 1
Administrative Divisions: Indian States

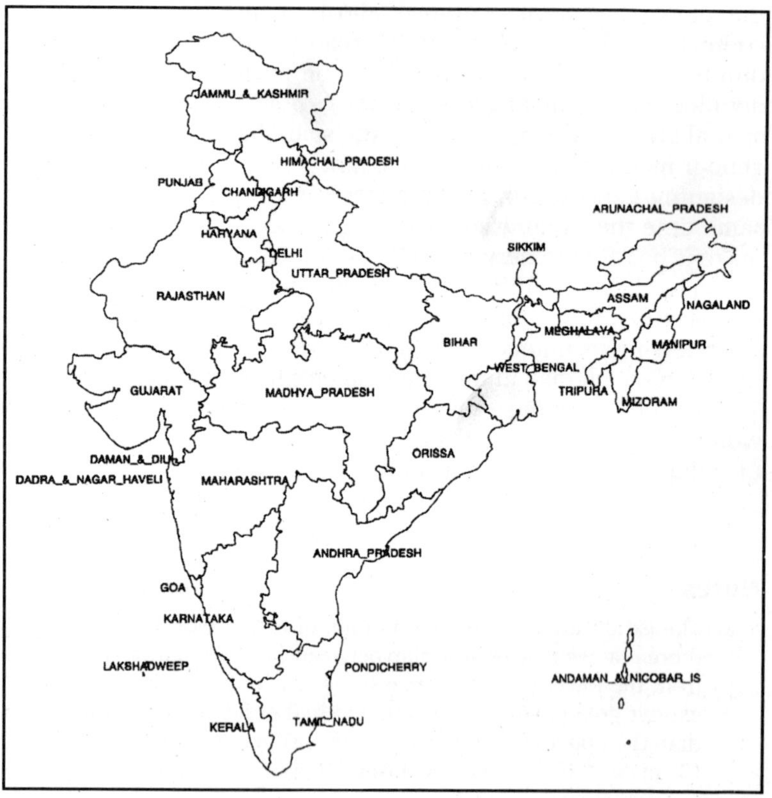

Map 2a

Administrative Divisions: North and East India Districts 1981

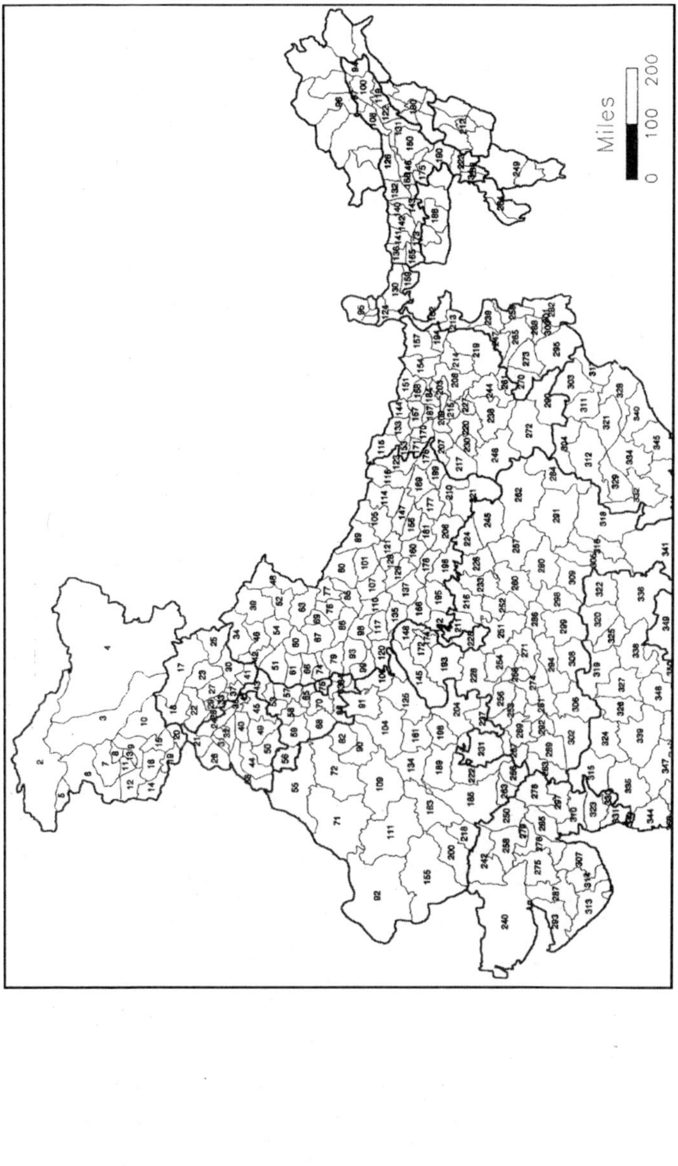

Map 2b

Administrative Divisions: South India Districts 1981

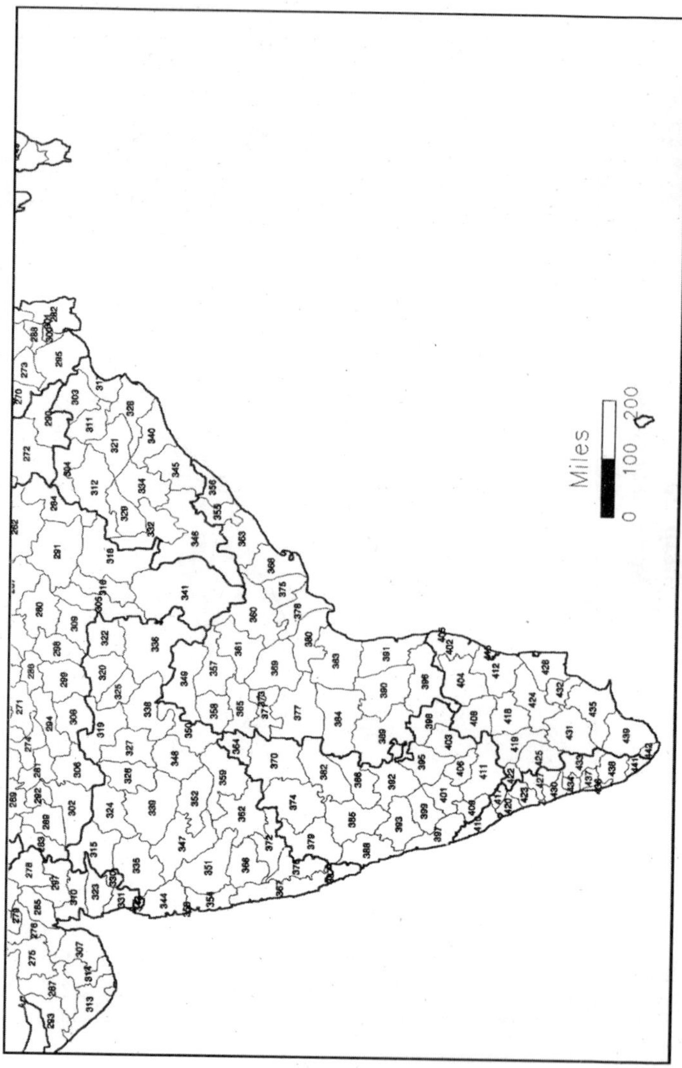

Andhra Pradesh

District	No.
Srikakulam	356
Vizianagaram	355
Vishakhapatnam	363
East Godavari	368
West Godavari	375
Krishna	378
Guntur	380
Prakasam (Ongole)	383
Nellore	391
Chittoor	396
Cuddapah	390
Anantapur	389
Kurnool	384
Mahbubnagar	377
Rangareddi	371
Hyderabad	373
Medak	365
Nizamabad	358
Adilabad	349
Karimnagar	357
Warangal	361
Khammam	360
Nalgonda	369

Arunachal Pradesh

District	No.
Arunachal Pradesh (total)	96

Bihar

District	No.
Patna	209
Nalanda	215
Nawada	227
Gaya	220
Aurangabad	230
Rohtas	217
Bhojpur	207
Saran	170
Siwan	171
Gopalganj	153
W. Champaran	115
E. Champaran	133
Sitamarhi	144
Muzaffarpur	167
Vaishali	187
Begusarai	203
Samastipur	184
Darbhanga	168
Madhubani	151
Saharsa	154
Purnia	157
Katihar	194
Munger	208
Bhagalpur	214
Santhal Pargana	219
Dhanbad	261
Giridih	244
Hazaribag	238
Palamu	246
Ranchi	272
Singhbhum	290

Goa, Daman & Diu

District	No.
Goa (total)	100

Gujarat

District	No.
Jamnagar	293
Rajkot	287
Surendranagar	275
Bhavnagar	307
Amreli	314
Janagadh	313
Kachchh	240
Banaskantha	242
Sabarkantha	250
Mahesana	258
Gandhinagar	279
Ahmedabad	276
Kheda (Kaira)	285
Panch Mahals	278
Vadodara	297
Bharuch (Broach)	310
Surat	323
Valsad (Bulsar)	331
The Dangs	330

Haryana

District	No.
Ambala	43
Kurukshetra	53
Karnal	57
Jind	58
Sonipat	65
Rohtak	70
Faridabad	84
Gurgaon	83
Mahendragarh	88
Bhiwani	68
Hisar	59
Sirsa	56

Himachal Pradesh

District	No.
Chamba	18
Kangra	22
Hamirpur	29
Una	28
Bilaspur	33
Mandi	27
Kullu	23
Lahul & Spiti	17
Shimla	30
Solan	37
Sirmaur	41
Kinnaur	25

Jammu & Kashmir

District	No.
Anantnag	9
Pulwama	13
Srinagar	8
Badgam	11
Baramula	7
Kupwara	6
Kargil	3
Ladakh	4
Doda	10
Udhampur	15

Kuthua	20
Jammu	19
Rajauri	16
Punch	12

Karnataka

Bangalore	403
Belgaum	379
Bellary	386
Bidar	364
Bijapur	374
Chikmangalur	399
Chitradurga	392
Dakshin Kannad	397
Dharwad	385
Gulbarga	370
Hassan	401
Kodagu (Coorg)	409
Kolar	398
Mandya	406
Mysore	411
Raichur	382
Shimoga	393
Tumkur	395
Uttar Kannad	388

Kerala

Cannanore	410
Wayanad	417
Kozhikode	420
Malappuram	423
Palghat	427
Trichur	430
Ernakulam	434
Idukki	433
Kottayam	437
Alleppey	436
Quilon	438
Trivandrum	441

Madhya Pradesh

Morena	145
Bhind	148
Gwalior	172
Datia	174
Shivpuri	193
Guna	228
Tikamgarh	211
Chhatarpur	216
Panna	233
Sagar	251
Damoh	252
Satna	226
Rewa	224
Shahdol	257
Sidhi	245
Mandsaur	231
Ratlam	267
Ujjain	269
Shajapur	253
Dewas	281
Jhabua	283
Dhar	289
Indore	292
West Nimar	302
East Nimar	306
Rajgarh	256
Vidisha	254
Bhopal	268
Sehore	274
Raisen	271
Betul	308
Hoshangabad	294
Jabalpur	260
Narsimhapur	286
Mandla	280
Chhindwara	299
Seoni	298
Balaghat	309
Surguja	262
Bilaspur	291
Raigarh	284
Raj Nandgaon	305
Durg	316
Raipur	318
Bastar	341

Maharashtra

Greater Bombay	353
Thane	344
Raigarh (Kolaba)	354
Ratnagiri	367
Nashik	335
Dhule	315
Jalgaon	324
Ahmadnagar	347
Pune	351
Satara	366
Sangli	372
Salapur (Sholapur)	362
Kolhapur	376
Aurangabad	339
Parbhani	348
Bid (Bhir)	352
Nanded	350
Osmanabad	359
Buldana	326
Akola	327
Amravati	319
Yavatmal	338
Wardha	325
Nagpur	320
Bhandara	322
Chandrapur	336

Manipur

Manipur (total)	212

Meghalaya

Meghalaya (total)	188

Mizoram

Mizoram (total)	249

Nagaland

Nagaland (total)	180

Orissa

Sambalpur	312
Sundargarh	304
Kendujhar	311
Mayurbhanj	303
Baleshwar	317
Cuttack	328
Dhenkanal	321
Phulabani (B.Khndml)	334
Balangir	329
Kalahandi	332
Koraput	346
Ganjam	345
Puri	340

Punjab

Gurdaspur	21
Amritsar	26
Firozpur	38
Ludhiana	40
Jalandhar	32
Kapurthala	31
Hoshiarpur	24
Rupnagar (Ropar)	35
Patiala	45
Sangrur	49
Bathinda	50
Faridkot	44

Rajasthan

Ganganagar	55
Bikaner	71
Churu	72
Jhunjhunu	82
Alwar	91
Bharatpur	106
Sawai Madhopur	125
Jaipur	104
Sikar	90
Ajmer	134
Tonk	161
Jaisalmer	92
Jodhpur	111
Nagaur	109
Pali	163
Barmer	155
Jalore	200
Sirohi	218
Bhilwara	189
Udaipur	185
Chittaurgarh	222
Dungarpur	263
Banswara	266
Bundi	198
Kota	204
Jhalawar	237

Sikkim

Sikkim (total)	95

Tamil Nadu

Madras	405
Chengalpattu	402
North Arcot	404
South Arcot	412
Dharmapuri	408
Salem	418
Periyar	419
Coimbatore	425
Nilgiri	422
Madurai	431
Tiruchchirappalli	424
Thanjavur	426
Pudukkottai	432
Ramanathapuram	435
Tirunelveli	439
Kanniyakumari	442

Tripura

Tripura (total)	264

Uttar Pradesh

Uttar Kashi	34
Chamoli	39
Tehri Garhwal	46
Dehradun	42
Garhwal	54
Pithoragarh	48
Almora	52
Nainital	63
Saharanpur	51
Muzaffarnagar	61
Bijnor	60
Meerut	66
Ghaziabad	74
Bulandshahr	79
Moradabad	67
Rampur	69
Budaun	86
Bareilly	76
Pilibhit	77
Shahjahanpur	85
Aligarh	93
Mathura	99
Agra	120
Etah	98
Mainpuri	117
Farrukhabad	110
Etawah	135
Kanpur	137
Fatehpur	178
Allahabad	206
Jalaun	166
Jhansi	192
Lalitpur	225
Hamirpur	195
Banda	196
Kheri	80

Sitapur	101
Hardoi	107
Unnao	129
Lucknow	128
Rae Bareli	160
Bahraich	89
Gonda	105
Bara Banki	121
Faizabad	147
Sultanpur	156
Pratapgarh	181
Basti	114
Gorakhpur	116
Deoria	123
Azamgarh	169
Jaunpur	177
Ballia	176
Ghazipur	199
Varanasi	210
Mirzapur	221
West Bengal	
Koch Bihar	159
Jalpaiguri	130
Darjiling	124
West Dinajpur	162
Maldah	213
Murshidabad	239
Nadia	259
24 Pargana	282
Calcutta	301
Haora	300
Hugli	288
Medinipur	295
Bankura	273
Puruliya	270
Barddhaman	265
Birbhum	247
Union Territories	
Andaman & Nicobar Islands	400
Chandigarh	47
Dadra & Nagar Haveli	343
Delhi	75
Lakshadweep	413
Pondicherry (total)	415

Map 3a

Selected Cities and Regions of India: Cities

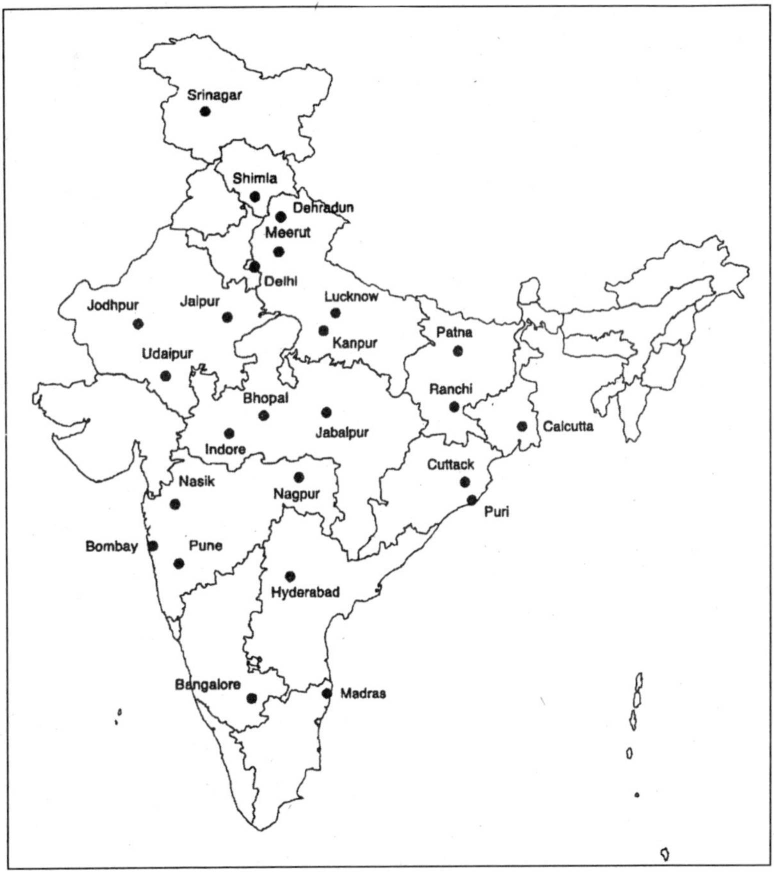

Map 3b

Selected Cities and Regions of India: Regions

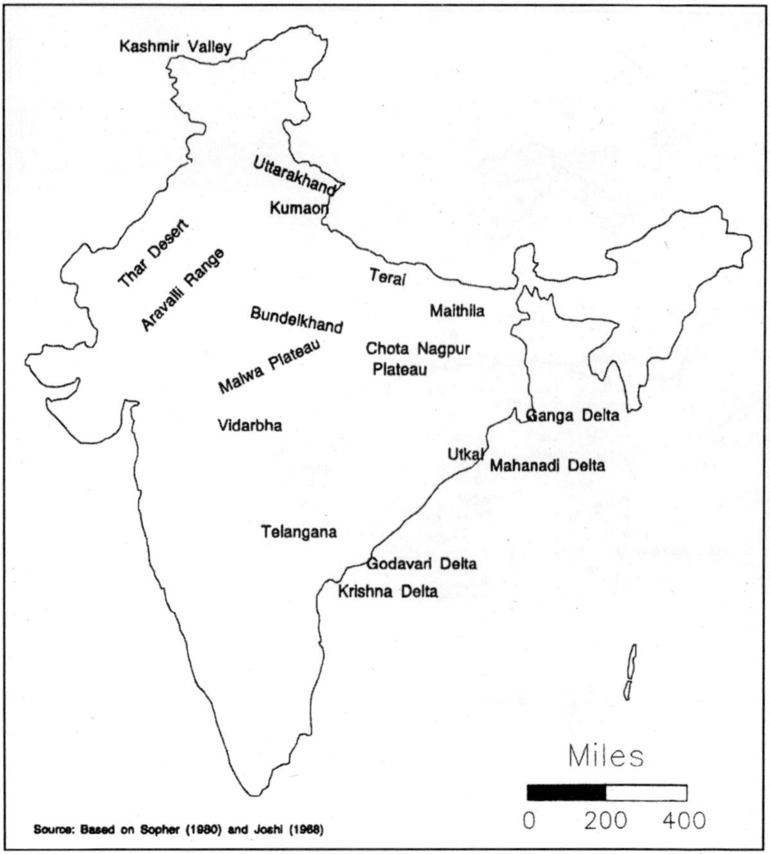

Map 4
Economic Status of Women 1991

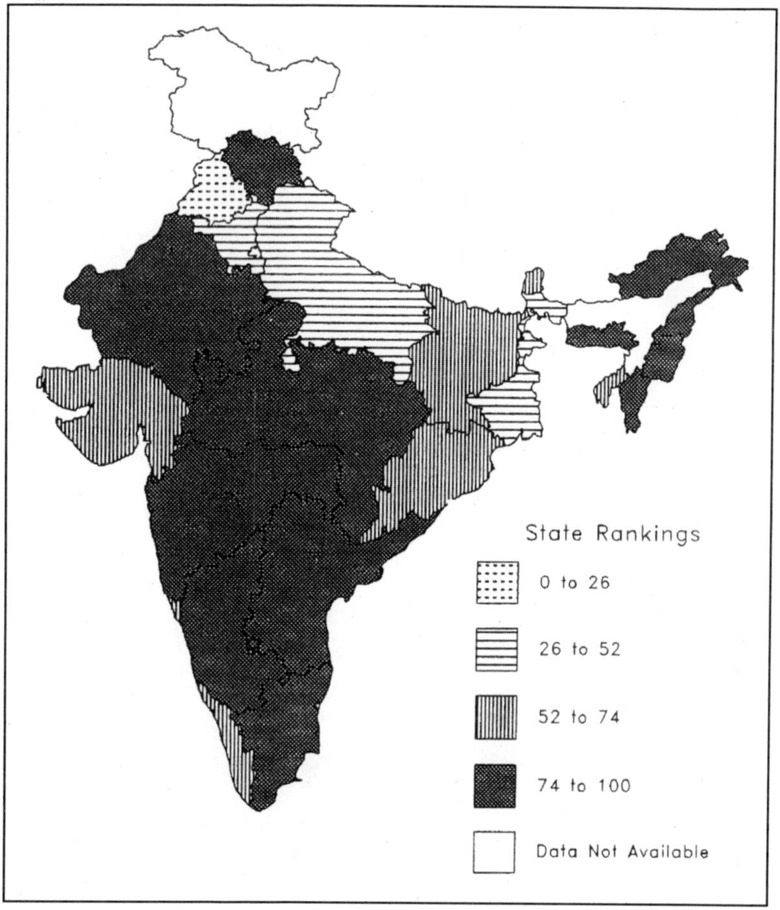

Map 5

Political Status of Women 1991

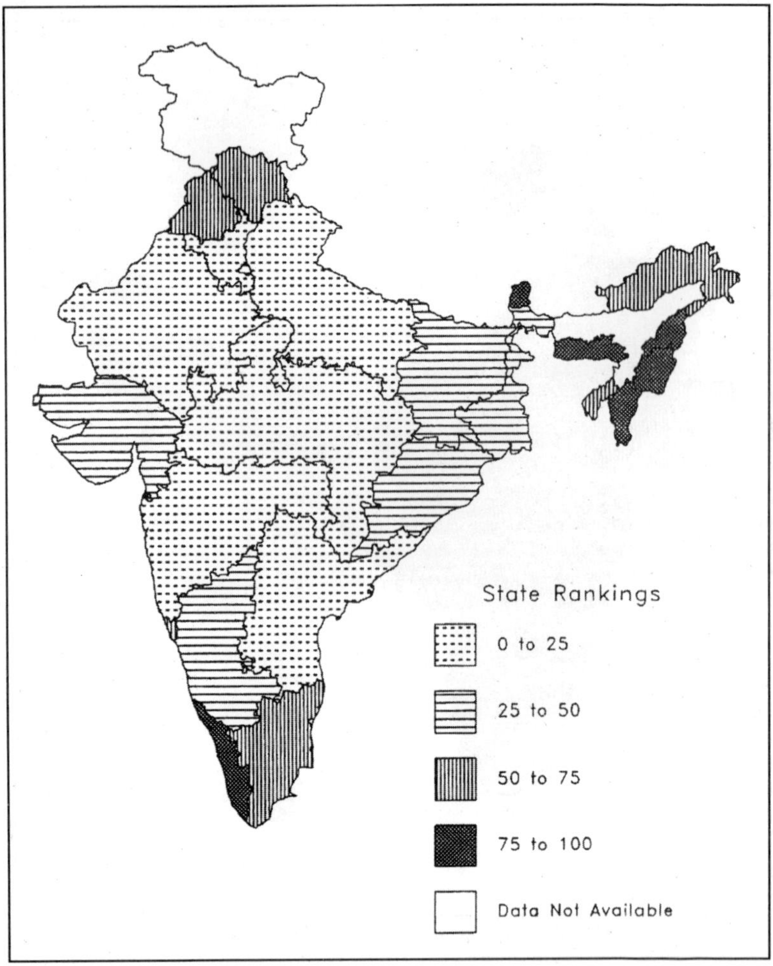

Map 6

Social Status of Women 1991

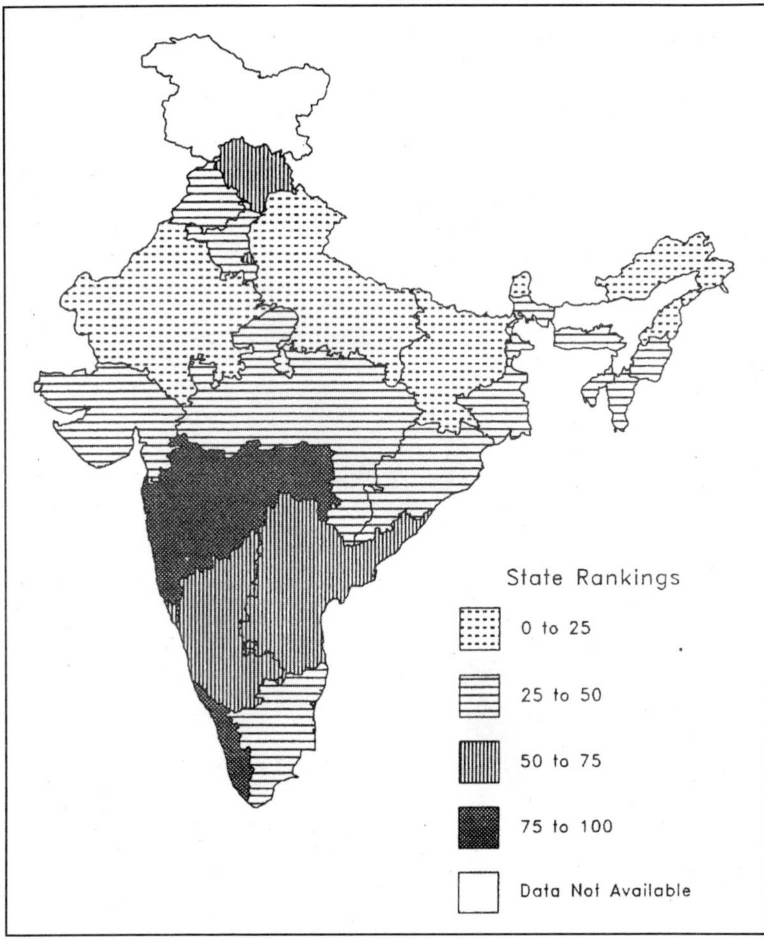

Map 7

Population Below Poverty Line 1987-88

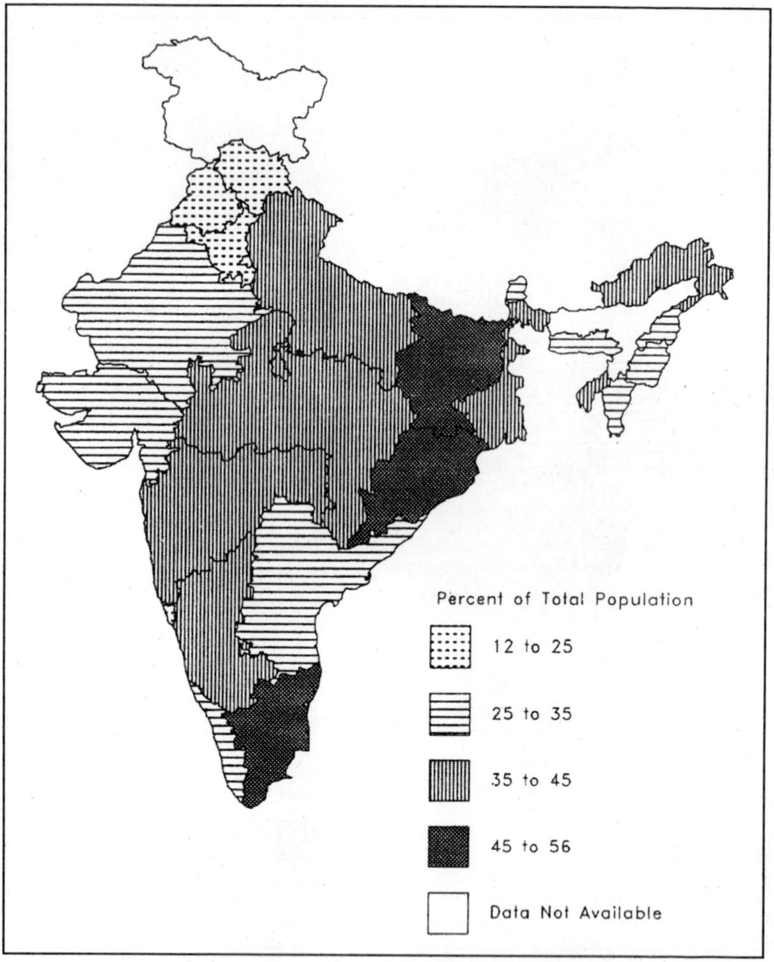

Map 8

Female Labor Force Participation Rate 1981

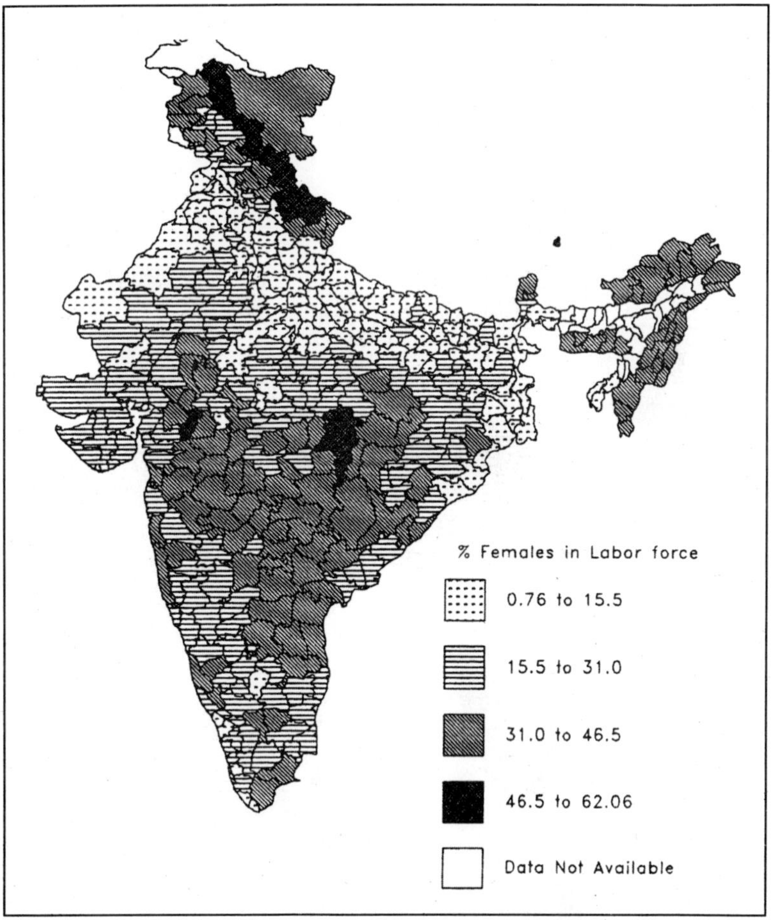

Map 9

Female Literary Rate 1981

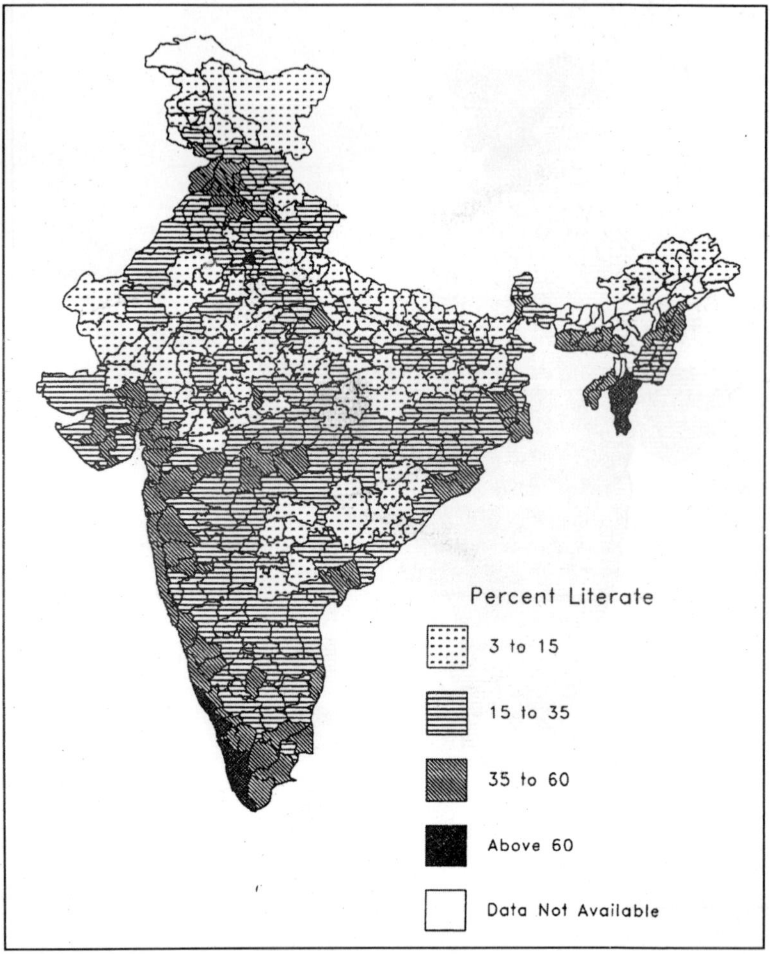

Map 10

Female Voter Participation 1977-1980

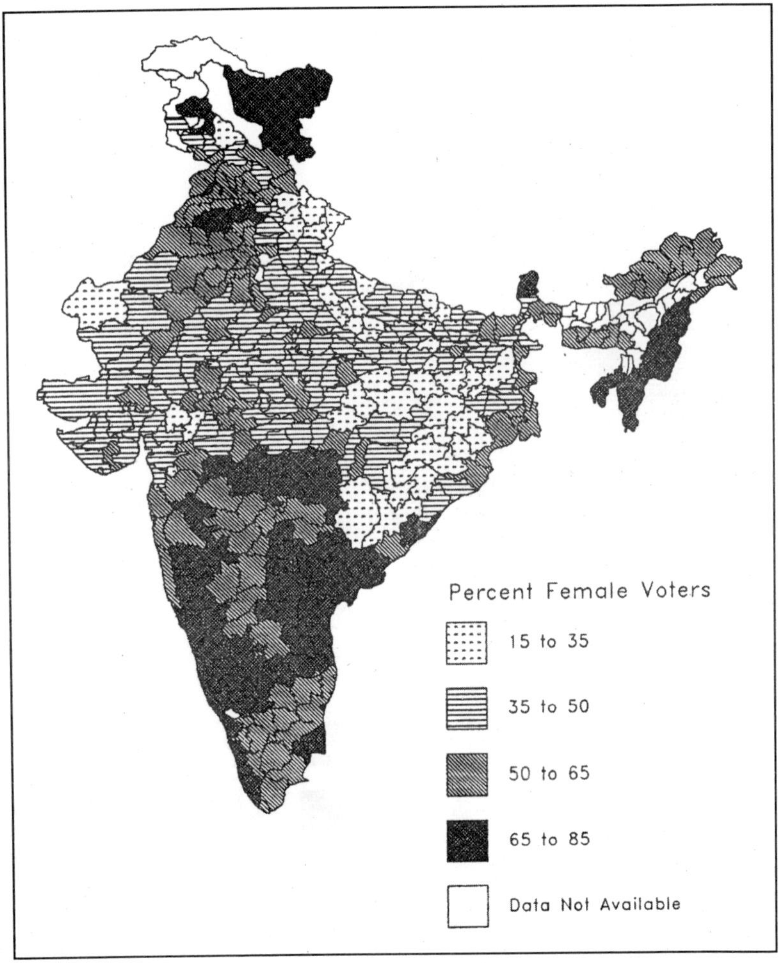

Map 11

Females Married Under 19 Years of Age 1981

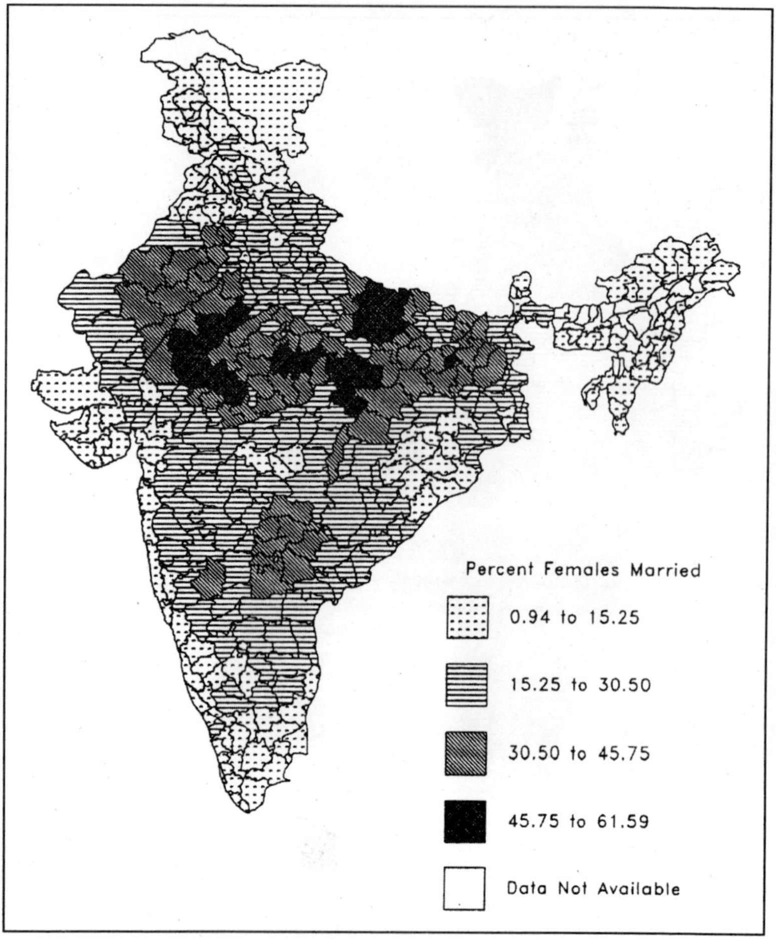

Map 12
Female Migration 1981

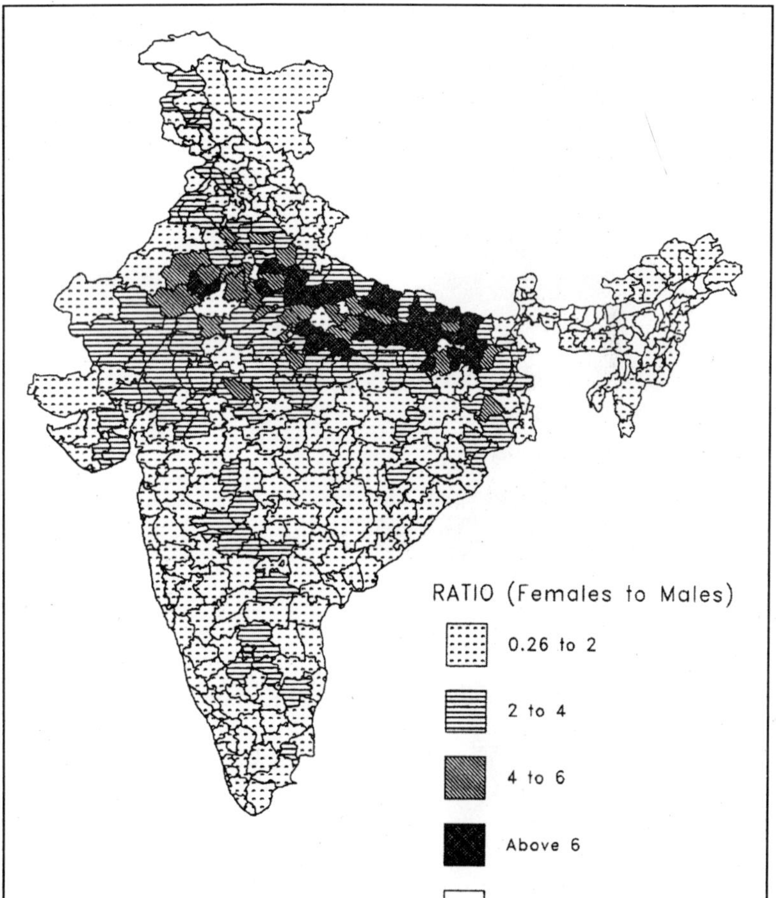

Map 13
Fertility Rate 1981

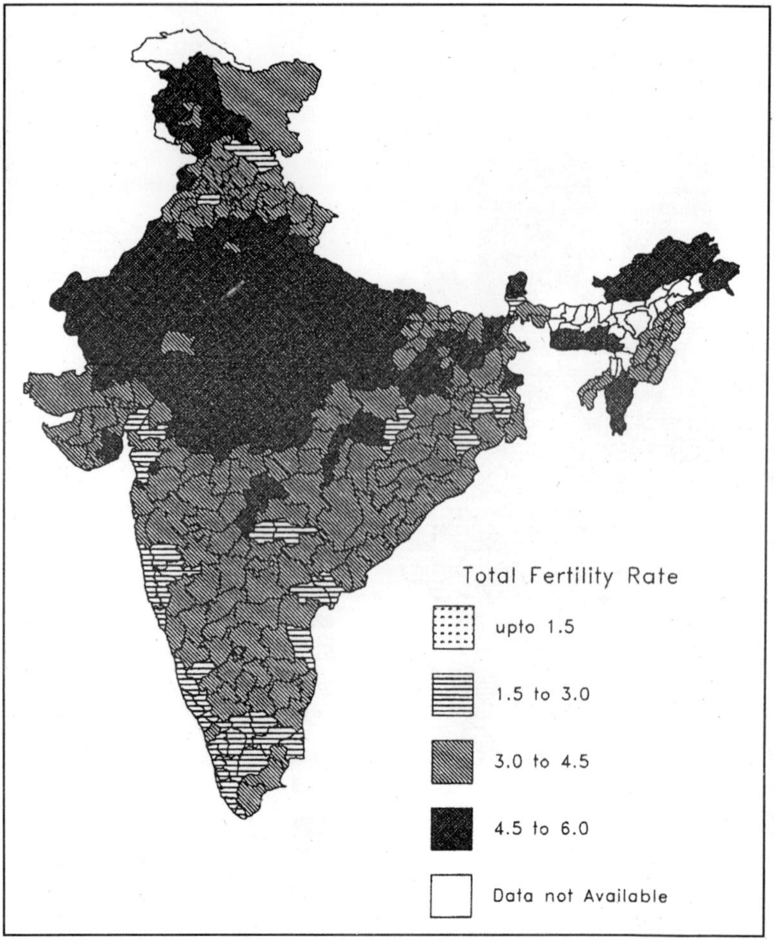

Map 14
Juvenile Sex Ratio

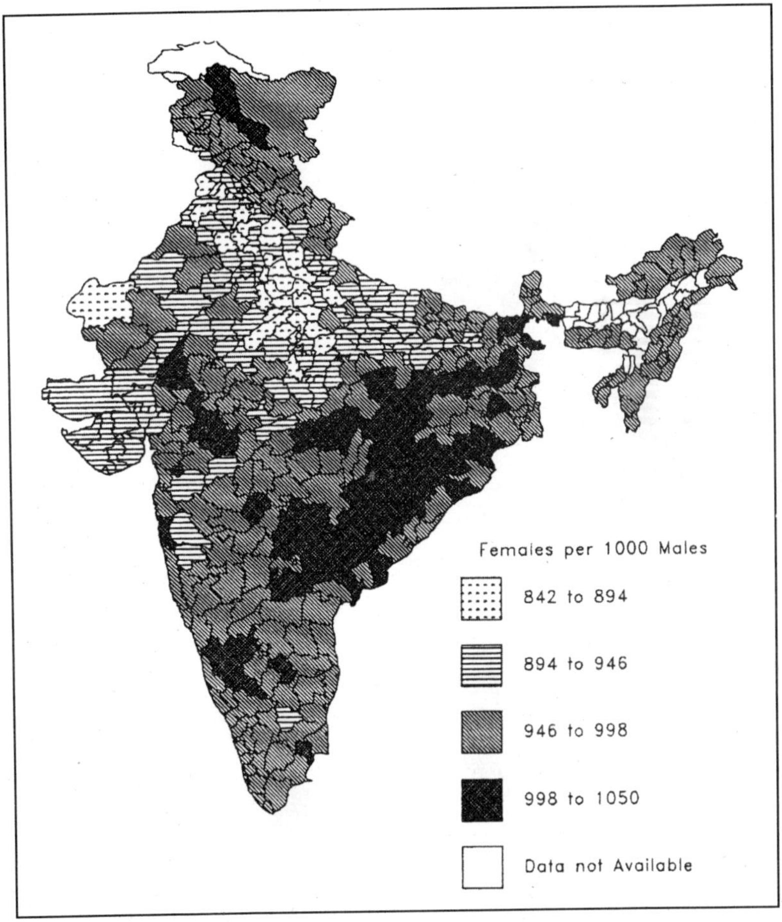

Map 15

Agricultural Product per Farm Worker 1981

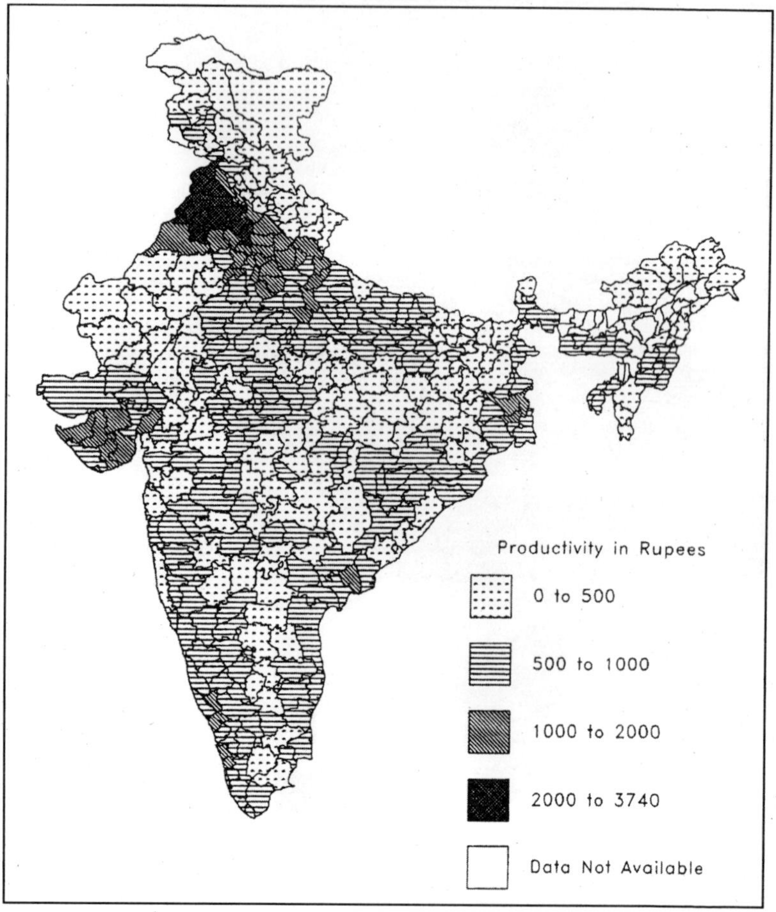

Map 16
Urban Population 1981

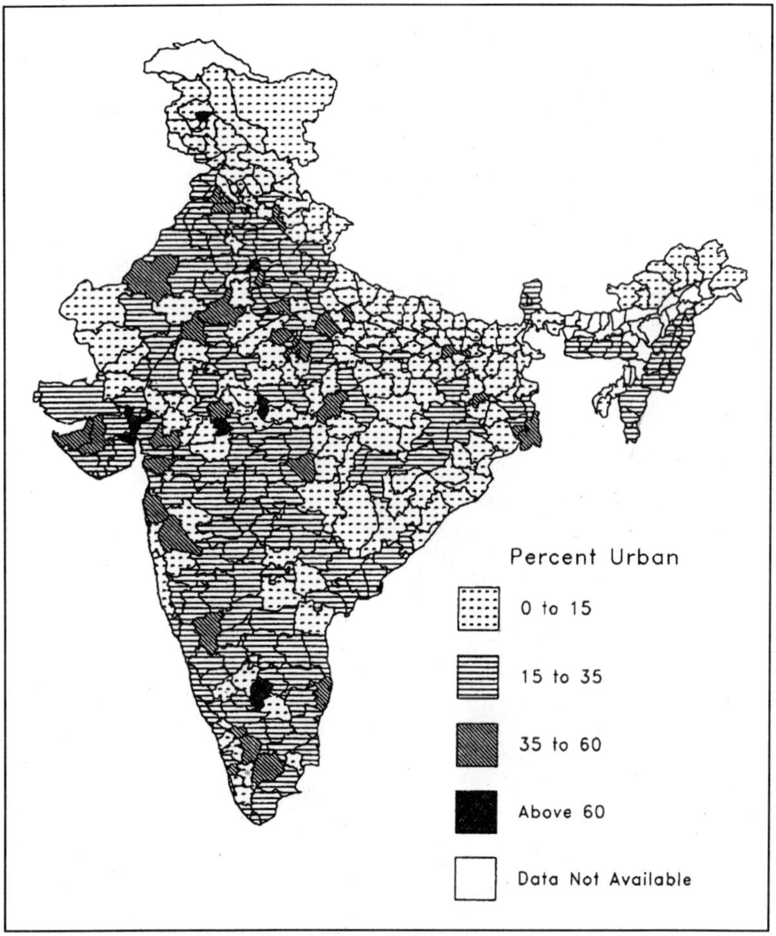

Map 17

Male Labor Force Participation Rate 1981

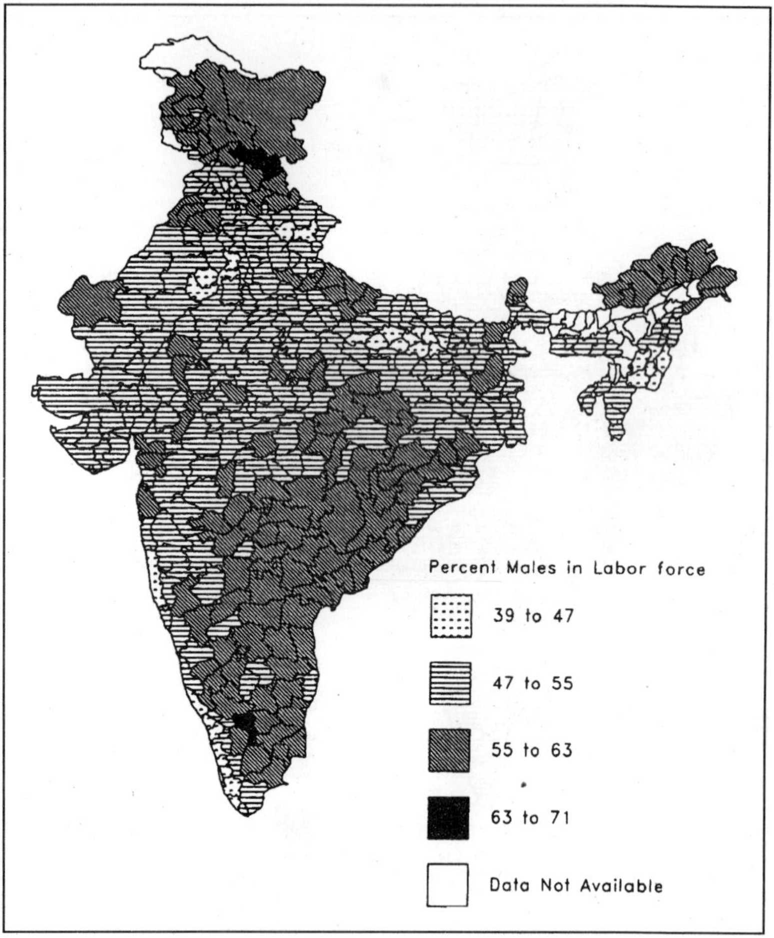

Map 18

Males in Non-Agricultural Workforce 1981

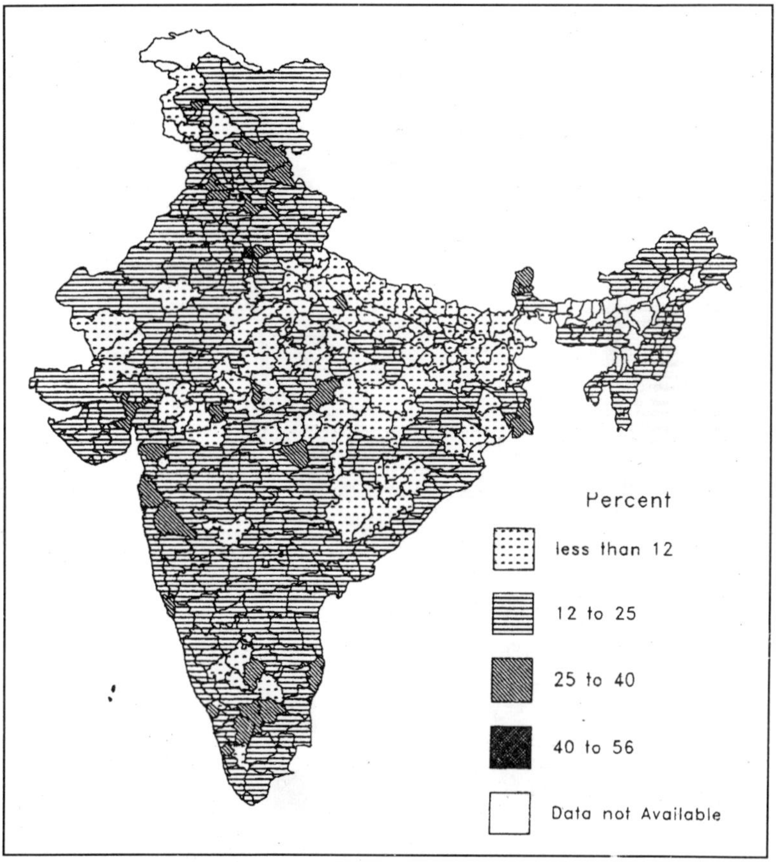

Map 19

Male Literacy 1981

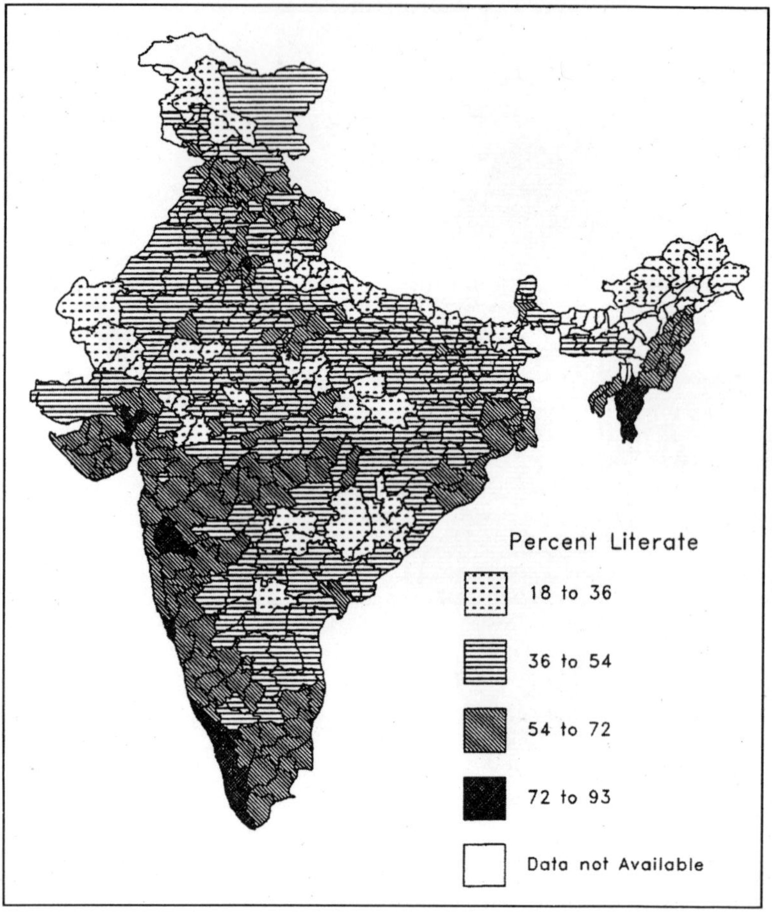

Map 20

Scheduled Caste Population 1981

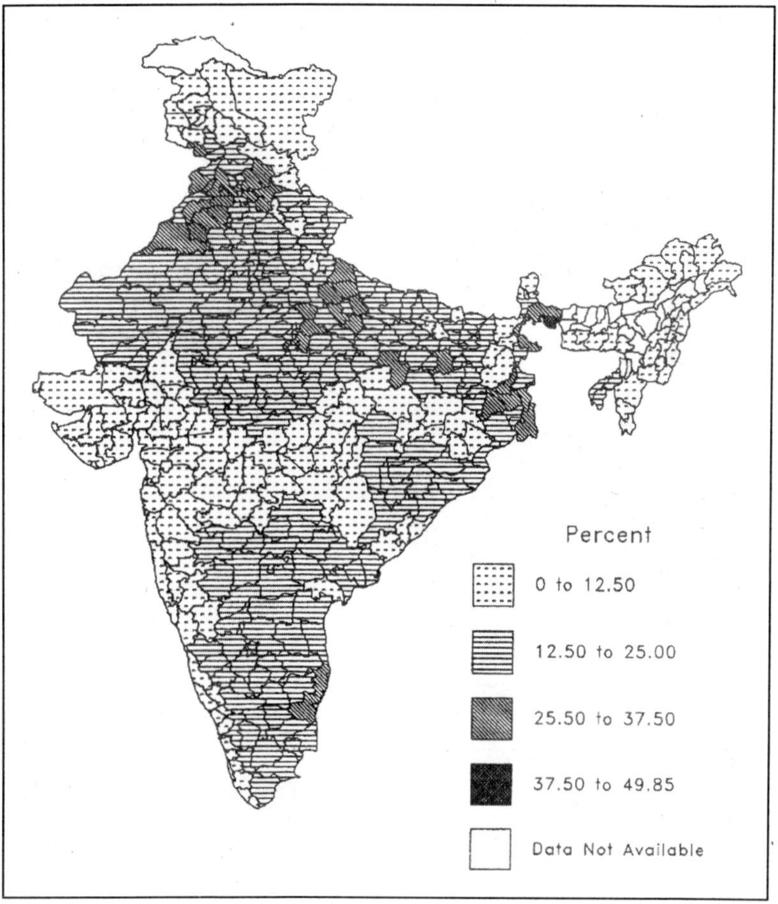

Map 21

Scheduled Tribe Population 1981

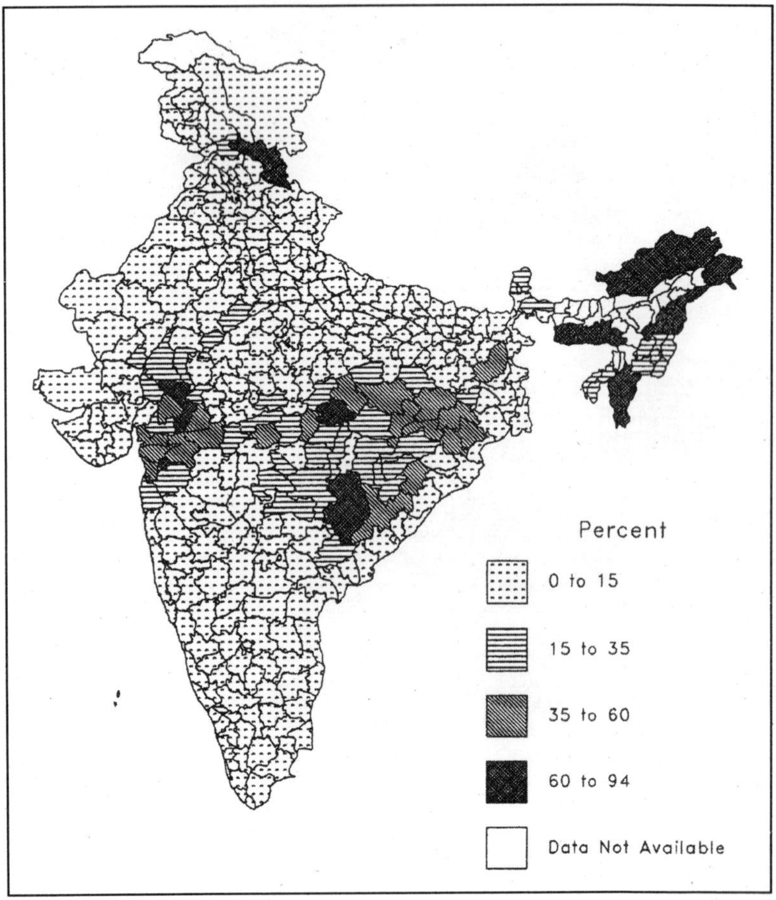

Map 22

Muslim Population 1981

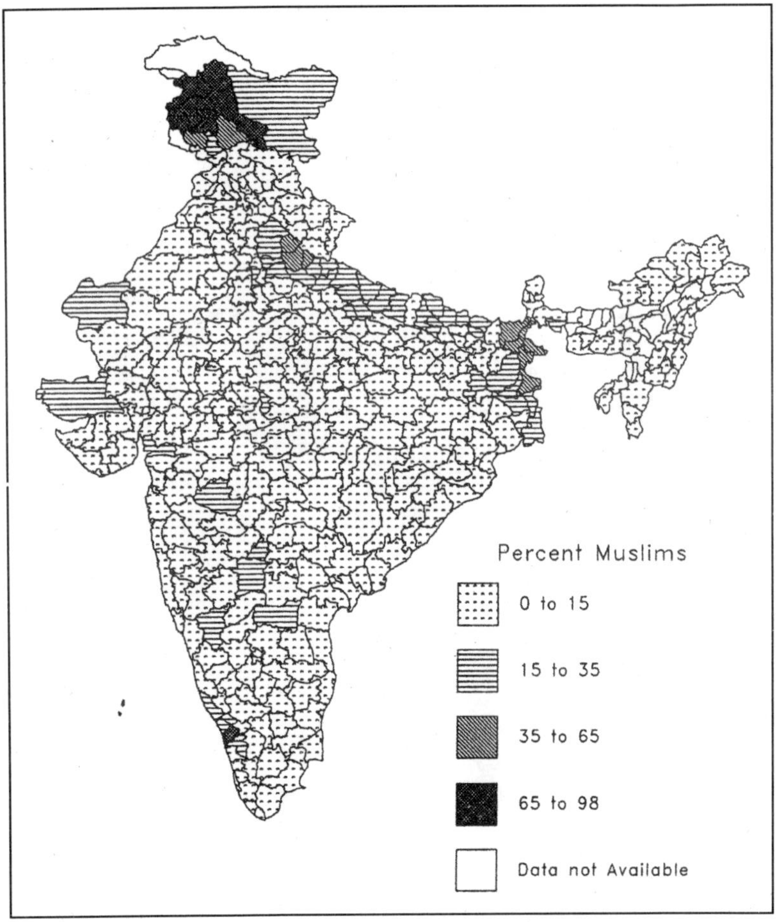

Map 23
Area Devoted to Rice Cultivation 1981

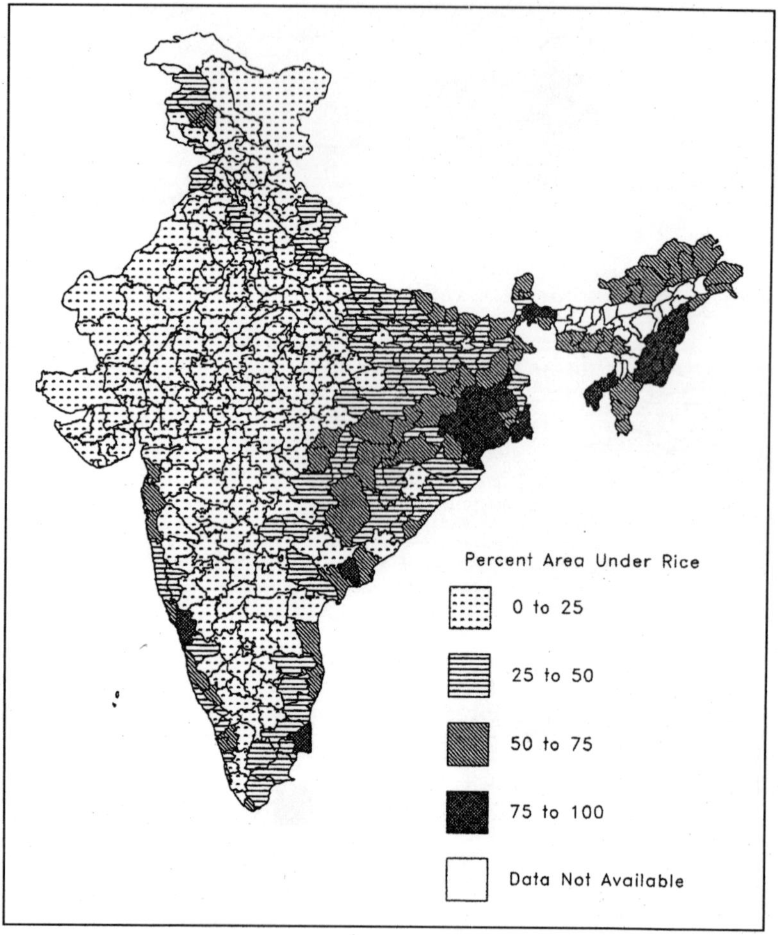

Map 24

Male Voter Participation 1977-1980

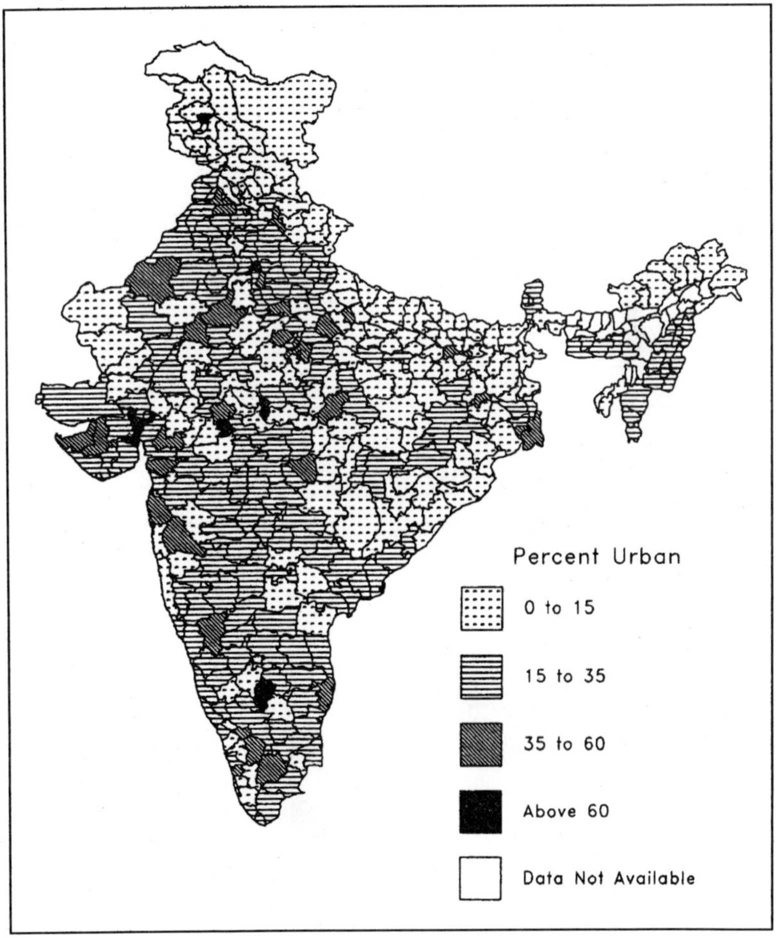

Map 25

Physical Accessibility Election Years 1977-1980

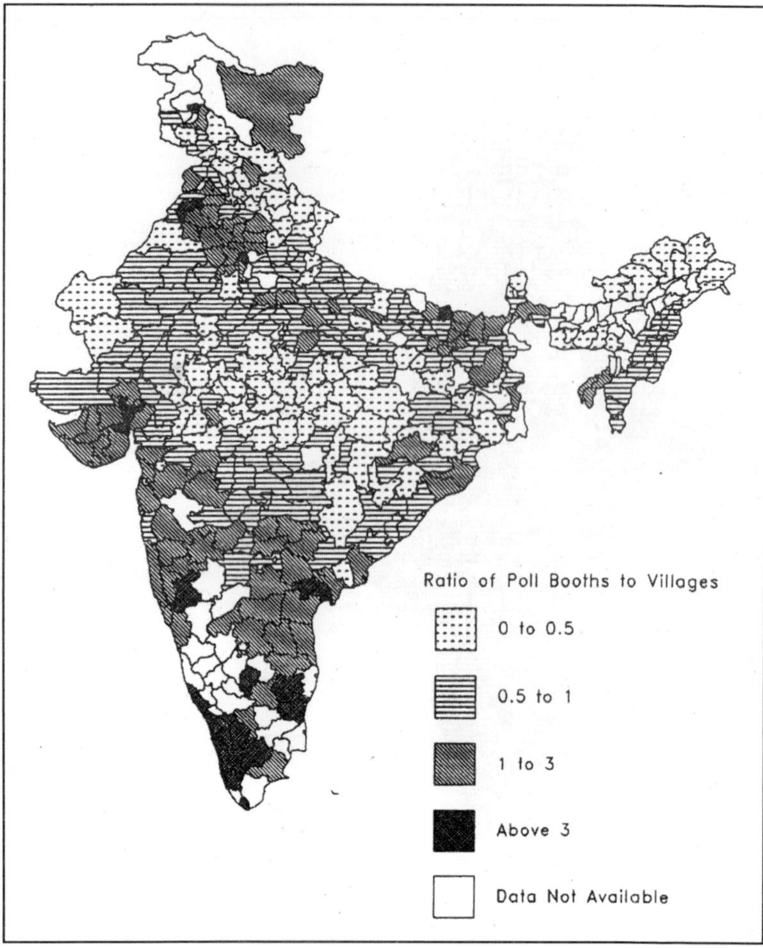

Map 26

Difference in Rural and Urban Female Work Participation 1981

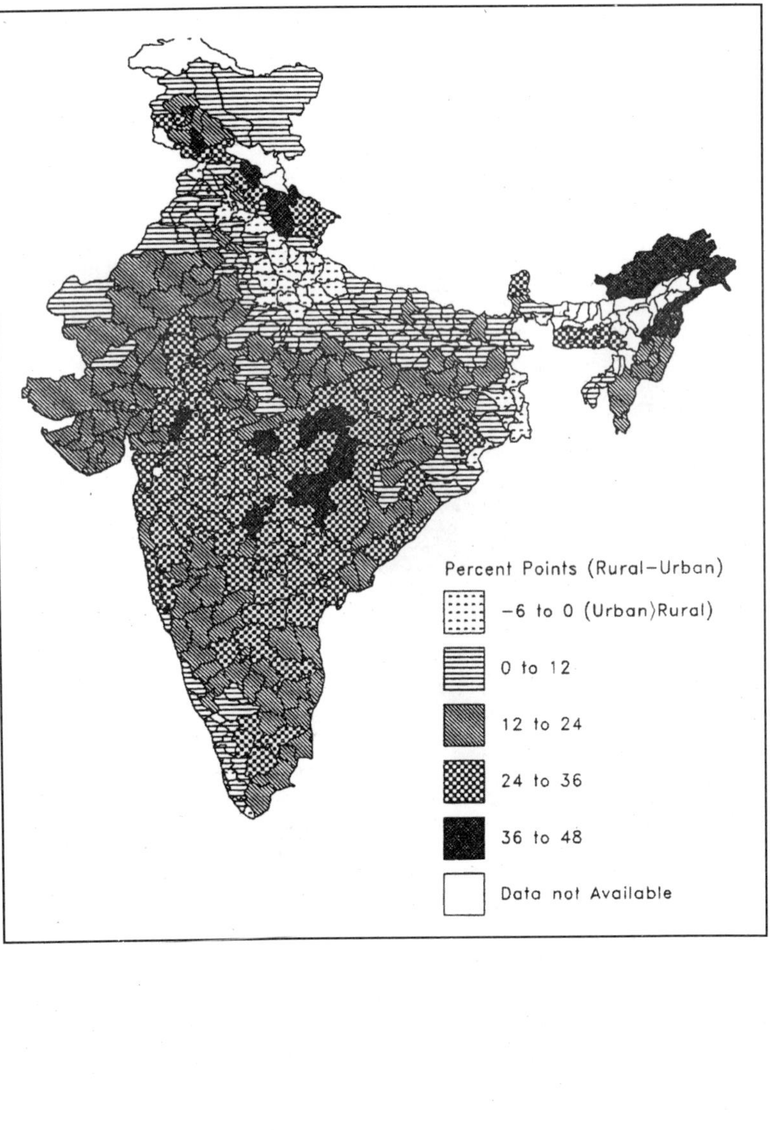

Map 27

Rural Scheduled Caste Population 1981

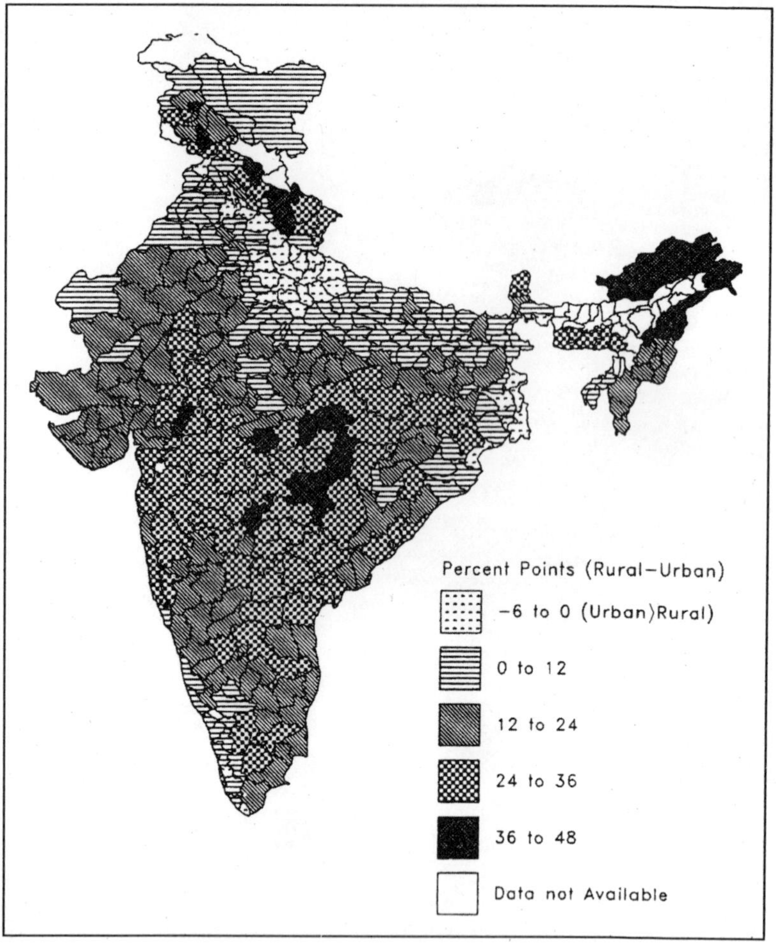

Map 28

Urban Scheduled Caste Population 1981

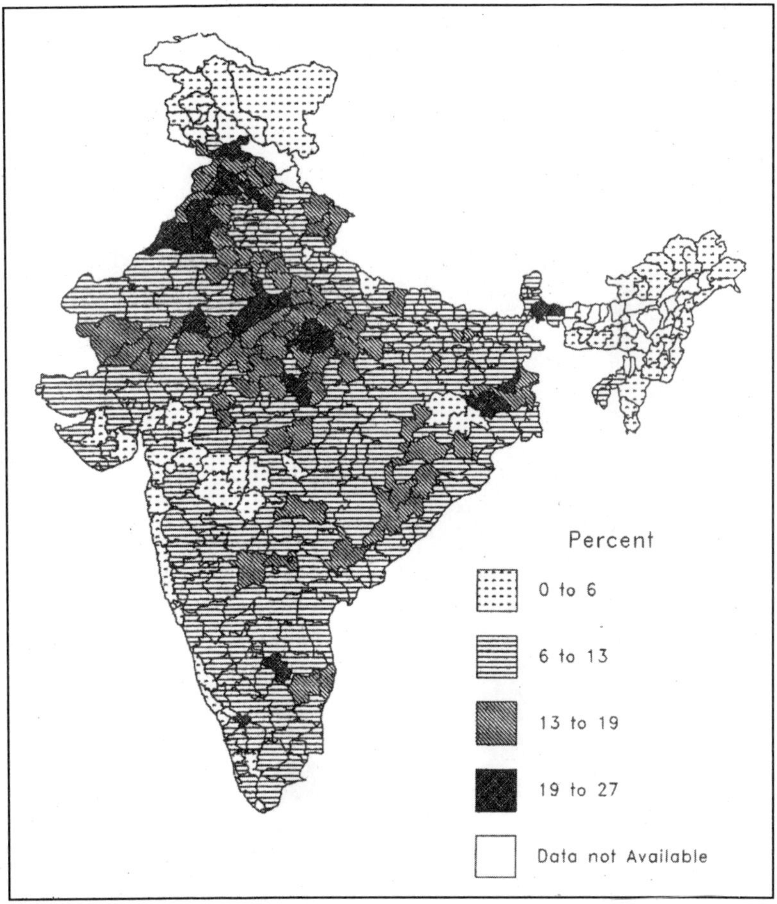

Map 29

Difference in Rural and Urban Female Literacy 1981

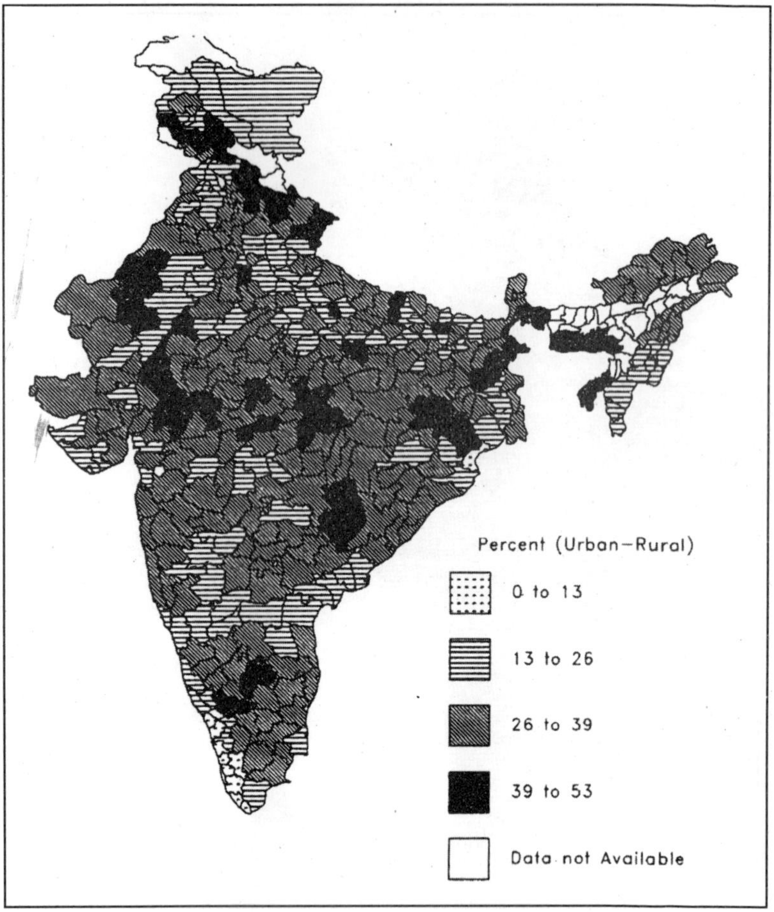

Map 30

Rural Scheduled Tribe Population 1981

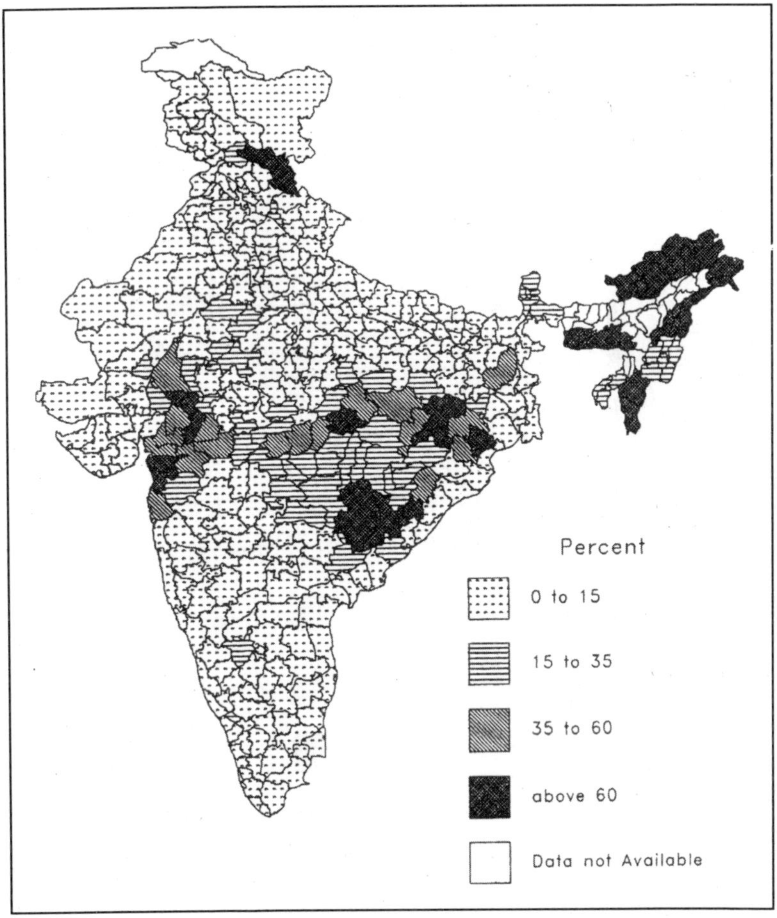

Map 31

Urban Scheduled Tribe Population 1981

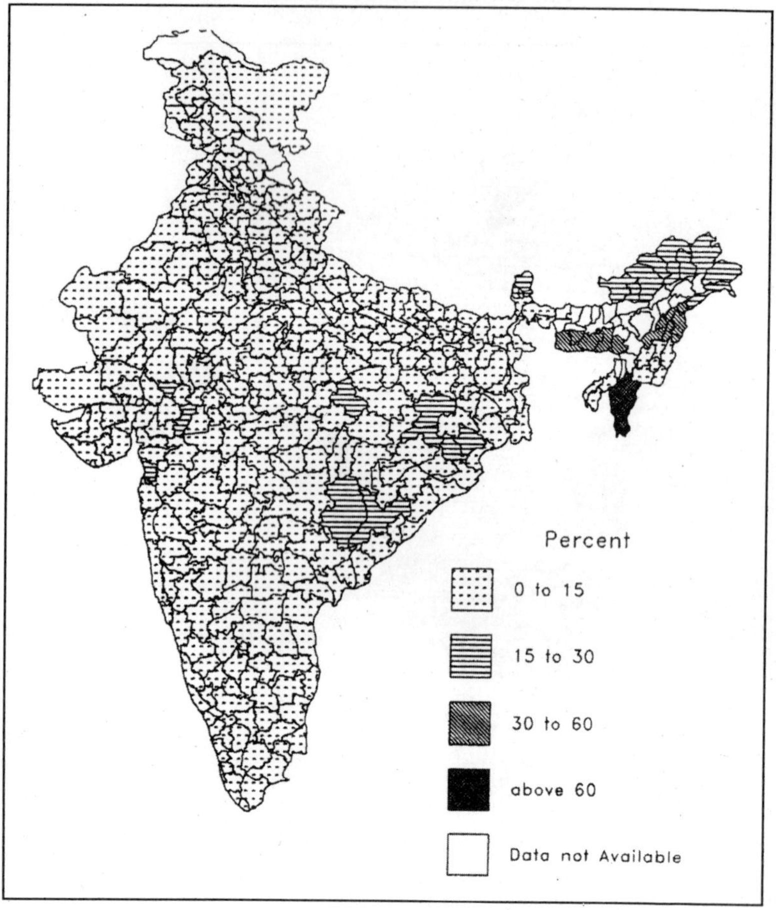

Appendix 2

Procedure of Calculation (Chapter 2)

1. Women's Share of the Labor Force (PFW)

$$\frac{\text{Total Female Workers (main + marginal)}}{\text{Total Workers (male + female)}} \times 100$$

Source: Registrar General and Census Commissioner (1991).

2. Sectoral Distribution of Female Labor Force (FPRIM, FSEC, FTERT)

$$\frac{\text{Female Workers in Primary, Secondary or Tertiary Sector}}{\text{Total Female Main Workers}} \times 100$$

Source: Registrar General and Census Commissioner (1991).

3. Female Labor Force Participation Rate (FLFPR)

$$\frac{\text{Female Workers (main + marginal)}}{\text{Female Population}} \times 100$$

Source: Registrar General and Census Commissioner (1991).

4. Ratio of Female Non-agricultural Wages to Male Non-agricultural Wages (NAGWG)

$$\frac{\text{Female Non-agricultural Wages}}{\text{Male Non-agricultural Wages}} \times 100$$

Source: Jose (1989).

5. Female Electors who Voted (FVOTE)

$$\frac{\text{Female Electors who Voted}}{\text{Male Non-agricultural Wages}} \times 100$$

Source: Election Commission of India (1996).

6. Women elected to Parliament (FLOK) is a binary variable, with states where women were elected coded as 1 and states where no woman was elected coded 0.

Source: Election Commission of India (1996).

7. Sexual Harassment in Public Places (FHAR)

$$\frac{\text{Number of Females Harassed}}{\text{Total Female Population}} \times 100{,}000$$

Source: Crime in India (1996).

8. Rate of Dowry Deaths (DWRY)

$$\frac{\text{Number of Dowry Deaths}}{\text{Total Female Population}} \times 100{,}000$$

Source: National Crime Records Bureau (1996).

9. Rate of Abuse by Husband and Family (ABUSE)

$$\frac{\text{Number of Females Abused}}{\text{Total Female Population}} \times 100{,}000$$

Source: National Crime Records Bureau (1996)

10. Average Age of Marriage

Source: Statistical Tables in *Demographic Zones in India* (Bose 1994, pp. 173).

11. Female Literates (FLIT)

$$\frac{\text{Female Literates}}{\text{Female Population } > 7 \text{ years}} \times 100$$

Source: Registrar General and Census Commissioner (1991).

12. Female Enrolment in Primary Schools (FENROL)

$$\frac{\text{Female Enrolled}}{\text{Total Enrolment}} \times 100$$

Source: GISTNIC Database (1997).

13. Sex Ratio (SEXRTO)

$$\frac{\text{Female Population}}{\text{Male Population}} \times 100$$

Source: Registrar General and Census Commissioner (1991).

Bibliography

Abdullah, T. and S. Ziedenstein. 1982. *Women in Bangladesh: Prospects of Change*. London: Pergamon.

Acharya, Sarthi. 1996. Women in the Indian Labor Force: A Temporal and Spatial Analysis. In *Women and Industrialization in Asia*, Susan Horton, (ed.) pp. 43–80. New York: Routledge.

Agnihotri, Indu and Vina Mazumdar. 1995. Changing Terms of Political Discourse: Women's Movement in India, 1970s–1990s. *Economic and Political Weekly* July 22: 1869–78.

Ahmed-Ghosh, Huma. 1994. Agricultural Development and Work Pattern of Women in a North Indian Village. In *Women and Work in South Asia*, Deepica Bagchi and Saraswati Raju, (eds.) pp. 74–98. New York: Routledge.

Andrews, Alice C. 1982. Toward a Status-of-Women Index. *Professional Geographer* 34(1): 24–31.

Anker, Richard and Hein Catherine. 1986. *Sex Inequalities in Urban Employment in the Third World*. New York: St. Martin's Press.

Baig, Tara Ali. 1976. *India's Women Power*. New Delhi: S. Chand and Co.

Banerjee, Nirmala. 1988. *Some Recent Trends in the Economic Activities of Indian Women.* Prepared for the National Commission on Self-Employed Women and Women in the Informal Sector, Center for Studies in Social Science, Calcutta.

Bardhan, Pranab K. 1974. On Life and Death Questions. *Economic and Political Weekly* 9: 1293–1304.

Bardhan, Pranab K. 1988. Sex Disparity in Child Survival in Rural India. *Rural Poverty in South Asia*, eds. T.N. Srinivasan and P.K. Bardhan, pp. 473–82. New York: Columbia University Press.

Barnett, Marguerite Ross. 1975. Cultural Nationalist Electoral Politics in Tamil Nadu. In *Studies in Electoral Politics in the Indian States*, Vol. IV, eds. Myron Weiner and John Osgood Field, pp. 70–108. Delhi: Manohar Book Service.

Basu, Alaka M. 1992. *Culture, the Status of Women and Demographic Behavior: Illustrated with the Case of India*. Oxford: Clarendon Press.

Benjamin, Roger W., Richard N. Blue and Stephen Coleman. 1971. Modernization and Political Change: A Comparative Aggregate Data Analysis of Indian Political Behavior. *Midwest Journal of Political Science* XV(2): 219–61.

Bennett, Lynn. 1992. *Women, Poverty, and Productivity in India*. EDI Seminar, Paper No. 43, Washington D.C.: World Bank.

Berreman, Gerald D. 1993. Sanskritization as Female Oppression in India. In *Sex and Gender Hierarchies*, (ed.) Barbara Diane Miller, pp. 366–92. Great Britain: Cambridge University Press.

Beteille, A. 1975. *Inequality and Social Change*. Delhi: Oxford University Press.

Bhasin, Kamla, (ed.) 1972. *The Position of Women in India*, Proceedings of a Seminar held in Srinagar, India. Bombay: Leslie Sawhny Program of Training for Development and Friedrich-Naumann-Stiftung.

Bhatt, Bharat L. 1980. India and Indian Regions: A Critical Overview. In *An Exploration of India: Geographical Perspectives on Society and Culture*, ed. David. E. Sopher, pp. 35–64. New York: Cornell University Press.

Bose, Ashish. 1994. *Demographic Zones in India*. Delhi: B.R. Publishing Corporation.

Boserup, Ester. 1970. *Women's Role in Economic Development*. London: George Allen & Unwin.

Bradley, Karen and Diana Khor. 1993. Toward an Integration of Theory and Research on the Status of Women. *Gender & Society* 7(3): 347–78.

Brydon, L. and S. Chant, (eds.) 1989. *Women in the Third World: Gender Issues in Rural and Urban Areas*. London: Edward Elgar.

Butler, David, Ashok Lahiri and Prannoy Roy. 1991. *India Decides: Elections 1952–1991*. New Delhi: Living Media India.

Buttimer, A. 1976. Grasping the Dynamism of the Lifeworld. *Annals of the Association of American Geographers* 66: 277–92.

Caldwell, John C. 1982. *A Theory of Fertility Decline*. London: Academic Press.

Calman, Leslie J. 1992. *Toward Empowerment: Women and Movement Politics in India*. Boulder, Colorado: Westview Press.

Cameron, Rondo. 1975. The Diffusion of Technology as a Problem in Economic History. *Economic Geography* 51: 217–30.

Centre for Criminology. 1990. *Second Islington Crime Survey,* Middlesex Polytechnic, Middlesex: Enfield.

Chandidas, R. 1972. Poll Participation Slump. *Economic and Political Weekly* 7(29): 1359–68.

Chinchilla, N. 1977. Industrialization, Monopoly Capital, and Women's Work in Guatemala. *Signs* 3(1): 38–56.

Cipolla, Carlo M. 1969. *Literacy and Development in the West*. Baltimore: Penguin Books.

Committee on the Status of Women in India. 1974. *Towards Equality: Report of the Committee on the Status of Women in India*. New Delhi: Ministry of Education and Social Welfare, Department of Social Welfare.

Corbridge, Stuart. 1991. Third World Development. *Progress in Human Geography* 15(3): 311–21.

Cornwell, Gretchen T. and Bih-Er Chou. 1986. *Women's Work, Status, and Fertility in the Context of Chinese Family Structure*. Paper presented at the Rockfeller Foundation. Workshop on Women's Status and Fertility, Mount Kisco, New York.

Das, Veena. 1976. Indian Women: Work, Power and Status. In *Indian Women: From Purdah to Modernity*, ed. B.R. Nanda, pp. 129–45. Delhi: Vikas Publishing House.

Dasgupta, Biplab and W.H. Morris Jones. 1975. *Patterns and Trends in Indian Politics: An Ecological Analysis of Aggregate Data on Society and Elections*. Bombay: Allied Publishers.

de Souza, Alfred. (ed.) 1975. *Women in Contemporary India: Traditional Images and Changing Roles*. Delhi: Manohar Book Service.

Department of Social Welfare. 1978. *Women in India: A Statistical Profile by Government of India*. New Delhi: Department of Social Welfare.

Desai, Neera. 1977. *Woman in Modern India*. Bombay: Vora Publication House.

Desai, Padma and Jagdish N. Bhagwati. 1973. Women in Indian Elections. In *Studies in Electoral Politics in the Indian States*, Vol. II, eds. Myron Weiner and John Osgood Field, pp. 165–175. Delhi: Manohar Book Service.

Dholakia, B.H. and R.H. Dholakia. 1978. Inter-state Variations in Female Labor Force Participation Rates. *Indian Journal of Labor Economics*, January.

Dikshit, R.D. 1995. *Geography of Elections: The Indian Context*. Jaipur: Rawat Publications.

Dikshit, R.D. and J.C. Sharma. 1982. Trends and Patterns in Voter Turn-out in Punjab, 1967–1980: An Ecological Analysis. *The National Geographical Journal of India* 29: 18–29.

Dixon, Ruth B. 1976. Measuring Equality between the Sexes. *Journal of Social Issues* 32: 19–32.

Dreze, Jean and Amartya Sen. 1995. *India: Economic Development and Social Opportunity*. New Delhi: Oxford University Press.

Duncan, S. 1989. Gender Divisions of Labor in Greater London. *Urban and Regional* Studies, University of Sussex Working Paper 73. Brighton, Sussex.

Duncan, S. 1991. The Geography of Gender Divisions of Labor in Britain. *Transactions,* Institute of British Geographers 16: 420–39.

Duvvury, Nata. 1989. Work Participation of Women in India: A Study with Special Reference to Female Agricultural Laborers, 1961 to 1981. In *Limited Options: Women Workers in Rural India*, pp. 63–107. New Delhi: Asian Employment Program (ARTEP), ILO.

Ehrenreich, Barbara. 1984. Life Without Father: Reconsidering Socialist-Feminist Theory. *Socialist Review* 73 (January-February), pp. 48–57; rpt. in *Women, Class, and the Feminist Imagination: A Socialist-Feminist Reader,* eds. Karen V. Hansen and Ilene J. Philipson, pp. 268–76. Philadelphia: Temple University Press, 1990.

Eisenstein, Zillah. 1977. Constructing a Theory of Capitalist Patriarchy and Socialist Feminism. *Insurgent Sociologist* 7(3): 3–17; rpt. in *Women, Class, and the Feminist Imagination: A Socialist-Feminist Reader*, eds. Karen V. Hansen and Ilene J. Philipson, pp. 114–45. Philadelphia: Temple University Press, 1990.

Eisenstein, Zillah. 1979. Constructing a Theory of Capitalist Patriarchy and Socialist Feminism. In *Capitalist Patriarchy and the Case for Socialist Feminism*, ed. Eisenstein, pp. 22–28. New York: Monthly Review Press.

Election Commission of India. 1969. *Handbook for Returning Officers*. New Delhi: Election Commission.

Election Commission of India. 1996. *Statistical Report on General Elections 1996 to the Lok Sabha,* Vol.I, National and State Abstracts. New Delhi.

Forbes, Geraldine. 1981. The Indian Women's Movement: A Struggle for Women's Rights or National Liberation? In *The Extended Family: Women and Political Participation in India and Pakistan*, ed. Gail Minault, pp. 49–82. Columbia, Missouri: South Asia Books.

Forbes, Geraldine. 1996. *The New Cambridge History of India IV. 2: Women in Modern India*. Cambridge: Cambridge University Press.

Frankel, Francine. 1977. Problems of Correlating Electoral and Economic Variables: An Analysis of Voting Behaviour and Agrarian Modernization in Uttar Pradesh. In *Studies in Electoral Politics in the Indian States,* Vol. III, eds. Myron Weiner and Osgood Field, pp. 149–93. Delhi: Manohar Book Service.

Freebody, Peter and Anthony R. Welch, (eds.) 1993. *Knowledge, Culture and Power: International Perspectives on Literacy as Policy and Practice*. Pittsburgh, PA.: University of Pittsburgh Press.

Galtung, Johan 1972. On the Relationship between Human Resources and Development: Theory, Methods, and Data. *Journal of Development Studies* 8: 137–53.

Gibson, A. and T. Fast. 1986. *Women's Atlas of the United States.* New York: Facts on File Publication.

GISTNIC (General Information Service Terminal-National Information Center). 1997. On-line Information Retrieval Service. Hyderabad: Government of India.

Golden, Hilda. 1955. Literacy and Social Change in Underdeveloped Countries. *Rural Sociology* 20: 1–7.

Goode, William J. 1963. *World Revolution and Family Patterns*. New York: Free Press.

Gosal, G.S. 1964. Literacy in India: An Interpretive Study. *Rural Sociology* 29(3): 261–77.

Gould, Peter and Rodney White. 1974. *Mental Maps*. Baltimore, Maryland: Penguin Books.

Government of India. 1966. *Report of the Education Commission 1964–66*. New Delhi: Ministry of Education.

Gulati, L. 1975. Female Work Participation: A Study of Inter-State Differences. *Economic and Political Weekly* 10(1–2): 35–42.

Gustafsson, Uwe. 1991. *Can Literacy Lead to Development?: A Case Study in Literacy, Adult Education and Economic Development in India*. Dallas, TX: The Summer Institute of Linguistics and The University of Texas at Arlington.

Hardgrave, Robert L. Jr. 1975. The Communist Parties of Kerala: An Electoral Profile. In *Studies in Electoral Politics in the Indian States*, Vol. IV, eds. Myron Weiner and John Osgood Field, pp. 163–223. Delhi: Manohar Book Service.

Harding, Sandra. 1986. *The Science Question in Feminism*. Ithaca: Cornell University Press.

Hate, Chandrakala A. 1969. *Changing Status of Women*, Bombay: Allied Publishers.

HMSO. 1989. *Domestic Violence: An Overview of the Literature*. London: HMSO.

Hodge, David C. 1995. Should Women Count? The Role of Quantitative Methodology in Feminist Geographic Research. *Professional Geographer* 47(4): 426.

Holcomb, B., J. Kodras and S. Brunn. 1990. Women's Issues and State Legislation: Fragmentation and Inconsistency. In *Geographic Dimensions of United States Social Policy,* eds. J. Kodras and J.P. Jones, pp. 178–99. London: Edward Arnold.

Holcomb, B. and J.P. Jones. 1990. Work, Welfare and Poverty among Black Female-headed Families. In *Geographic Dimensions of United States Social Policy,* eds. J. Kodras and J.P. Jones, pp. 200–17. London: Edward Arnold.

Horton, Susan, (ed.) 1996. *Women and Industrialization in Asia*. New York: Routledge.

Howes, Stephen. 1992. *Purchasing Power, Infant Mortality and Literacy in China and India*. London: London School of Economics.

Indian Council of Social Science Research. 1975. *Status of Women in India: A Synopsis of the Report of the National Committee on the Status of Women, 1971–1974*. New Delhi: Indian Council of Social Science Research.

Issac, Thomas T.M. and Michael Tharakan P.K. 1995. Kerala: Towards a New Agenda. *Economic and Political Weekly,* August 5–12: 1993–2004.

Jacobson, Doranne. 1976–77. Indian Women in Process of Development. *Journal of International Affairs* 30(2): 211–242.

Jain, Devaki, (ed.) 1975. *Indian Women*. New Delhi: Publication Division, Ministry of Information and Broadcasting, Government of India.

Jain, D. 1985. The Household Trap: Report on a Field Survey of Female Activity Patterns. In *Tyranny of the Household: Investigative Essays on Women's Work*, eds. D. Jain and N. Banerjee. Delhi: Shakti Books.

Jamison, Stephanie W. 1996. *Sacrificed Wife/ Sacrificer's Wife: Women, Ritual, and Hospitality in Ancient India*. New York: Oxford University Press.

Jeffery, Patricia and Roger Jeffery. 1996. *Don't Marry me to a Plowman! Women's Everyday Lives in Rural North India*. Boulder, Colorado: Westview Press.

Johnston, R.J. 1992. *Multivariate Statistical Analysis in Geography*, New York: Longman Group Limited.

Johnston, R.J., D. Gregory and D.M. Smith, (eds.) 1994. *The Dictionary of Human Geography*. Oxford: Basil Blackwell.

Jones, Kathleen B. 1993. *Compassionate Authority: Democracy and Representation of Women*. New York: Routledge.

Jose, A.V. 1989. Female Labor Force Participation in India: A Case of Limited Options. In *Limited Options: Women Workers in Rural India,* ed. A.V. Jose, pp. 1–29. New Delhi: Asian Employment Program (ARTEP), ILO.

Joshi, Ram. 1968. Maharashtra. In *State Politics in India*, ed. Myron Weiner, pp. 177–214. Princeton, New Jersey: Princeton University Press.

Kannabiran, Vasanth and Kalpana Kannabiran. 1997. From Social Action to Political Action: Women and the 81st Amendment. *Economic and Political Weekly*, February 1–7, XXXII(5): 196–97.

Karve, Irawati. 1968. *Kinship Organization in India*. New York: Asia Publishing House.

Kishor, Sunita. 1993. May God give Sons to All: Gender and Child Mortality in India. *American Sociological Review* 58(2): 247–65.

Krishan, Gopal and Madhav Shyam. 1973. Spatial Perspectives on Progress of Female Literacy in India: 1901–1971. *Pacific Viewpoint* 14: 203–6.

Krishan, Gopal and Madhav Shyam. 1974. Patterns of City Literacy. *Economic and Political Weekly* 9(20): 800.

Kumar, Radha. 1993. *A History of Doing: An Illustrated Account of Movements for Women's Rights and Feminism in India, 1800–1900*. New Delhi: Kali for Women.

Kumar, Radha. 1995. Political Women and Women's Politics in India. In *A Rising Public Voice: Women in Politics Worldwide*, ed. Alida Brill, pp. 59–72. New York: The Feminist Press at the City University of New York.

Kumari, Abhilasha and Sabina Kidwai. 1994. *Illusion of Power: The Women's Vote*. New Delhi: Friedrich-Ebert-Stiftung.

Kumari, Ranjana and Anju Dubey. 1994. *Women Parliamentarian: A Study in the Indian Context*. New Delhi: Har Anand Publications.

Kurrien, John. 1990. *The Education of Girls and Women in India*. Background paper prepared for the World Bank WID Assessment, New Delhi.

Lawson, Victoria. 1995. The Politics of Difference: Examining the Quantitative/Qualitative Dualism in Post-Structuralist Feminist Research. *The Professional Geographer* 47(4): 449–57.

Lee, David and Ronald Shultz. 1982. Regional Patterns of the Status of Women in the United States. *Professional Geographer* 34(1): 32–41.

Lee, D., R. Stewart and D.G. Winter. 1979. The Geography of Female Status: A World-wide View. *Transition* 9: 2–7.

Levi-Strauss, Claude. 1969. *The Elementary Structures of Kinship*. Boston: Beacon Press.

Libbee, Michael J. and D.E. Sopher. 1975. Marriage Migration in Rural India. In *People on the Move: Studies on Internal Migration*, eds. Leszek A.Kosinski and R. Mansell Prothero. London: Methuen.

Liddle, Joanna and Joshi, Rama. 1986. *Daughters of Independence: Gender, Caste and Class in India*. New Delhi and London: Zed Books Ltd.

Malhotra, Anju, Reeve Vanneman and Sunita Kishor. 1995. Fertility, Dimensions of Patriarchy, and Development in India. *Population and Development Review*, 21(2): 281–305.

Mandelbaum, David G. 1988. *Women's Seclusion and Men's Honor: Sex Roles in North India*. Tucson: University of Arizona Press.

Mascia-Lees, Frances. 1984. *Toward a Model of Women's Status*. New York: Lang.

Mason, Karen Oppenheim. 1989. The Impact of Women's Social Position on Fertility in Developing Countries. In *Demography as an Interdiscipline*, ed. J. Mayone Stycos, pp. 19–42. New Brunswick: Transaction Publishers.

Mattingly, Doreen J. and Karen Falconer-Al-Hindi. 1995. Should Women Count? A Context for the Debate. *Professional Geographer* 47(4): 427–35.

Mazumdar, Vina. 1979. *Symbols of Power: Studies on the Political Status of Women in India*. Bombay: Allied Publishers.

McDowell, Linda. 1991. The Baby and the Bath Water: Diversity, Deconstruction and Feminist Theory in Geography. *Geoforum* 22(2): 123–33.

McDowell, Linda. 1993. Space, Place and Gender Relations: Part 1. Feminist Empiricism and the Geography of Social Relations. *Progress in Human Geography* 17(2): 157–79.

McLafferty, Sara L. 1995. Counting for Women. *Professional Geographer* 47(4): 436–42.

McLafferty, Sara L. and V. Preston. 1991. Gender, Race and Commuting among Service Sector Workers. *Professional Geographer* 43: 1–15.

McMillan, Alistair and Kanchan Chandra. 1998. Post-Poll: Who Voted for Whom? *India Today International*, March 16, 1998.

Mead, Margaret 1948. *Male and Female*. New York: Dell Publishing Co.

Mies, Maria. 1980. *Indian Women and Patriarchy: Conflicts and Dilemmas of Students and Working Women*. New Delhi: Concept Publication.

Mies. Maria. 1991. Women's Research or Feminist Research? The Debate Surrounding Feminist Science and Methodology. In *Beyond Methodology: Feminist Scholarship as Lived Experience*, eds. M. Fonow and J. Cook, pp. 60–84. Bloomington: Indiana University Press.

Miller, Barbara D. 1981. *The Endangered Sex: Neglect of Female Children in Rural India*. Ithaca: Cornell University Press.

Mishra, Subhash. 1998. Death Wish. *India Today International*, April 27, pp. 26–29.

Misra, Kalpana. 1997. Indian Feminism and the Post-Colonial State. *Women & Politics* 17(4): 25–45.

Mitchell, Juliet. 1974. *Psychoanalysis and Feminism*. New York: Pantheon Books.

Mitra, Ashok. 1961. *Levels of Regional Development in India*. Census of India, Vol. 1, Part 1A(I). Delhi: Controller of Publications, Government of India.

Momsen, J. and J. Townsend, (eds.) 1987. *Geography and Gender in the Third World*. London: Hutchinson.

Moore, Mick. 1973. Cross-cultural Surveys of Peasant Family Structures: Some Comments. *American Anthropologist* 75(3): 911–14.

Morgen, Sandra. 1990. Conceptualizing and Changing Consciousness: Socialist-Feminist Perspectives. In *Women, Class, and the Feminist Imagination: A Socialist-Feminist Reader*, eds. Karen V. Hansen and Ilene J. Philipson, pp. 277–91. Philadelphia: Temple University Press, 1990.

Mukhopadhyay, Maitrayee. 1984. *Silver Shackles: Women and Development in India*. Oxford: Oxfam.

Nagraj, K. 1989. Female Workers in Rural Tamil Nadu: A Preliminary Study. In *Limited Options: Women Workers in Rural India*, pp. 108–202. New Delhi: Asian Employment Program (ARTEP), ILO.

Nanda, B.R., (ed.) 1976. *Indian Women: From Purdah to Modernity*. New Delhi: Vikas Publishing House.

National Crime Records Bureau. 1996. *Crime in India, 1994*. New Delhi: Ministry of Home Affairs.

National Institute of Urban Affairs (NIUA). 1987. *Women Vendors in India's Urban Centers*. Research Study Series No. 22. New Delhi: NIUA.

Nayyar, Rohini. 1989. Rural Labor Markets and Employment of Women in Punjab-Haryana. In *Limited Options: Women Workers in Rural India*, New Delhi: Asian Employment Program (ARTEP), ILO.

Olsson, G. 1980. *Birds in Egg: Eggs in Bird*. London: Pion.

Omvedt, Gail. 1980. *We Will Smash the Prison! Indian Women in Struggle*. London: Zed Press.

Painter, K. 1991. *Wife Rape, Marriage and the Law*. Manchester: Manchester University.

Pampel, Fred C. and Kazuko Tanaka. 1986. Economic Development and Female Labor Force Participation: A Reconsideration. *Social Forces* 64: 599–619.

Papanek, H. 1976. Women in Cities: Problems and Perspectives. In *Women and World Development,* eds. Irene Tinker, M. Bramsen, and Mayra Buvinic, pp. 54–69. Washington D.C.: Overseas Development Council.

Papanek, H. 1979. Development Planning for Women: The Implications of Women's Work. In *Women and Development In South-east Asia*, eds. R. Jahan and H. Papanek, pp. 170–201. Dacca: Bangladesh Institute of Law and International Affairs.

Parthasarthy, G. and G.D. Rama Rao. 1974. *Employment and Unemployment of Rural Labor and the Crash Programme*. Waltair, India: Andhra University Press.

Patel, Tara. 1984. *Development of Education among Tribal Women*. Delhi: Mittal Publications.

Philipson Ilene J. and Karen V. Hansen. 1990. An Introduction. In *Women, Class, and the Feminist Imagination: A Socialist-Feminist Reader*, eds. Karen V. Hansen and Ilene J. Philipson, pp. 3–40. Philadelphia: Temple University Press, 1990.

Poonacha, Veena. 1993. On the Edge of Silence: Gender within Human Rights Discourse. *Economic and Political Weekly* October 9, pp. 2192–94.

Premi, Mahendra K. 1979. *Patterns of Internal Migration of Females in India*. Occasional Paper No. 15, Center for the Study of Regional Development, Jawaharlal Nehru University, New Delhi.

Presser, Harriet B. and Sunita Kishor. 1991. Economic Development and Occupational Sex Segregation in Puerto Rico. *Population and Development Review* 17: 53–85.

Quinn, N. 1977. Anthropological Studies of Women's Status. *Annual Review of Anthropology* 6: 181–225.

Raju, Saraswati. 1994. Gender and Caste Inequities in Work-Force Participation in Urban India: A Socio-Spatial Interpretation. In *Women and Work in South Asia*, eds. Deipica Bagchi and Saraswati Raju, pp. 74–98. New York: Routledge.

Rao, M.S.A. 1957. *Social Change in Malabar*. Bombay: Popular Book Depot.

Rao, M.S.A. 1978. Tobacco Development and Labor Migration: Planning for Labor Welfare and Development. *Economic and Political Weekly* 13(29): 1183–6.

Rao, Usha N.J. 1983. *Women in a Developing Society*. New Delhi: Ashish Publishing House.

Raza, Moonis. 1990. *Education, Development, and Society*, New Delhi: Vikas Publishing House.

Reddy, D.N. 1975. Female Work Participation: A Study of Interstate Differences, a Comment. *Economic and Political Weekly* 10(23): 902–5.

Registrar General and Census Commissioner. 1981. *Final Population Totals: Brief Analysis of Primary Census Abstract*, Series 1, Paper 2 of 1982. New Delhi: Ministry of Home Affairs.

Registrar General and Census Commissioner. 1991. *Final Population Totals: Brief Analysis of Primary Census Abstract,* Paper 2 of 1992. New Delhi: Ministry of Home Affairs.

Richter, William L. 1975. Electoral Patterns in Post-Princely India. In *Studies in Electoral Politics in the Indian States*, Vol. II, eds. Myron Weiner and John Osgood Field, pp. 1–77. Delhi: Manohar Book Service.

Rosenzweig, Mark R. and T. Paul Shultz. 1982. Market Opportunities, Genetic Endowments and the Intrafamily Distributions of Resources: Child Survival in Rural India. *American Economic Review* 72: 803–15.

Rubin, Gayle. 1976. The Traffic in Women: Notes on the "Political Economy" of Sex. In *Toward an Anthology of Women*, ed. Rayna Rapp Reiter, pp. 157–210. New York: Monthly Review Press; rpt. in *Women, Class, and the Feminist Imagination: A Socialist-Feminist Reader*, eds. Karen V. Hansen and Ilene J. Philipson, pp. 74–113. Philadelphia: Temple University Press, 1990.

Rudolph, Lloyd and Susanne Rudolph. 1967. *The Modernity of Tradition: Political Development in India*. Part I. Chicago: University of Chicago Press.

Safilios-Rothschild, C. 1980. A Class and Sex Stratification Theoretical Model and its Relevance for Fertility Trends in the Developing World.

In *Determinants of Fertility Trends: Theories Re-Examineu*, eds. Charlotte Hohn and Rainer Mackensen, pp. 189–202. Liege: Ordina Editions.

Safilios-Rothschild, C. 1982. Female Power, Autonomy, and Demographic Change in the Third World. In *Women's Roles and Population Trends in the Third World*, eds. R. Anker, M. Buvinic, and N. Youssef, pp. 117–32. London: ILO.

Sahoo, B. and B.K. Mahanty. 1978. Female Participation in Work in Orissa: An Interdistrict Comparison. *Indian Journal of Labor Economics* 20(4): 40–50.

Sathar, Zeba, Nigel Crook, Christine Callum and Shahnaz Kazi. 1988. Women's Status and Fertility in Pakistan. *Population and Development Review* 14(3): 415–32.

Sawant, S.D. and R. Dewan. 1979. Rural Female Labor and Economic Development. *Economic and Political Weekly* 24(26): 1091–9.

Schlegel, A. 1977. Toward a Theory of Sexual Stratification. In *Sexual Stratification*, ed. A. Schlegel, pp. 1–40. New York: Columbia University Press.

Schuth, Katarina. 1980. Village Literacy and its Correlates: A Mysore Case Study. In *An Exploration of India Geographical Perspectives on Society and Culture*, ed. David E. Sopher, pp. 191–212. Ithaca, New York: Cornell University Press.

Seager, J. and A. Olson. 1986. *Women in the World: An International Atlas*, New York: Simon and Schuster.

Sengupta P. 1968. Formation of Economic Regions by Population Characteristics and Resource Development. In *Census of India 1961*, Monograph Series Vol. 1, No. 8, *Economic Regionalization of India: Problems and Approaches*, pp. 89–98. New Delhi.

Sharma, Mariam. 1985. Caste, Class, and Gender: Production and Reproduction in North India. *The Journal of Peasant Studies* 12(4): 57–89.

Sharma, O.P. and Robert Rutherford. 1987. *Recent Literacy Trends in India*. New Delhi: Registrar General and Census Commissioner of India.

Sharma, O.P. and Robert Rutherford. 1990. *Effect of Female Literacy on Fertility in India*. New Delhi: Registrar General and Census Commissioner of India.

Sharma, Ursula. 1980. *Women, Work and Property in North-West India*. New York: Tavistock Publications Limited.

Shortridge, B.G. 1987. *Atlas on American Women*. New York: Macmillan.

Shukla, D.M. 1988. *Political Socialization and Women Voters: A Case Study of Kodarma Constituency, Bihar*. New Delhi: Anmol Publications.

Singh, Andrea M. 1975. The Study of Women in India: Some Problems in Methodology. In *Women in Contemporary India*, ed. Alfred de Souza, pp. 189–218. New Delhi: Manohar Book Service.

Singh, Andrea M. 1984. Rural-to-Urban Migration of Women in India: Patterns and Implications. In *Women in the Cities of Asia: Migration and Urban Adaptation*, eds. J.T. Fawcett, S. Khoo, and P. Smith, pp. 81–107. Boulder, Colorado: Westview Replica Edition.

Singh, A.M. and A. Kelles-Viitanen. 1987. *Invisible Hands: Women in Home Based Production*. New Delhi: Sage Publications.

Sinha, N.J. 1975. Female Work Participation: A Comment. *Economic and Political Weekly* 10(16): 672–4.

Sivard, Ruth Leger. 1985. *Women: A World Survey*. Washington D.C.: World priorities.

Smith, David M. 1973. *The Geography of Social Well-Being in the United States: An Introduction to Territorial Social Indicators*. New York: McGraw Hill Book Company.

Sopher, David E. 1980. Sex Disparity in Indian Literacy. In *An Exploration of India Geographical Perspectives on Society and Culture*, edited by David E. Sopher, pp. 130–90. Ithaca, New York: Cornell University Press.

SPSS Inc. 1996. *SPSS Base 7.0 for Windows: User's Guide*, pp. 355–57. Chicago: SPSS Inc.

Srinivas, M.N. 1977. The Changing Position of Indian Women. *Man* 12(2): 221–38.

Stein, Dorothy. 1988. Burning Brides: The Perils of Daughterhood in India. *Pacific Affairs* 61(3): 465–85.

Sundaram, K. 1989. Interstate Variations in Work Force Participation Rates of Women in India. In *Limited Options: Women Workers in Rural India,* ed. A.V. Jose, pp. 30–62. New Delhi: Asian Employment Program (ARTEP) ILO.

Tinker, I. and M. Bramsen. 1976. The Adverse Impact of Development on Women. In *Women and World Development*, eds. I. Tinker, M. Bramsen and Mayra Buvinic, pp. 22–34. Washington D.C.: Overseas Development Council.

UNESCO. 1984. *Literacy Situation in Asia and the Pacific: India*. Bangkok, Thailand: UNESCO.

UNESCO. 1986. *Education of Girls in Asia and the Pacific: Report of the Regional Review Meeting on the Situation of Education of Girls for Universalization of Primary Education.* Bangkok, Thailand: UNESCO.

UNESCO. 1987. *Universal Primary Education for Girls: India*. Bangkok Thailand: UNESCO.

United Nations. 1980. *Review and Evaluation of Progress Achieved in the Implementation of the World Plan of action: Employment*. Paper prepared for the World Conference of the United nations Decade for Women, Copenhagen, Denmark, July 14–30, 1980. A/CONF. 94/8.

United Nations. 1991. *Human Development Report*. New York: Oxford University Press.

United Nations. 1995. *Human Development Report*. New York: Oxford University Press.

Valentine, G. 1989. The Geography of Women's Fear. *Area* 21: 385–90.

Van Allen, Judith. 1984. Capitalism Without Patriarchy. *Socialist Review* 77: 81–91, rpt. in *Women, Class, and the Feminist Imagination: A Socialist-Feminist Reader*, eds. Karen V. Hansen and Ilene J. Philipson, pp. 292–300. Philadelphia: Temple University Press, 1990.

Van Dusen, R.A., and E.B. Sheldon. 1976. The Changing Status of American Women: A Life Cycle Perspective. *American Psychologist* 31: 106–16.

Vanneman, Reeve and Douglas Barnes. 1992. Indian Development District Database. Unpublished Codebook available from the *Center on Population, Gender and Social Inequality*, University of Maryland, College Park.

Varma, Sudhir. 1997. *Women's Struggle for Political Space: From Enfranchisement to Participation*. Jaipur: Rawat Publications.

Wadley, Susan. 1977. Women and the Hindu Tradition. *Signs* 3 (Autumn): 113–25.

Walby, S. 1986. *Patriarchy at Work: Patriarchal and Capitalist Relations in Employment.* Cambridge: Polity.

Walby, S. 1989. Theorizing Patriarchy. *Sociology* 23: 213–34.

Weiner, Myron. 1975. Preface. In *Studies in Electoral Politics in the Indian States*, Vol. II, eds. Myron Weiner and John Osgood Field, pp. ix-xiv. Delhi: Manohar Book Service.

Weiner, Myron. 1980. *India at the Polls, 1980: A Study of the Parliamentary Elections.* Washington D.C.: The American Enterprise Institute for Public Policy Research.

Weiner, Myron and John Osgood Field. 1975. How Tribal Constituencies in India Vote. In *Studies in Electoral Politics in the Indian States*, Vol. II, eds. Myron Weiner and John Osgood Field, pp. 78–164. Delhi: Manohar Book Service.

Weiner, Myron and John Osgood Field. 1977. India's Urban Constituencies. In *Studies in Electoral Politics in the Indian States*, Vol. III, eds. Myron Weiner and John Osgood Field, pp. 1–121. Delhi: Manohar Book Service.

Whyte, Martin King. 1978. *The Status of Women in Pre-Industrial Societies*. Princeton, N.J.: Princeton University Press.

World Bank. 1995. *World Development Report, 1995.* Oxford: OUP.

Young, Iris. 1980. Socialist Feminism and the Limits of Dual Systems Theory. *Socialist Review* 50–51: 169–87.

Zelditch, Morris Jr. 1968. Social Status. In *International Encyclopedia of the Social Sciences,* ed. David L. Sills. New York: Macmillan.

Index